W9-ABZ-047

THE LONG WAR

*Dictatorship and Revolution in
El Salvador*

THE LONG WAR

Dictatorship and Revolution in El Salvador

JAMES DUNKERLEY

JUNCTION BOOKS

© 1982 James Dunkerley
Reprinted 1983

Verso Editions
15 Greek Street London W1

First published in Great Britain by
Junction Books 15 St John's Hill
London SW11 1TN

ISBN 0 8052 7166 X

All rights reserved. No part of this publication may be reproduced,
transmitted or stored in a retrieval system, in any form or by any means,
without permission in writing from the publisher.

Typeset by Elephant Productions
Printed and bound by Whitstable Litho Ltd.,
Whitstable, Kent.

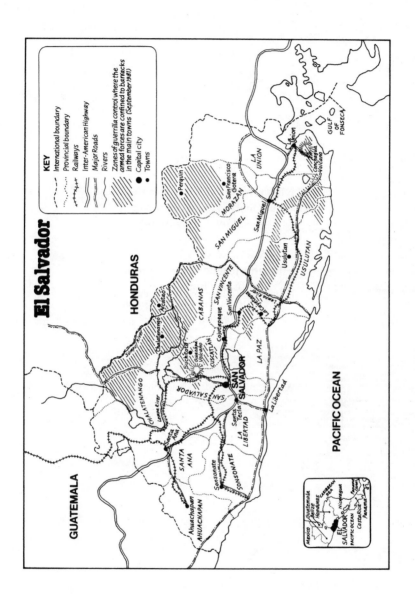

El Salvador

GUATEMALA

HONDURAS

PACIFIC OCEAN

GULF OF FONSECA

KEY
- International boundary
- Provincial boundary
- Railways
- Inter-American Highway
- Major Roads
- Rivers
- Zones of guerrilla control where the armed forces are confined to barracks in the main towns (September 1981)
- ● Capital city
- ● Towns

CHALATENANGO

SANTA ANA

AHUACHAPAN

SONSONATE

LA LIBERTAD

SAN SALVADOR

CABAÑAS

CUSCATLAN

SAN VICENTE

LA PAZ

SAN MIGUEL

MORAZAN

LA UNION

USULUTAN

Ahuachapan

Santa Ana

Sonsonate

Chalatenango

Suchitoto

Cojutepeque

San Vicente

SAN SALVADOR

Santa Tecla

La Libertad

Perquin

San Francisco Gotera

San Miguel

Usulutan

La Union

Lempa River

Torola River

Lempa River

Jiboa River

Santa Ana Volcano

Guazapa Volcano

San Miguel Volcano

Conchagua Volcano

To the memory of Mercedes Recinos,
killed in Chalatenango on 27 May 1979,
one of tens of thousands

that this plague of tears compel
not pity but victory
over the barbarities of capital,
the treason of reform

CONTENTS

INTRODUCTION

Although this book contains more than its fair share of footnotes, it is the product not only of study and political conviction but also outrage. There is nothing especially commendable in this; indeed, angry books are often extremely hard to read and far from edifying. However, it is more than likely that many of the people who pick up this book will have shared, at some time and in some form, that sense of deep disgust and anger that I experienced one sunny day in August 1981. On my way home from work I picked up *Meridiano*, the midday paper of La Paz, Bolivia, to read that the armed forces of El Salvador were using guillotines to execute their prisoners. Some months later I saw the detailed *denuncia* of the workers of 'Quality Meats of Central America' which described how the victims were first stunned with an electric needle and then decapitated with the modern equipment of the slaughterhouse.

After reflection of the type that is not the privilege of those likely to have their lives ended in such a manner it became plain that this event stood apart from countless other instances of murder in cold blood in El Salvador precisely because of the needless trouble taken to kill. It was an almost cartesian act, undertaken with care and precision; the calculated nature of the butchery betokened a distinct sadism. Objectively there is nothing to distinguish this from the more common practice of the Salvadorean security forces of dragging sleepy peasants and workers into the cold night and beating, raping and burning them with cigarettes before they are shot and dismembered with machetes. However, I was reminded of the incident when listening to Luis De Sebastián of the *Frente Democrático Revolucionario* speak in London in October 1981. De Sebastián forcefully made the point that the barbarism in El Salvador was not unique to that country nor the sole responsibility of the indigenous forces of reaction; this Moloch is

1

equally the product of the earnest desk-ridden managers of 'counter-insurgency' employed in Washington (or London, Tel Aviv, Pretoria, Moscow). No doubt the compilers of those neat manuals on anti-guerrilla warfare would be better pleased with operations that are undertaken under conditions of maximum hygiene in an abattoir than in the customary style of peasant violence.

This would all be idle speculation were it not for the millions of US dollars pumped into the Salvadorean repressive apparatus and the vast resources given over to train its personnel. It may have become somewhat hackneyed to insist on the parallel with Vietnam, but in this sense at least it stands up very well. As in Vietnam, 'freedom', 'democracy' and 'stability' can only be defended in El Salvador by means that are their very opposite. As in Vietnam, the vileness of the measures taken against faceless 'communists' progressively reveals the ideals of liberal democracy to be unrealisable; the ideological construction of individual liberty becomes the rationale for atrocity on a massive scale. The contradiction at the heart of the ideal nurtured by monopoly capitalism has been made so acute by the ferocity of the struggle that it takes the form of a transparent hypocrisy, a phenomenon conducive as much to anger as to understanding.

Yet, while the violation of human rights is an extremely tangible and terrifying activity, these rights are themselves ideals; even as defined in the UN Charter they remain unrealised in every nation on the face of the globe. A 'human right' represents the margin of inhumanity; if we wish to understand how and why this margin is traversed or, very frequently, completely discarded we have to move into the terrain of history and politics in a manner that questions the very notion that such rights exist *sui generis*, evacuated of any ideological bias. This becomes even more manifestly the case when the norm of a 'human right' in its political and strictly juridical sense (right to life, freedom from torture, extralegal encarceration, etc.) is expanded to include 'social' rights, such as those to an adequate calorie and protein intake, pure drinking water, medical care, guaranteed wages, employment, control over one's body and sexuality, etc. It is, therefore, no good simply to view El Salvador as the site of exceptional inhumanity; indeed, as De Sebastián suggests, in a number of respects this does not just obscure but is positively regressive.

The aim of this book is not to tabulate the incidence of barbarism in El Salvador but to locate it in a social and political context. The most transparent flaw of the text as a piece of history is that it has no determinate conclusion; the manuscript was concluded at the end of March 1982 when the outcome of the struggle was neither known nor sensibly prophesiable in any but the most general terms. However, to have waited until the battle is decisively lost or won would have been to seek a spurious succour in events rather than engage with them.

This becomes more obvious if one views the civil war in El Salvador not just in its own terms but as a 'moment' in a regional upsurge that is gripping all of Central America. This aspect is underlined by the enormous impact of the Nicaraguan revolution, but it is also evident in the continuing political crisis and progressive polarisation in Guatemala, the growing confusion and instability in Honduras, and the deepening economic crisis in Costa Rica, hitherto the most becalmed nation in the region. Clearly, the decision taken in Washington to 'make a stand' in El Salvador accounts for the extra-ordinary ferocity and extended nature of the war there even compared with Nicaragua. However, there is much to suggest that the revolution that is brewing in Guatemala could result in a conflagration greater still in its effects on the human condition and balance of political power in Central America.

The mandarins of the State Department have, as a consequence, speedily dusted down the domino theories of yore. Although these are suffused with all manner of incomprehensible jargon and have been stretched to idiotic lengths, they do at least register a recognition of the international dimension of the conflict that was not for some time paralleled on the left. It has not been possible to give this aspect its proper due here but it is worth noting that revolution is not being 'exported'. It has been nurtured in the social conditions of states that comprise a region that is politically balkanised but of a relatively homogeneous economic and social fabric. If the peculiarities of Nicaragua under the Somoza dynasty proved to be the weakest link in the chain, and the small size, high population and remarkable omnipotence of the local oligarchy in El Salvador provided an obvious sequitur, there is nothing so remarkable in the physiognomy of the other countries that would confer upon them some kind of immunity.

The 19 million people who inhabit the five core states of Central America (Costa Rica, El Salvador, Guatemala, Honduras and Nicaragua) live in backward capitalist states which rely upon agri-culture for 72 per cent of their exports and at least 25 per cent of their GDP. Although they have over the years become known as 'Banana Republics', it is upon coffee that they depend, coffee beans accounting for 45 per cent of total exports against 7 per cent for bananas. While the nature of the plant has certainly determined the precise character of agricultural organisation, it has not resulted in any escape from the tragi-comic rite implied in the Anglo-Saxon terminology imposed upon these countries. Not only do these states remain extremely poor– registering balance of payments deficits constantly throughout the 1970s, which ended with a regional external debt of nearly $6 billion– but they are also founded upon social systems that preserve and accelerate a grossly imbalanced internal structure of wealth and power. In 1977 the per capita GDP of the five states was $424 but even this paltry figure does not denote the real income of the mass of the population. In 1970 the bottom 50 per cent of the population received only 13 per cent of the total income, averaging $54 per head, whereas the top 5 per cent enjoyed 31 per cent of earnings, at $1,760 per capita.

Given the almost absolute reliance upon agriculture, it is not surprising to find that the pattern of income relates very closely with the pattern of land ownership. In 1961 the rural population of Central America numbered some 6.67 million people, 27,700 of whom were connected with commercial farming, 2.95 million holding plots of less than four hectares in size, a million with less than one hectare and 1.53 million possessing no land whatsoever. In the subsequent decades the population has rocketed and the imbalance in ownership increased with landlessness, unemployment and, more acutely, underemploy-ment all rising substantially. The quality of life of the poor of Central America has not reflected in any positive sense the massive technological advances made in the capitalist metropolis over these years, making the indices of their deprivation even more abhorrent. A Central American may expect to live for 55 years if he or she survives for twelve months, during which time the incidence of mortality is 10 per cent against 0.8 per cent in Sweden and 1.4 per cent in Britain. Since only 15 per cent of the population had access to a piped sewerage system in 1971 it is no anomaly that 15 per cent of all deaths can be attributed to easily curable gastro-entiritis and other diarrhoeal diseases. There were only 6,134 doctors to deal with this situation. This is an average of one for every 2,869 people, necessitating a threefold rise to meet the minimum requirements of the World Health Organisation, but this is itself an artificial ratio since a great many doctors work in lucrative private practices in the cities.

One could multiply the examples until they become a frozen statistical litany, but the point to be registered here is that El Salvador is very much of a type both in its historical development and in its current social condition. I have attempted to draw this aspect out impressionistically in the early chapters but to maintain it throughout would require a wholly different book; a book that will, no doubt, soon be written as social and political conflict trespasses the inherited colonial boundaries resurrected in 1841, when the transient experiment of a Federal Central American Republic finally collapsed under the weight of the contradictions bestowed upon it by the epoch. Today these contradictions have been reversed: the struggle is for national liberation but it pays scant respect to formal frontiers and cannot be resolved in a lasting manner without a fundamental reintegration of the region as a whole.

Some of these points are considered in the Conclusion, which also attempts to draw together more general political characteristics of the present struggle. The rest of the book is organised in a broadly chronological format with the chapters falling into a number of identifiable sections. The first (Chapters 1 to 3) covers political developments up to 1961, placing particular emphasis on the revolution of 1932. The second (Chapters 4 and 5) considers in greater detail the nature of contemporary economic organisation and its social consequences as well as the political background up to 1972, at which point polarisation underwent a marked acceleration. The third section (Chapters 6 to 8) covers what might be termed the prologue to the revolution over the years 1972 to 1979, looking at the rise of the left, the crisis of the military regime, and the influence of the Nicaraguan revolution. The fourth and final section (Chapters 9 and 10) analyses in greater detail the period from October 1979 to March 1982, taking in the collapse of the first reformist junta and the consolidation of the two opposing camps followed by the onset of unrestrained civil war in the context of a rapid return to the Cold War on the international plane.

Although the text displays a number of personal eccentricities, this should not be allowed to hide the fact that many people have helped to nurse it into existence. My colleagues at the Universities of London and Liverpool contributed by taking a benign interest and respecting the time devoted to what was formally an 'extra-mural' project. To my ex-*compañeros de trabajo* at the Latin America Bureau, Jan Karmali and Jenny Pearce, I owe my introduction to Central America and ceaseless discussions of its politics from which I continue to learn a great deal. In Washington I was helped beyond the call of duty by Laurence and Lynette Whitehead, Reggie and Emily Norton, Roberto Alvarez,

Cynthia Arson of IPS and Heather Foote of WOLA. I am also very grateful to Carolyn Forchè, whose investigative enterprise is only matched by the flair with which she presents the results. Various sections of the book could not have been written without the help of Oscar Avila, Hermione Harris, Roberto Vargas and Salvador Moncada, none of whom will agree entirely with the analytical line, and some of whom will dispute it vehemently, but all of whom gave generously that it might take shape. Much of the text was prepared in the home of Alberto and Chela Aguilar, although they did not know it; their boundless generosity will have to be repaid more fully in another way. Nor is there enough here to make good my debt to Bill Schwarz, Dylan Woolcock and Ana Maria Aguilar, who are the sort of friends everybody should have. Were this another type of book it would be dedicated to Penny and Dylan; they will understand why it is not.

1
THE RISE OF THE OLIGARCHY

The Dueñas, the Reglados, the Hills, the Meza Ayaus, the De Solas, the Sol Millets, the Guirolas, the Alvarez, the Meléndez, the Menéndez Castros, the Deiningers, the Quinoñez, the Garcia Prietos, and the Vilanovas: this oligarchy runs the lives of three million mestizos.

Marcel Neidergang, *The Twenty Latin Americas*

They remain as always, rude and superstitious, obtaining their simple food and scanty dress at a cost of great work. Without social needs, without a wish to improve their condition . . . they do not pursue progress nor do they seem to consider the wellbeing of their descendants . . .

'Los Indios', *Diario Oficial del Gobierno,* 23 August 1855

For the last century economic and political power in El Salvador have been concentrated in the hands of an oligarchy that has a good claim to be one of the smallest, most omnipotent, pugnacious and reactionary in the world. It is not, as popular opinion would have it, comprised solely of 'fourteen families', although in the early years of this century it had a core of fourteen family groups with some 65 families in all. In 1974, 67 family firms exported coffee on a commercial scale while an inner group of 37 enterprises dominated the production of coffee, sugar and cotton (see Appendix Two.)

The key to the formation of this veritable aristocracy and to the development of the social structure of El Salvador, as well as that of most of Central America, lies with coffee. It was the introduction of this plant and its transformation into the region's leading export crop in the mid-nineteenth century that hauled the gaggle of isolated isthmian provinces into the world market and provided the conditions for the subordination of feudal, pre-capitalist economic relations that had endured under the Spanish colony. Coffee became the axis around

which the contemporary class structure evolved, giving meaning to the
fledgling nation states. These had hitherto existed almost by default,
sundered from Spain by the impact of the insurrections in Mexico,
divided up along the judicial boundaries of the old imperial system;
despite the voluntarism of the republican ideologues, they were almost
exclusively dependent upon the economic base and administrative
apparatus inherited from the colony.[1]

The consolidation of coffee and the emergence of the new
republican oligarchies was a slow and uneven process, dependent not
solely on a shift in agricultural patterns but also an extended political
contest between the forces of conservatism – tied to the old colonial
apparatus, defenders of clericalism, and supporters of protectionism
and monopoly – and those of liberalism – secularist, exponents of free
trade and positivism, enemies of the 'backward' communal lands of the
indigenous populations. It was also, of course, determined by the
topographical nature and social composition of each state. Thus, Costa
Rica, which possessed only a very small indigenous population and
large tracts of uncultivated land, was able to adapt to coffee early,
starting to export in the late 1830s and consolidating the new liberal
order with the dictatorship of Tomás Guardia (1871–82) after 30 years
of relatively even distribution of lands through free concessions and
cheap sales. The development of a strata of medium farmers and the
'openness' of the Costa Rican ruling class should, nevertheless, be put
in context: 33 of the 44 presidents since independence have been
descendants of three families, one of which (Vázquez de Coronado)
has contrived to produce some 18 presidents and no less than 230
parliamentary deputies. In Nicaragua and Honduras, where the
topography was less well suited to coffee, the shift from a virtually
autarkic reliance upon cattle-raising, forestry and small-scale mining
was long delayed. Honduras never experienced an authentic liberal
revolution and adopted coffee only after its banana enclave was well
established. Nicaragua, on the other hand, was the last to enter the
liberal fold with the robust dictatorship of José Santos Zelaya (1893–
1909) presiding not so much over a major transfer of power between
elites as a shift in the orientation of the established oligarchy.

Resistance to liberalism was strongest in Guatemala, where
independence failed to dislocate the entrenched forces of conservatism.
Under the plebeian dictator Rafael Carrera (1839–65), these continually
intervened in the other states to uphold clerical privilege, monopoly
and the forced labour systems until the market for its principal export,

the vegetable colorant cochineal, was badly hit by the discovery in Europe of a coal-based dye in 1856. The liberal revolution of 1871 and the dictatorship of Justo Rufino Barrios (1873–85) proved irreversible, giving Central American liberals the hegemonic base that Carrera had long provided for conservatism. Yet, the rise of the new coffee oligarchy in Guatemala showed very clearly that the new elites were liberal only in name and attachment to economic doctrine. The scarcity of suitable land and lack of labour required a major programme of expropriation of lands belonging not only to the Church but also to the indigenous communities, and the introduction of new vagrancy and forced labour laws, if anything more onerous than those of the colonial era. Hundreds of thousands of peasants were dispossessed of their traditional holdings to create a fluid market in land and labour which was propelled both by the capital and modern techniques of foreign settlers (principally Germans) and the directly coercive measures that today still persist in many parts of Guatemala. The government tended as a consequence towards highly authoritarian and extended dictatorship: Manuel Estrada Cabrera (1899–1920) and Jorge Ubico (1930–44).

The brave verbiage of 'progress' and 'modernisation' that accompanied the rise of the liberal oligarchies cannot be dismissed in entirety. In some senses Central America was indeed transformed. The expansion of coffee benefited considerably from the capital and expertise of European immigrants; new roads and railways were built to connect plantations with ports (Costa Rica 1854; Panama 1855; Guatemala 1884; Nicaragua 1900); US and European steamship lines opened new routes first on the Pacific coast and then on that of the Atlantic; by 1880 the telegraph connected Central America with the main industrial centres of the world, where it took its place in the ledgers of banks, stock exchanges, railway and steamship companies. Until the short recession following the First World War the oligarchies faced few threats and underwent little change, buoyed up by the flourishing market in coffee. However, outside provision for production on the large plantations and transport to the ports, infrastructure improvements were negligible and made no impact on the fabric of society. The state, limited to the collection of export taxes and the maintenance of the army, grew at a snail's pace. Society as a whole remained in virtual stasis, locked into a productive system that necessarily concentrated wealth, fortified the backwardness and impoverishment of the mass of the population dedicated to subsistence agriculture, imposed a regime on the haciendas no less brutal and generally more exploitative than that of colonial days, and introduced few alterations in the mechanics of political control by which one section of the ruling class was exchanged for another.

While it conformed to this broad pattern, the development of the coffee economy and the liberal state in El Salvador manifested particular characteristics which in many respects made it an extreme case. As in Guatemala, liberalism only established its hegemony after a long period of conflict with the radical regime of Rafael Zaldívar (1876–85) coming to power a full 50 years after independence. However, this period was not one of conservative domination, as in Guatemala, but one of recurrent insurrection and civil war, in which neither party gained the upper hand and power was exchanged at regular intervals. The liberals were too weak to sustain their federalist project and the conservatives were obliged constantly to rely upon Carrera's assistance. The result was major disruption of the economy and society, and a power vacuum that proved to be highly dangerous to the landlord class as a whole. This was vividly exemplified by the major peasant revolt of 1833 in the region of Los Nonualcos, the bloodiest of a series of agrarian rebellions that occurred throughout the nineteenth century. Protesting at the illegal continuation of forced labour on the estates, increased taxation, press-gang conscription into the plethora of roving armies, and consistent pressure on their lands due to the inexorable demands of the slash and burn techniques of the indigo growers, both *indios* and *ladinos* (those of mixed race) took up arms. Led by Anastasio Aquino, a worker on an indigo estate in Santiago Nonualco, the ramshackle 'Army of Liberation' inflicted a number of defeats upon creole forces, and within ten days was apparently in a position to march unopposed on San Salvador. But, in common with many peasant jacqueries, the lack of a coherent political leadership combined with a preference to stay on familiar territory led to Aquino's forces holding back from an assault on the country's seat of power, allowing the government army time to rebuild its strength. Within six weeks of its outbreak the rebellion was decisively defeated. The revolt displayed few indications of purely ethnic antagonism and a far greater orientation towards a crude social justice, with expropriated lands and property being diligently recorded and handed over to the poor. Needless to say, the republican authorities paid scant attention to the possible merits of this insurrectionary counter-culture when they embarked upon a bloody repressive campaign. Aquino himself was captured after three months, summarily decapitated and his head put on public display in a cage. Celebrated as El Salvador's first rebel hero, his example hung over the creole elite like a cloud until it was surpassed both in scale and consequence 99 years later.

The system against which Aquino rebelled was one based firmly in the cultivation of the indigo plant, which had been the most important crop of the colonial era. Indigo continued to be the country's main export until the 1870s, but although it was less immediately damaged by the discovery of artificial dyes than was Guatemalan cochineal, its market was in marked decline from the early 1860s. Despite this, and the fact that coffee had been grown on a commercial scale since 1840, the indigo planters proved highly reluctant to shift to the new crop. The main reason for this was that, unlike indigo, which was a low-cost quick-yield plant, coffee took five years to produce fruit and required major investment. Moreover, coffee grows best above 1,500 feet, restricting its potential cultivable area in a region already densely populated and worked by the peasantry. Thus, it was the state rather than individual landlords that prompted the transformation of the Salvadorean economy. The pioneer liberal regime of General Gerardo Barrios, himself an indigo planter, took the first major initiative in 1859 with a reduction of production taxes, exemption of the coffee labour force from military service, and some discrete distribution of land to those who undertook to grow coffee on at least two-thirds of their holdings. These modest measures, combined with the progressive stagnation of the indigo trade, saw coffee rise from 1 per cent of exports in 1859 to 33 per cent in 1875.[2] Its potential was obvious but it was equally evident that it could not expand further without a qualitative alteration in rural organisation.

This was undertaken in one feverish five-year period by the Zaldivar administration, which launched a major offensive against the *ejidos* (municipal commons) and *comunidades* (communal lands) belonging to the indigenous population and poor *ladinos*. By transferring these lands from communal to private ownership the state succeeded in bringing into the market the most valuable assets for coffee production: land and labour. The laws of 1879, 1881 and 1882 which abolished collective property were versed in the unambiguous prose of liberalism:

The existence of lands under the ownership of the *comunidades* impedes agricultural development, obstructs the circulation of wealth, and weakens family bonds and the independence of the individual. Their existence is contrary to the economic and social principles that the Republic has accepted.[3]

Since the 1879 agricultural census showed some 742,000 acres as being held in *ejido* and at least 750,000 acres in *comunidades*, over a quarter of the cultivable land in the republic would have been formally affected by these decrees and there is little doubt that their social impact was considerable. We still lack a detailed and authoritative study of the process of expropriation, but it is evident that despite concerted peasant resistance there was a notable expansion of large, privately-owned landholdings and a concentration of ownership, particularly in the central zone. There was also general confusion and no lack of violence. The west of the country experienced a series of uprisings, the origins of which were only too apparent when it was reported that peasants had cut off the hands of judges 'as punishment for having redistributed land, dispossessing the old owners'.[4] There was no need to adopt the Guatemalan example of forced labour laws since the expropriations naturally provided a vast pool of unemployed labour, unique in Central America. Nevertheless, it rapidly proved necessary to pass vagrancy laws and set up a regular army (1886) precisely to control this mass of landless workers and counteract the wave of squatting, crop-burning and theft to which it made recourse in its plight.

By the last decade of the century, coffee exports were four times those of indigo; the new rural bourgeoisie was well on the way to consolidating itself. In 1880 the first bank was established although El Salvador only acquired its own currency three years later, having previously used those of its neighbours and the US. In 1882 the first railway was built (from Sonsonate to Acajutla), to be followed in 1888 by the telegraph. Although very small in size, the landed bourgeoisie was neither homogeneous in origin nor unified in its political attachments. Its nucleus was constituted by a number of traditional republican families that had transferred their interests from indigo to coffee: Alfaro, Dueñas, Palomo, Regalado, Orellana, Escalón, Prado and Meléndez. To this group was added a new generation of immigrant planters, arriving in the last quarter of the nineteenth century and providing a valuable infusion of capital and technique that was to obviate the need for direct foreign investment in cultivation until 1910 and keep it very low even after 1945. The new arrivals came to stay and moled their way into the established aristocracy with such skill that by

1920 half the country's richest families were of foreign extraction. They imposed their stamp so firmly on Salvadorean society that their names resonate as firmly in the 1980s as they did seventy years ago: Alvarez, Bloom, Canessa, Daglio, D'Aubuissón, De Sola, Deininger, Duke, Freund, Goldtree-Liebes, Gotuzzo, Hill, Sol Millet and Wright.

It was not until the first years of the century that the internal balance of the oligarchy had reached a state where it was possible to apportion political power with a modicum of consistency. Between 1850 and 1900 there were 47 heads of state, only 5 of whom completed their legal term. The coup d'etat continued to be the principal means of changing administrations until well into the present century, with political power remaining highly vulnerable to the caprice of some prominent caudillo. A dispatch sent to Washington by the US ambassador in July 1906 recounts an incident typical of the time:

> On the 5th, General Regalado, Commander of the Salvadorean army, commenced one of his drunken orgies, ordered out a Hotchkiss gun, and fired two shells at the Presidential Palace, loudly proclaiming his government a den of thieves whom he desired to wipe out ... The morning of the 6th he left for the Guatemalan border where he had previously stationed 1,400 troops, and attacked a Guatemalan outpost. [President] Escalón did all in his power to get him to return to the Capital ...[5]

Such episodes continued to occur but with diminishing regularity as the military received a fifth of a national budget boosted by a threefold rise in coffee revenue between 1901 and 1914.[6] This expansion, which also had the effect of increasing state employment to the highest in Central America, enabled a faction of the oligarchy to assume direct and unchallenged political control for the only time in its 100-year sway. For a period of nearly 20 years the presidency was the exclusive domain of the Meléndez–Quinoñez clan, the members of which elected and appointed each other in positively Costa Rican style and with no regard whatsoever to the careful and detailed stipulations of the adult male suffrage statute of 1885:

Carlos Meléndez	9/2/1913 – 28/8/1914
Alfonso Quinoñez (brother-in-law of Carlos Meléndez)	28/9/1914 – 28/2/1915
Carlos Meléndez	1/3/1915 — 21/12/1918

Alfonso Quinoñez	21/12/1918 — 28/2/1919
Jorge Meléndez (brother of Carlos)	1/3/1919 – 28/2/1923
Alfonso Quinoñez	1/3/1923 – 28/2/1927
Pio Romero Bosque (imposed by the family)	1/3/1927 – 28/2/1931

The arrogance of these smooth exchanges of power between siblings was no mere aberration but a faithful representation of the extra-ordinary power built up by the families of the oligarchy in the first three decades of the century. Of a population of under 1.5 million, only 5 per cent of which was considered 'white' and 80 per cent of which lived in the countryside, the 'fourteen families' marked themselves out by controlling 75 per cent of a coffee crop that rose in value from $3.3 million in 1901 to $22.7 million in 1924. Between 1918 and 1928 alone the area under coffee rose by 50 per cent. As the San Salvador daily *La Patria* pointed out in September 1929, 'where formerly there was yuca, tobacco, bananas and many other crops, today one sees only coffee, coffee, coffee'.[7]

This natural tendency to maximise production in times of high prices exerted considerable pressure on the subsistence economy and those sectors of the rural bourgeoisie farming sugar and henequen (only 17 of the 65 leading families), but it also revealed the extent to which the Salvadorean economy depended on a single crop, the failure of which promised the complete collapse of the state and social control. The manner in which the oligarchy accumulated its fabulous wealth was totally reliant upon the constant expansion of the world economy and strict containment of domestic class conflict. By the end of the 1920s neither of these conditions existed and El Salvador was plunging into a social and political crisis that was to mark a major watershed in its history and sow the seeds of the revolutionary movement that arose in the 1970s.

2
THE CRISIS OF THE 1930s

We'd like this race of the plague to be exterminated ... It is necessary for the government to use a strong hand. They did it right in North America ... by shooting them in the first place before they could impede the progress of the nation.

A *ladino* from Juayúa, spring 1932[1]

Bolshevism? It's drifting in. The working people hold meetings on Sundays and get very excited. They say, 'we dig the holes for the trees, we clean the weeds, we prune the trees, we pick the coffee. Who earns the money then?' ... Yes, there will be trouble one of these days.

Hacendado James Hill, 1925[2]

Soldiers: break the barracks discipline imposed on you by the bourgeoisie through their representatives, the officers! Assert the right to elect your own chiefs, to name common soldiers from the ranks! Place yourselves at the orders of the Executive Committee of the Communist Party which at the impending hour of triumph will distribute the lands and *fincas* of the rich among you and your brothers of the country! Workers of the World Arise!

Communist Party handbill, January 1932[3]

The impact upon Central America of the crash of 1929 and the years of acute depression that followed should be seen against the background not only of the consolidation of the agro-exporting oligarchies but also the rise to economic and political domination of the region by the US. Of all the countries in the Caribbean and Central America, El Salvador was perhaps the least directly affected by this, but it nevertheless registered many of the consequences of the new imperialist mandate.

Although the US had historically claimed Latin America to be its legitimate sphere of interest from the days of the Monroe Doctrine

15

(1823), it had only made slight advances in displacing European influence throughout the nineteenth century. The Clayton–Bulwer treaty of 1850 had established the capacity of the US to negotiate with the British in so far as it provided for joint control of any isthmian route and declared that neither nation would exercise dominion over any part of Central America, but this accord remained a dead letter. The British continued to hold on to their colony of British Honduras (Belize) and although by the end of the century this had lost its importance as a trading centre, they still controlled most of the region's foreign commerce and made periodic incursions to adjust political affairs, particularly on the Atlantic coast. Survivals of this presence may still be found on the map: Bluefields, Bragman's Bluff (now Puerto Cabezas, Nicaragua), Greytown (now San Juan del Norte, Nicaragua). However, the strongest legacy lies in the English-speaking population of the Moskito Coast in Nicaragua, so culturally distinct from the hispanic inhabitants of the interior that they have come to pose an acute problem for the Revolution. Thus, the British remained in the vanguard of the European invasion for much of the period, but by the first years of the century they faced a powerful challenge from Germany, which by 1913 controlled 21 per cent of the region's commerce against 17.6 per cent held by British entrepreneurs.

The First World War changed this pattern completely: US monopoly capital, undergoing massive expansion from the last decades of the nineteenth century, rapidly displaced the hegemony of the war-torn European powers. In 1913 US investment in Central America stood at $30 million against British interests of $188 million; by 1930 the US figure had risen to over $227 million, while British investments had dropped to $131 million.[4] This growth was consistent with US assumption of control over foreign investment in Latin America as a whole, its share rising from 17 per cent in 1914 to 40 per cent in 1929.[5] In El Salvador US investment rose tenfold between 1913 and 1930 while British investment fell by 15 per cent, to less than a third of North American holdings.[6] US economic interests were highly important but they have always been subordinate in the Caribbean and Central American region to strategic and military requirements. This was clear from early on and has seldom been deemed worthy of only discreet diplomatic handling; direct financial and military intervention were from the start of the US mandate the methods used to hold the boisterous local states in check. The most outstanding cases are, of course, the annexation of Puerto Rico and the occupation of Cuba following the military expulsion of the Spanish (1898), and the heavy-handed support for the revolution that split Panama from Colombia (1903) and provided the site for a trans-isthmian canal so crucial to the US, which had hitherto been considering constructing such a canal through the Nicaraguan lake system. In these cases the permanent stationing of US troops or direct US administration was to remain a major political issue, partially resolved in the case of Panama by the 1977 canal treaty but still outstanding in Puerto Rico and, with the retention of the Guantánamo military base, in Cuba.

The untempered imperialist ethos of Theodore Roosevelt was in later years refined somewhat in what was to enter popular parlance as 'dollar diplomacy', by which control depended heavily upon direct administration of the client states' financial affairs.[7] On numerous occasions the appearance of warships or the threat of landing troops served as an adequate complement to the instructions of bankers and customs officials in shunting recalcitrant puppets back into line, but often these methods did not suffice and the first decades of the century saw a series of interventions and occupations by the marines:

Cuba 1898–1902; 1906–9
Dominican Republic 1912; 1916–24
Haiti 1915–34
Mexico 1915
Nicaragua 1912–25; 1926–33
Panama 1903; 1908

It is worth quoting at some length from a memorandum produced by an Under-secretary of State in 1927 to give an insight into the nature of US policy towards Central America in these years and to demonstrate that, despite changes of form, its real substance has altered little since then:

The Central American area down to and including the Isthmus of Panama constitutes a legitimate sphere of influence for the United States, if we are to have due regard for our own safety and protection . . . Our ministers accredited to the five little republics . . . have been advisers whose advice has been accepted virtually as law . . . we do control the destinies of Central America and we do so for the simple reason that the national interest dictates such a course . . . There is no room for any outside influence other than ours in this region. We could not tolerate such a thing without incurring grave risks. At this moment a deliberate attempt to undermine our position and set aside our special relationship in Central America is being made. The action of Mexico in the Nicaraguan crisis is a direct challenge to the United States . . . Until now Central America has always understood that governments which we recognize and support stay in power, while those which we do not recognize and support fall. Nicaragua has become a test case. It is difficult to see how we can afford to be defeated.[8]

The very great importance of Nicaragua in the campaign to halt the disintegration of the oligarchic mandate in the face of deep-seated social and political crisis is signalled by the fact that the two names thrown up by the six-year struggle have become established as incarnations of the Central American traditions of national liberation and atrophied dictatorship: Sandino and Somoza. The eventual defeat of Sandino's celebrated but always isolated guerrilla struggle to eject the marines from the country and establish an authentic liberal democracy was achieved by the infusion of unprecedented quantities of aid, equipment and troops, the adoption of extensive counter-insurgency tactics and an exhaustive programme of training a domestic constabulary force in the National Guard, whose members acted first as the sepoys and then as the replacements of the US Marine Corps.[9] However, the eradication of the national liberation movement was only fully consolidated with the rise to power of the Guard's commander, Somoza, whose facility with the English language and compliance with the dictates of Washington ensured both his rapid promotion and a subsequent tolerance when he used his military monopoly to turn Nicaragua into little less than a family fiefdom. Three years after Sandino's death in 1934, Somoza strolled through an 'election', winning 107, 201 votes against 108. His marriage into the wealthy Sacasa family bestowed upon him the social standing to complement control of the Guard but hardly gave legitimacy to such measures as the personal tribute of 1½ cents on each pound of exported beef or 5 per cent of public salaries. By these means power remained in the family for 42 years; the US had created a veritable dynasty, the nature of which was to impel its downfall and create a critical fissure in US control of the region. The degree to which Washington perceived the possible ramifications of its actions may be judged from the fact that in 1932 the ambassador to Managua said of Somoza, 'no-one will labour as intelligently or as consciously to maintain the non-partisan character of the *Guardia*'.[10]

Yet, despite the fact that Somoza would make recourse to the support of fascist squads in the late 1930s, continually antagonise neighbouring states, and threaten to precipitate popular revolt with his excesses in the mid-1940s, he provided the US with its most ardent and dependable ally in the region until the Guatemalan counter-revolution of 1954. Nowhere else in Central America was the crisis of the 1930s resolved in such a lasting manner. In Costa Rica, ever the exception, it was met by a number of reforms and a realignment of political power away from the traditional oligarchy, but in Honduras and Guatemala with long dictatorships until the mid-1940s.[11] In Honduras, the regime of Tiburcio Carías Andino (1932–48) made no effort to supply itself with a veneer of legitimacy by calling elections and, supported by a pact between the major banana enterprises, suppressed a string of badly-organised liberal rebellions with ease. Yet, the Carías regime was always less severe than the monolithic Guatemalan dictatorship of Jorge Ubico (1932–44), who within a year of his election embarked upon a comprehensive repression of the left, eradicating all vestiges of opposition for a decade. Ubico himself proclaimed, 'I have no friends, only domesticated enemies', and the septuagenarian motorcycle enthusiast of English extraction kept Guatemala 'as orderly as an empty billiard table' for thirteen years with a steady flow of executions, exiles and long prison sentences.[12] Throughout the 1930s Ubico had only one peer in Central America: the Salvadorean General Maximiliano Hernández Martínez, who came to power late in 1931, consolidated himself with the suppression of the 1932 rebellion, and established a dictatorship that was to outlive him by many years.

The rising of 1932 is perhaps the single most important event in Salvadorean history; it is indelibly etched into the nation's collective memory both as a momentous occurrence in itself and as the matrix through which all succeeding developments have been understood. 1932 is a black myth, for the right as a hideous example of communist revolution, for the left as a heroic failure drowned in blood. For both sides of El Salvador's polarised society the uprising encapsulates the being of their enemy and, as such, it is impossible to deny its centrality to the present civil war.

By 1930 important fissures had appeared in the oligarchy's political control of the country. Although President Pio Romero Bosque (1927–31) had been placed in power by the Meléndez–Quiñoñez clan, he deviated from his predecessors in permitting a guarded liberalisation of the political structure, a process that was to terminate in November 1930 with what was arguably the sole clean, and therefore popular, election in the country's history. By the standards of the western democracies this election was highly dubious in terms of its democratic credentials, but for Central America it was remarkable in so far as Pio Romero desisted from nominating a successor, throwing the oligarchy into confusion as six candidates, all bar one of distinctly rightist hue, entered the lists. This confusion was further deepened when the poll was won with surprising ease by the liberal candidate Arturo Araujo, a dissident landowner from Suchitoto. Araujo had trained as a lawyer and engineer in Liverpool and Zurich, was deeply impressed by his contacts with the British Labour Party, and strongly attached to the ideas of the local *vitalismo* movement. *Vitalismo,* devised and earnestly propounded by the writer Alberto Masferrer, who for a while served in Araujo's cabinet, held that social justice could only be attained by establishing and meeting minimum standards in nutrition, housing, hygiene and education within an almost algebraic organisation of labour and leisure. This hodge-podge of nineteenth-century positivism and that rarified idealism so persistently nurtured by the rigid Thomist curriculum of Latin American universities was utterly impracticable in the El Salvador of 1931, and is popularity was strictly limited to a closed group of professionals and maverick landlords. None the less, it indicated a drift in those circles towards a timorous and mutant reformism as a result of the shifting conditions of economic and political life in the 1920s, marked by a notable upturn in worker and student opposition to the entrenched oligarchy.

As early as 1917 President Quiñoñez had perceived the need to co-opt certain sectors of the workforce as well as relying on the contingents of the National Guard posted on each major estate and paid directly by the *hacendados* to enforce order and discipline. Dipping adventurously into the distant but vibrant motifs thrown up by the burgeoning European communist movement, Quiñoñez created the *Liga Roja*, which espoused some vague egalitarian sentiments but in practice acted as a network of vigilante groups, armed and paid by the regime to fix votes, disperse demonstrations and report on subversive developments in the artisanal workshops and rural plantations. By the early 1920s this discontent was growing apace. In 1922 the *Liga Roja* and the National Guard killed a large number of people, the majority of them women market sellers, who were protesting against the effects on prices of changes in the exchange rate of the *colón.* This massacre increased the tempo of unrest and accelerated the formation of the trade union movement. The basis for this was still limited, with manufacturing production representing only 15 per cent of GDP and the urban working class confined to groups of railway workers, printers, cobblers, bakery workers and carpenters. The printers had organised themselves as early as 1912 and the railway workers in 1915, but by 1917 there were only 40 small and unco-ordinated workers' groups. Nevertheless, in 1918 the *Confederación de Obreros de El Salvador* (COES) came into tenuous existence and by 1924 had attained sufficient momentum to become, in its new form as the *Federación Regional de Trabajadores de El Salvador* (FRTS), an important member of the new regional *Confederación Obrera Centroamericana*, providing a framework for the growing radicalism of isolated knots of workers struggling to obtain the eight-hour day, minimum wage agreements and some form of political voice. Conscious of these developments, Pio Romero, who was an adept of the 'scientific organisation of labour', attempted to head off mobilisation by decreeing in 1928 and 1929 limits to the number of hours to be worked and provisions for accident compensation for certain groups of workers. However, these measures were not applied to the rural sector, had little effect in the towns, and did nothing to appease those scattered individuals who were rapidly moving towards an understanding of the conditions of the country's masses in terms of its political structure and were looking for direction towards communism.

The veteran communist Miguel Mármol describes in his memoirs, which were written up by Roque Dalton and remain one of the ignored classics of the Latin American communist movement, how the cobblers were particularly strongly influenced by the new radical currents affecting the region and how growing numbers of urban workers were being drawn into heated ideological debates over anarcho-syndicalism and communism or Leninism. According to Mármol, the 1920s were a time when the artisans of San Salvador were selling 'bolshevik shoes', 'bolshevik sweets' and even 'bolshevik bread'.[13] The FRTS headquarters received propaganda from as far afield as Argentina, France, Italy, the US and Holland as well as Mexico, much of it coming from communist parties. Pamphlets by Lossovsky, Bukharin and Lenin were made the subjects of evening classes, leading to the establishment of a local branch of the Guatemalan-based Anti-Imperialist League in 1927. An attempt to set up a Communist Party was made in 1925 but remained still-born, and it was not until the arrival in 1929 of the Mexican communist Jorge Fernando Anaya, who was fluent in Nahuatl and had been responsible for the formation of the Aztec Farmers' Union in his home country, that the party – the *Partido*

Comunista de El Salvador (PCS) – was brought into stable existence. It was very small, lacked programmatic and organisational consistency to the extent that the Third International conceded it only observer status, and remained highly dependent upon the experience and support of the Guatemalans and the Caribbean area office of the International, situated for what one can only assume to be extra-Caribbean reasons in New York. Despite all this, the PCS grew very quickly and within 18 months of its formation had come to the forefront of national political struggle.

The backdrop to these developments was the virtual collapse of the economy following the crash of 1929. The price of coffee, which accounted for 85 per cent of exports, fell 45 per cent in six months and was eventually to drop by 57 per cent. Between 1930 and 1932 export revenue from the commodity dropped from 34 million *colones* to ¢13 million; in 1931 national income was half that of 1928.[14] Credit folded, the *colón* collapsed, gold exports were prohibited, vast tracts of land were left unplanted and many coffee bushes left to rot. The daily wages of plantation workers fell from 30 to 15 *centavos*, while nearly a third of peasant tenants were thrown off their lands for indebtedness or simple lack of work. The state itself lost 30 per cent of its revenues and began to default on its payments, with the wages of the civil service and army months in arrears.

In April 1930 the FRTS, now securely controlled by the PCS, collected 50,000 signatures for a petition demanding a 'workers' law' guaranteeing existing contracts and a minimum wage. The traditional May Day march in San Salvador attracted 80,000 supporters when the city's population numbered only 90,000. It was followed by a succession of demonstrations to demand unemployment centres, a campaign of which the daily *La Patria* remarked, 'The shoemakers, railway workers, store employees, managers of the *fincas*, small landowners, everyone, in short, except the aristocracy of the capital, is in the streets.'[15] Pio Romero lost no time in decreeing the prohibition of all demonstrations and banned the printing and circulation of left-wing propaganda. All pretence to liberalism was dropped. In September a 'white terror' reigned in Sonsonate, where more than 600 peasants were arrested by the National Guard which, since its establishment in 1911, had been transformed from a relatively popular police force composed largely of artisans into the principal tool of repression for the state and the landlords. Between November 1930 and February 1931 around 1,200 activists were jailed, and while many of these were certainly members of the PCS (including many of its leading militants, such as Juan Pablo Wainwright, Miguel Mármol, Modesto Ramírez and Agustín Farabundo Marti), a great many more were not. The regime, however, had immersed itself so fully in an anti-communist crusade that such fine distinctions were limited to the work of the hyperactive secret police. By November 1930, *La Patria*, whose leftist credentials may be judged from the fact that it considered Araujo's refined *vitalista* friends to be 'dangerous . . . crackpots', was complaining that,

> 'Communist' is today a facile expression that is used to condemn any act that is approved by persons who fear the laws of God and man. It is customary in the Republic to call communist any demand for justice. If Santa Tecla agitates for more humane electricity rates, the extortioners are ready to call that demand 'communist' . . . If the unemployed ask for work and better wages they are immediately labelled 'communists'.[16]

It was under these circumstances that the luckless Araujo took power in the spring of 1931. His government was to last nine months, losing the services of the prophet of *vitalismo*, Masferrer, within a matter of weeks, when it became quite apparent that the regime was bankrupt, corrupt and unable to exercise any independent authority. When Araujo rejected an offer of ¢500,000 from a group of *cafetaleros* to devalue the *colón* to $2.50 the oligarchy moved to boycott a regime that it had anyway deeply distrusted. However, Araujo met equally entrenched opposition from the workers and peasants. There were major peasant strikes in April and May, and in July the repression of a student demonstration led to the establishment of martial law. This brought the army to the fore and signalled the end for the bemused liberal president. The officer corps was discontented after three months without pay and deeply worried by the growing unreliability of its conscripts which it attributed directly to the actions of the 'Labour Party', despite having studiously avoided backing any candidate in the elections.[17] In November the San Salvador garrison declared itself on strike in order to obtain its back-pay. Ten days later, on 2 December, a coup which had been planned since September was staged by a group of colonels in the city. Only a third of the military sided with the government and after three days of fighting, in which no civilians participated, a military junta took power.

Within two days this junta had named as president Araujo's Minister of War, General Maximiliano Hernández Martínez. Martínez had dropped out of the 1930 electoral race after having made a number of populist speeches which had served to strengthen his reputation as something of an eccentric. Like many officers, he was of humble background, but differed substantially from his peers in his adhesion to the causes of temperance, vegetarianism and theosophy. Dubbed by the aristocracy as *el indio chiflado* ('the crazy indian') and by the populace as *el brujo* ('the wizard'), Martinez espoused views on the transmigration of human souls and reincarnation that led him to place more importance on the life of an ant than that of a human being: 'let my enemies reincarnate when I am dead'. The new president of El Salvador made a practice of staring directly at the sun daily and had installed on the roof of the palace large vats of coloured water that after a period of 'ageing' in the sun he sold off as potions capable of curing almost every ailment from toothache to heart disease. Preferring to be called *el Maestro* to *Presidente*, Martinez presided over a truly bizarre palace regime and conformed perfectly to the lineage of local dictators for whom absolute power allowed full reign to personal whim. Yet none of these peculiarities explain his actions in January 1932 or afterwards; those responded faithfully to the requirements of a social class confronted with a major challenge to its domination.

The December coup accelerated popular mobilisation, which was concentrated largely in the centre and west of the country, from Santa Ana to Ilopango. The PCS had for over a year been agitating in these zones, backed by the radicalism of the rural teachers and gaining acceptance with the peasantry with its 'popular universities', held clandestinely at night and of particular importance in Ahuachapán, Izalco and Juayúa. However, it still lacked the mass base and popularity to do this under its own name, and the bulk of the work was undertaken in the name of the SRI (*Socorro Rojo Internacional*, International Red Aid), a broad front organisation, whose purpose was, according to its propaganda,

> to defend all workers who are persecuted by imperialism, capitalist governments, and all other agencies of oppression . . . proportioning its legal aid and material means to those workers and their families by means of agitation and publicity and organised demonstrations . . . The aid of SRI is also extended to the families of the fallen and persecuted in the revolutionary struggle . . . All persons, whatever their politics, race or nationality, who fill in the card of admission and are in accord with the ends of the organisation.[18]

The SRI received little money from abroad, and its success in building up an active periphery was largely due to the work of Agustin Farabundo Marti, who was the acknowledged leader of the PCS and the most celebrated radical figure in the country. Marti *(el Negro)* was one of a band of necessarily cosmopolitan agitators who traversed Central America in the 1920s and 1930s. This career was forced on him when he was exiled in the middle of his university studies (which included challenging his philosophy professor to a duel after a dispute over the nature of cognition) after a demonstration in 1920. Joining the 'Red Battalions' in Mexico, Marti later worked in Honduras and Guatemala as a baker, bricklayer and farm labourer. He played a leading role in founding the ill-fated *Partido Socialista Centroamericano* in 1925, and in his many short-lived returns to El Salvador helped organise the left-wing discussion groups that were to form the still-existing AGEUS *(Asociación General de Estudiantes Universitarios Salvadoreños)* and provide the socialist backbone of the FRTS. In 1928, having gained release from one of a number of spells in jail with a hunger strike that acutely embarrassed the Pio Romero regime, Marti worked for the SRI and the Anti-Imperialist League in New York, taking a tortuous route that covered the majority of the states of Central America to join Sandino, for whom he acted as personal secretary. This liaison is given great prominence by the contemporary forces of national liberation in Nicaragua and El Salvador, but in fact it ended badly when Marti attempted to convert Sandino to communism. In July 1929 Marti returned to Mexico, later explaining his break with Sandino to the Uruguayan poetess Blanca Luz Blum in unequivocal terms:

> My break with Sandino was not, as is sometimes said, for divergence of moral principles or opposing norms of conduct . . . He would not embrace my communist programme. His banner was only that of national independence . . . not social revolution. I solemnly declare that General Sandino is the greatest patriot in the world.[19]

It is thought that Marti perhaps suffered a nervous collapse after this episode, for his movements are hard to trace for a while and he complained of exhaustion. Whatever the case, by early 1931 he was back in El Salvador, twice jailed (again being released only after a hunger strike and popular agitation) and taking a leading role in directing the campaign of the PCS, despite the fact that he differed from many of his comrades in his admiration for the now-disgraced Trotsky, whose image adorned the red star Martí always wore on his lapel.

The role played by the PCS in the insurrection of 22 January 1932 was, in the event, neither decided nor directed by Martí. Indeed, while, after long and sometimes acrimonious debate, the party's executive committee as a whole decided on the plans, it did not direct the actual uprising. It would be a misnomer to call the 1932 rebellion a 'communist' uprising since the PCS had scarcely any control over it once it had begun, failing to give it direction and a communist programme.[20] In fact, in most areas it was snuffed out so quickly it did not acquire any political physiognomy beyond a democratic radicalism which is latent in all such mobilisations, including those that do come under the direction of a communist leadership.

The decision of the PCS to participate in the municipal and congressional elections called by the new Martínez government for the first two weeks of January 1932 was itself hotly contested within the party, the youth wing led by Miguel Mármol opposing it on the grounds that there was little time for preparation, that the government would without doubt indulge in extensive rigging of the polls, and that the level of mobilisation and violence in the countryside had gone beyond the point where an electoral campaign could serve any useful purpose.[21] This opposition was overcome when Martí backed the party's intellectuals, arguing that the election would deepen contact with the masses and that the military were not yet sufficiently blackened in the popular eye for there to be whole-hearted support for an insurrection. However, it was agreed to press ahead with the organisation of a general strike on the coffee estates.

The experience of the first poll, 3 to 5 January, clearly rendered the electoralist strategy inoperative. The National Guard imposed tight control on the vote, the press was closely censored, isolated *tomas* (land occupations) were repressed with scores of deaths, the early victories of the PCS in San Salvador either openly annulled or reversed by fraud, the next round of elections due in a week's time cancelled, and a state of siege imposed. In some areas, such as Ahuachapán, the peasantry was so close to open rebellion that the party was forced to send out special commissions to persuade them not to make piecemeal attacks on barracks which would have precipitated an immediate military counter-offensive. On the night of 7 January it was agreed unanimously to prepare for an armed insurrection on 16 January, the short time being necessary to maintain surprise. However, the following week the date was put forward, first to 19 January and then to 22 January, with disastrous results. Martí had himself supported these postponements to enable further organisation of the rebellion amongst the army regiments in the city. But on 18 January the regime discovered the plans for this, shot many of its ringleaders and jailed Martí along with two students, Luna and Zapata, who were assisting him. Faced with the loss of their leader, the discovery of their plans, and the impossibility of raising critical support from the troops, the leadership of the PCS argued once again over whether to continue; the insurrectionary tendency, led by Mármol, winning out on the argument that to draw back would spell certain disaster while to proceed still offered the possibility of victory.[22]

Thus, the rebellion broke out with the PCS leadership lacking its principal figurehead and having made only the most rudimentary military preparations. Moreover, the regime was forwarned: within the first hours of the rising the remaining leaders of the party were captured, and in San Salvador itself the revolt never got off the ground. Its main foci were in the western departments of Sonsonate and Ahuachapán, centring on the towns of Izalco, Juayúa and Nahuizalco. In these *pueblos* the leadership of the insurrection was taken not by the party but by the local indigenous *caciques* (strongmen) who were able to muster support through family ties and their semi-official positions of authority. In Izalco, the *cacique* José Feliciano Ama, who was himself far from poor and had actually opposed Araujo's candidature in the elections, led the easy capture of the town on the night of 22 January. A number of *hacendados*, police officers and local government employees (as elsewhere, these were usually telegraphists) were killed in the attack, but the number of deaths was no more than half a dozen and the principle activity of the *campesinos* was to loot the stores and make merry. To the north west, the town of Juayúa was taken with similar ease, there being no National Guard and only two policemen stationed there to face the rebels who were well-armed with weapons left by Araujo in his retreat to Guatemala following the December coup. According to documents captured after the revolt some 484 people made donations to the rebel forces, suggesting that support was forthcoming from more than ordinary *peons*. Again, the insurrection followed the pattern of rough popular justice: the *alcaldes* (mayors), leading *hacendados*, and government officers were the main victims although much energy was spent in apprehending the widely-despised farm foremen *(mayordomos)*. Wealthy women were obliged to grind flour whilst fireworks were set off and the town's band made to play for the celebrations as the peasants prepared to march on Nahuizalco on the road to Sonsonate.

To the west, in Ahuachapán, the rising was strongly resisted by the garrison, attacked frontally three times on the night of the 23rd after much blowing of horns and beating of sticks. Despite the fact that many of the troops and some of the officers were sympathetic to the PCS, the army, stiffened by a rapidly-organised civilian militia, held out. At nearby Tacuba the staunchly communist Cuenca family took the leadership of the rising, but in other centres, where the PCS rather than the *caciques* was to the fore, things did not go well. Around San Salvador there were movements in Colón, Santa Tecla, Soyapango and Ilopango (the easternmost point of the insurrection), none of which went beyond the execution of a handful of especially hated landlords and the precipitate declaration of the *República Soviética*. By the night of the 23rd the only secure base held by the rebels was Juayúa. Earlier in the day 70 had died in an unsuccessful battle to take Sonsonate, where the rebels had driven the National Guard back to the barracks but, possessing only a few antiquated rifles and machetes against machine-guns, were soon forced into a chaotic retreat.[23]

By the 24th the government forces were moving to the counter-offensive. Martinez appointed General José Tomás Calderón to head the repression and encouraged the formation of civilian vigilante groups – *Guardias Cívicas* – which took the form of 'brotherhoods', held fascist-like ceremonies and soon proved to be the most active and unrestrained forces of the counter-revolution. In the towns, voting lists and informants were used to identify PCS militants and sympathisers, who were hunted down and shot in batches. It was in this campaign that Miguel Mármol miraculously survived four volleys from a firing squad; almost without exception his comrades perished. Nothing was left of the party's organisation, the entire left was smashed and the executions continued for weeks.

However, it was in the countryside that the repression took on massive proportions, becoming a veritable pogrom within a matter of hours. In Izalco the *cacique* Ama was handed over to the local populace who lynched and then tore him to pieces. All bar two of the Cuenca family in Tacuba were executed. In Juayúa houses were fired and peasants gunned down as they fled. Later all families were ordered to present themselves for the allocation of safe-conducts and then shot. According to one eye-witness, 985 people were killed in Nahuizalco on one day (13 February) alone. All *indios con machetes* were deemed guilty of subversion and, when apprehended, executed without question or any pretence at judicial process; many women and children died alongside them after digging their own graves. There is, of course, no sure way of calculating the precise extent of this slaughter. The lowest estimate given by a serious source is 10,000 dead, some claim 40,000 were exterminated, but the figure most commonly cited is 30,000.[24] In a sense precision is meaningless; an extraordinarily large number of people were killed in what can only be described as a wave of terror. The frightened Salvadorean oligarchy and its military allies were quite palpably prepared to resort to genocidal remedies to defend their position. Their most articulate spokesman was the military chief of Sonsonate, Colonel Marcelino Galdamez, who declared,

> Communism is a tree shaken by the wind. The moving tree causes the seeds to fall; the same wind carries the seed to other places. The seed falls on fertile soil. To be done with communism it is necessary to make the ground sterile.[25]

Martínez contented himself with a dour recapitulation of his mandate: 'The state has made laws that all citizens must obey. You ignored them and the government was obliged to punish you to avoid great damage to the entire country.'[26] The right-wing paper *Prensa Gráfica* went significantly beyond this in its call for,

> honourable labouring men of every centre of El Salvador to organise themselves . . .into militias patterned on the Italian fascio, the Spanish armed corps *(somatenes)* or the patriotic youth groups of Action Française, for the defence at any time of our families and homes against the deadly and ferocious attacks of the gangs of villains that fill the ranks of the Red Army that hopes to drown in blood the free and generous nation left to us by our ancestors.[27]

The victims of this 'Red Army' can be enumerated with some accuracy since they were given wide publicity. A rigorous analysis of the sources by Thomas Anderson yields a maximum possible figure of 30 civilians and 50 military personnel.[28]

On 29 January Martí and his young aides Luna and Zapata were tried. The communist leader declared at the military hearing that it was a trial of one class by another and that the students were middle-class idealists who should be spared; it was to no avail. That night Martí recounted to the others stories of his campaigns with Sandino and embarked upon a heated argument with the priest at the last confession. Luna and Zapata received the last sacraments from Padre Ramírez, who 'urged them to die "in communion with God". On hearing this word, Marti is said to have raised his eyes to heaven with a smile of bitter irony and repeated the beautiful, and for him meaningless, word "God" . . .'[29]

The Salvadorean armed forces master-minded and effected the counter-revolution by themselves although they had confident expectations of outside support should things go wrong. On 21 January, *El Diario de El Salvador* had firmly stated,

> Should the communists take control of the nation, the US will intervene in the management of our public affairs . . . if the government does not show its ability to subdue disorders intervention will certainly result . . . our country is within the sphere of influence of the most powerful nation on earth.[30]

Upon news of the uprising three US and two Canadian warships had been ordered into Salvadorean waters, a platoon of marines from the Canadian destroyer *Skeena* landing at the request of the British vice-consul on the afternoon of the 24th but hurriedly re-embarking after Martinez protested. The craft of the US 'Special Services Squadron' also had orders 'to be prepared to land troops', but since, as Martínez informed them, 'calm was restored' and the US did not anyway recognise his government because it had come to power through a coup, they were summarily withdrawn.[31]

On the other side, the PCS had not even received an answer from the Caribbean Bureau of the International to its request for advice over the insurrection. However, we may guess at its probable content had it been sent on the basis of an article written by O. Rodriguez in *Communist*, the journal of the US Communist Party, in March 1932. Rodríguez praised 'the heroic struggles of the workers and peasants of El Salvador, under the leadership of the CP', identified the rising as 'a landmark in the development of the revolutionary upsurge in the Caribbean countries and in the whole of Latin America', but blamed the leadership of the PCS for its failure to prepare the masses, while noting that, 'one of the chief lessons of the Salvadorean uprising is the danger of putchist and "left" sectarian tendencies . . .'[32] It is interesting to note in this regard that the International had not yet moved from its 'ultra-left' phase of rejection of united fronts against fascism with non-communist forces to its mirror-opposite in the 'Popular Front', where alliances were made with bourgeois and petty bourgeois forces involving extensive concessions in programme. Nevertheless, the independence of the PCS and the 'oppositionist tendencies' held by Marti required a firm response. It was to be 40 years before the PCS again considered armed struggle. Henceforth party leaders would evoke the heroism of 1932 and stress the leading role of the PCS but desist from serious critical analysis.[33] After two years of frantic and confused activity the broken and disorientated party limped quietly into the full fold of Stalinism. Yet, to understand the failure of 1932 exclusively in terms of the party's lack of a mass membership, its incapacity to develop a clear and consistent line along with an organised system of cells full of disciplined cadre would be an error. Above all else, these absences reflected a greater weakness: an urban working class that was so tiny and young that it could not yet form the nucleus of a mass revolutionary movement. No amount of voluntarism, in which the PCS was manifestly not lacking, could overcome this structural impediment.

A close reading of the events of 1932 cannot discount the argument that by calling the January elections, Martinez actively sought to provoke an uprising to facilitate a categorical settling of accounts with the radicalised peasantry and artisanate. Whatever the case, the resolution of the oligarchy's short but severe crisis led to a discernable restructuring of political power within the dominant bloc. From now on the military as an institution would conduct political affairs through a series of dictatorships. This was the price the landed bourgeoisie paid. But if the exigencies of the revolt obliged it to make a partial withdrawal from government, this affected only the highest posts and the clientilist economy attached to them; the oligarchy surrendered not one inch of its economic and social power, nor was it required to. Methods changed but the system remained intact.

3
MILITARISM READJUSTED

[Under Colonel Osorio] El Salvador has a frank programme of true social progress and is already well along the road to making itself a small nation's example of democracy in action.

US Ambassador Biddle Duke, 1952[1]

[The election was] wholly farcical. Crowds of paid voters were openly hauled from one voting booth to another in government trucks . . . Foreign correspondents visiting the outlying voting stations were given ballots and told, amidst great jollity, to go ahead and vote. I kept mine for years as a souvenir.

Paul Kennedy of the *New York Times*, on the 1956 poll[2]

Martínez ruled for twelve years under the shadow of 1932. There were occasional coup scares each time he announced that he was re-standing for 'election' but no significant interruption of or threat to the government of his specially-created *Pro-Patria* party. Trade unions and all but the very tamest political organisations were outlawed; those that possessed any independence only managed an ephemeral clandestine existence and to little effect. University autonomy was violated when necessary, and repression remained all-encompassing. In response to the continuing economic crisis, Martínez was obliged to make a number of departures from liberal orthodoxy, declaring a moratorium on debts, imposing some tariffs to protect certain artisanal trades, devaluing the colón, and even legalising a small number of squats. In order to regularise much-sought credit, the *Banco Hipotecario* was set up in 1935, followed by the *Cajas de Crédito Rural* in 1943. These adjustments (especially the devaluation) were thoroughly acceptable to the landed bourgeoisie; they did nothing to alter the pattern of ownership or production, which remained stagnant throughout most of the *martinato*. There was no inflationary expansion of the state, no indulgence in populist experiments, even of the most authoritarian type, as in some Latin American states. There was no need for them; the ruling class had 'solved' its political problem by the most emphatic method on offer. Although it certainly generated a number of contradictions and conflicts within the military and the oligarchy, the Martínez dictatorship might well have lasted longer than it did had it not been for the impact of the Second World War, the economic and political effects of which destabilised all the Central American dictatorships instituted in the crisis of the 1930s.[3]

Consistent with his dependence upon Germany and Italy in training the military, his style of rule, and the still significant German presence in Central America, Martínez – who was an unashamed admirer of Hitler and Mussolini – declared in June 1940 that it was a 'national crime' to express sympathy for the Allies. When Italy declared war, 200 blackshirts held a triumphant procession through the streets of San Salvador. But it was impossible to maintain this stance, if only for economic reasons. In 1930 the US purchased 14.9 per cent of Salvadorean coffee exports; by 1943, the US held 96.4 per cent of the market. Trade routes to Europe were cut, and US control of the hemisphere was uncontestable; the era of US hegemony had indisputably arrived. Martínez was forced to 'change sides', and although this was to some extent sweetened by the expropriation of German-owned estates – carried out on a much larger scale in Guatemala and Costa Rica – it opened the country to a flood of propaganda propounding the merits of democracy and the ills of fascism. This had inevitable results, especially amongst the middle class, students and junior officers.

With another election due, discontent grew throughout the spring of 1944. On 2 April – Easter Sunday – junior officers allied to sectors of the professional middle class launched a coup, which was suppressed only after two days of heavy fighting throughout the country. In some districts the rebel officers had distributed arms to civilians, and there were many casualties. Having momentarily regained control, Martínez made the mistake of 'applying the law' and proceeding to the execution of the leading conspirators. But the conditions were not those of 1932; there was widespread outcry, with the urban workers, the middle sectors, the petty bourgeoisie and the students coming out on strike to protest against the executions and the dictatorship. In this they had the tacit support of many entrepreneurs and some landlords who perceived the need for some relaxation of the system before it imploded. On the advice of the US Ambassador, Martínez quickly handed over power to General Andrés Ignacio Menéndez and fled the country on 7 May: 'The curtain has fallen. I have played my last game of chess. I shall now devote my life to agriculture and spiritual activity in Theosophy.'[4] Retiring to Honduras, the ex-dictator set up as a modest *hacendado* and was soon afterwards hacked to death with a machete by his *mayordomo*.

Menéndez' careful avoidance of repression during his interregnum, the very great heterogeneity of the social forces supporting the strike movement, and the conspicuous lack of a radical leadership combined to limit the scope of the mobilisation. The removal of Martínez was seen as a popular triumph in itself, and no assault was made on the dictatorship's apparatus, which remained intact but somewhat subdued, as if mesmerised by the caution and lack of direction of a popular movement that was still manifestly recovering from years of absolutist rule. Menéndez astutely called new elections, in which popular support went overwhelmingly to the candidature of Dr Arturo Romero, whose *Partido Unión Demócrata* (PUD) forwarded a vague programme of reforms in populist style. Exploiting the relaxation of control, the trade unions reorganised themselves and expanded their memberships with remarkable speed under the aegis of the *Unión Nacional de Trabajadores* (UNT), which gave added impetus to Romero's campaign.

This 'democratic interlude' lasted less than five months, being abruptly brought to a halt by a coup on 21 October. The move was undertaken by Colonel Osmín Aguirre y Salinas, who had overthrown Araujo in 1931 and played a leading role in the 1932 repression. The coup received the support not only of interim President Menéndez himself but also the US embassy, the still-intact bureaucracy of Martínez and the majority of the oligarchy, for whom the *romerista* campaign had begun to look alarmingly like that of Araujo 13 years previously. The election went ahead as planned, but without Romero, who had been shipped off to Costa Rica. It was won by General Salvador Castaneda Castro, an old Martínez hand and head of the aptly-named, highly financed, but remarkably anonymous *Partido Agrario*. In December the supporters of Romero attempted to reverse the situation with an 800-man invasion from Guatemala, led by dissident officers and supported by many liberals, including the octagenarian Miguel Tomás Molina, who personified the tenuous Salvadorean liberal tradition in having been a member of the 1886

Constituent Assembly and the leading opponent to Quiñoñez in the 1922 elections. The invasion was planned to coincide with another rising of officers in the interior, but this failed to materialise and the rebels were forced to return to Guatemala having been beaten back at Ahuachapán. With this defeat the PUD collapsed and joined the overcrowded cemetery of redundant political parties. Popular mobilisation receded and Castaneda Castro was able to revive the *martinato* in an altogether colourless regime which, while it did not adopt the extremes of repression of its predecessor, faithfully reproduced it in every other way.

The state of siege continued for four years, but when the guileless Castaneda attempted to have himself re-elected in the autumn of 1948 he succeeded in provoking many of the changes sought by the dissident bourgeois forces that had supported the 1944 movement against Martinez. This was certainly no full *apertura* (opening) but rather a realignment of the forms of political control with a reduction in the reliance upon pure repression and an incorporation of democratic motifs within the the dictatorial framework. The 'revolution' of 14 December 1948 that removed Castaneda Castro on the pretext of his 'unconstitutional behaviour' was, therefore, a belated readjustment and modernisation of the *martinato*. It had to be imposed on the most entrenched sectors of the landlord class and the military high command, but it offered nothing new to the country's workers and peasants. The system established in December 1948 was, with some modifications, to last until 1979.

The principal architect of this system was Major Oscar Osorio, who emerged as the 'strongman' of the new military junta and suppressed with a mix of diligent manoeuvre and open threat the personal ambitions of his military colleagues and the overtly liberal aspirations of their original civilian allies. In 1949 Osorio established the *Partido Revolucionario de Unificación Democrática* (PRUD), the model for all succeeding official parties in its toleration of a tame opposition within tightly circumscribed limits. Under the constitution of 1950 the long-standing liberal principles around which oligarchic rule had been constructed were reformulated to allow for a modicum of state intervention in order to 'assure all the inhabitants of the country an existence worthy of a human being', to guarantee 'the social function' of property, and to regulate relations between labour and capital through limits on the working day, the right of association, collective contracts and a formal minimum wage. The constitution even provided for land reform, but this, like many of its stipulations, never saw the light of day; what mattered was that things were proclaimed, not that they were realised. All the major social items of the charter were restricted to the urban sphere; rural organisation was strictly outlawed and relations on the land were left unchanged. The oligarchy could be made to concede the importance of commerce and light manufacturing, in which it was beginning to make some investment, but its real power-base on the land was scrupulously respected. In order to fortify this project of encouraging the transfer of landed capital into import-substituting industry, Osorio introduced tax exemptions for manufacturing, repealed Martínez' mildly protectionist measures, and began to invite foreign capital to invest in industrial concerns.

These measures were presented with a good deal of demagogy as El Salvador's adoption of the social advances made by the Mexican and Guatemalan revolutions. The PRUD was able to consolidate its hold on power, attract the support of the bulk of the landed bourgeoisie, and settle down as the organ of traditional governmental clientilism and corruption. Its wafer-thin populist guise enabled a degree of co-optation of the urban masses, but without impeding repression of militant opposition as, for example, in 1952, when the left was attacked with a vehemence comparable to that of Martínez. The uneasiness of the junior officers was soaked up and the path laid for untroubled succession through the carefully nurtured veneer of democratic procedure, which was never allowed to prejudice the operation of the regime's ultimate safeguard, the *Ley de Defensa del Orden Democrático y Constitucional*, a statute that simply provided for the suppresion of all democratic guarantees.

The attitude of the US to these developments was one of unrelieved enthusiasm since they contrasted very favourably with the authentic reform movement underway in neighbouring Guatemala, which by 1953 – the height of the Cold War – was perceived as the greatest threat to hemispheric security, a threat that was to occasion an intervention on a par with Nicaragua in the 1920s and 1930s and the Bay of Pigs in Cuba in 1961. Osorio was to play a supporting part in the organisation of the CIA-backed counter-revolution despite having invoked the gains of its 'revolution' to build his own regime.

It is sometimes said that when Guatemala sneezes El Salvador catches a cold, but in 1944 the reverse had been true. The seven months of mobilisation and relative freedom in El Salvador helped to precipitate the overthrow of the Guatemalan dictator Ubico on 20

October, one day before the Salvadorean coup of Colonel Aguirre. Unlike the Salvadorean episode, that in Guatemala survived, gained momentum, and developed into a major reformist experiment. At its head were nationalist field officers, urban professionals and students, small business interests and an anti-Ubico faction of the landed bourgeoisie. This original alliance was not to last for long, but at no stage of the 'revolution' (1944–54) were property relations threatened, and neither did the organised working class come to political leadership. Indeed, for much of the period the reformist regime held back from any substantial measures. The first president, the university professor Juan José Arévalo, espoused what he called 'spiritual socialism', which 'does not aim at ingenious distribution of material goods . . . [but] to liberate men psychologically, to return to all the psychological and spiritual integrity that has been denied them by conservatism and liberalism'.[5] There was in Arévalo more than a touch of Masferrer's *vitalismo*.

Arévalo did grant universal suffrage (except to illiterate women – a substantial proportion of the population) and devoted a third of the national budget to welfare, introducing social security, abolishing the old vagrancy laws, and providing a labour code (1947) that protected basic union rights although it made no provisions for unionisation on *fincas* employing less than 500 workers, severely limiting its effect. On the other hand, Arévalo constantly refused to introduce an agrarian reform, stating that, 'in Guatemala there is no agrarian probem; rather, the peasants are psychologically and politically restrained from working the land. The government will create for them the need to work, but without harming any other class.'[6] It is difficult to see how anyone except the peasants could take exception to this kind of talk, but Arévalo still suffered 23 coup attempts against his regime. After the 1950 elections he was succeeded by a much more concerted figure in Colonel Jacobo Arbenz, one of the leaders of the 1944 coup and a man of open sympathies with the left. Coming very quickly under pressure from the domestic right and the US, Arbenz accelerated the pace of reform and, although he never brought its members into the cabinet, permitted the existence and occasionally sought the advice of the young and increasingly popular Communist Party, the *Partido Guatemalteco de Trabajadores* (PGT).

The turning point came with the Arbenz regime's agrarian reform law of June 1952. This measure provided for the expropriation of holdings of over 223 acres when they included large tracts of unused land. Within two years some 1,000 planatations, covering 2.7 million acres, had been affected by the law and approximately 100,000 peasants had received redistributed land. It was hardly surprising that Guatemala's largest landowner, the United Fruit Company (UFCO), which possessed over 550,000 acres and cultivated only 15 per cent of them, should be hit by this measure. But what troubled the company most was the Guatemalan government's offer of compensation, which was assessed in terms of the firm's previous absurdly low tax returns.

The Arbenz government was subjected to an extensive campaign of destabilisation centred on a remarkably well-organised propaganda campaign in the local and US press from the middle of 1950. After Arbenz came to power, the *New York Times* began to publish articles regularly with such titles as 'How Communism Won Control in Guatemala', while *Readers' Digest,* the *Chicago Tribune* and the *New York Herald Tribune* all rushed to the vociferous defence of UFCO, condemning 'Moscow Domination' in the country and warning of a 'Soviet takeover' of the entire region. The ingenious position of the State Department – and it is one that is still full of vitality today – was that Arbenz was treating the PGT, 'as an authentic domestic political party and not as part of the world-wide Soviet Communist conspiracy'.[7]

In March 1953, Adolf A. Berle, an unofficial liaison officer between the Eisenhower administration and various Central American regimes, produced a memorandum for the US government that established the terms of the final intervention and could well be mistaken for similar briefs prepared by the State Department with respect to El Salvador 30 years later:

> The United States cannot tolerate a Kremlin-controlled Communist government in this hemisphere. It has several possible alternatives:
>
> (1) American armed intervention – like that of 1915. This is here ruled out except as an extremely bad last resort, because of the immense complications which it would raise all over the hemisphere.
>
> (2) Organizing a counter-movement, capable of using force if necessary, based on a cooperative neighboring republic. In practice this would mean Nicaragua . . . The course of action I should recommend is slower, less dramatic, but I think more complete. This is to work out a Central American 'Political Defense' action, using the three states El Salvador, Nicaragua and Costa Rica as chief elements . . .[8]

In mid-1953 the Eisenhower government decided to overthrow

Arbenz. It handed over the direction of the operation to the Dulles brothers: John Foster, Secretary of State, and Allen Welsh, Director of the CIA, both of whom had important interests in UFCO. The Dulles, who had themselves led the anti-Arbenz lobby and were surrounded by hardline anti-communist republicans, set in motion a campaign which brought in the diplomatic service, the marines and the CIA, deepening the propaganda attacks and destabilising the government from within, primarily through the sabotage of strategic installations. Plans were drawn up with the aid of the neighbouring states and military training provided for ex-patriot rightists. By early 1954, the Guatemalan government had substantial evidence of the plots for its overthrow and had already withdrawn from the Organisation of American States (OAS) as a result of the involvement of several Central American governments in a failed conspiracy in 1953. In January 1954, the new US Ambassador to Guatemala, John Peurifoy, who had previously made Greece 'safe for democracy', warned with a singular lack of diplomacy that, 'Public opinion in the US might force us to take some measures to prevent Guatemala from falling into the lap of international communism. We cannot permit a Soviet Republic to be established between Texas and the Panama Canal.'[9]

In May, Washington found a pretext to bring hostilities into the open when a shipment of Czech arms reached Guatemala, which had been subject to an arms boycott from all US 'allies' since 1948. Plans for the invasion were brought forward, Dulles openly denounced Arbenz in public forums, and the CIA's 'Radio Liberty' stepped up its broadcasts into the country. On 18 June, a mercenary force of some 200 men under the command of Colonel Castillo Armas invaded from Honduras. This force rapidly became bogged down, and it is generally accepted that the invasion only succeeded thanks to aerial bombardments made by CIA planes flown by North Americans and nationalist Chinese. The US was able to use the fact that Castillo Armas' land-force was composed largely of Guatemalans to deflect Arbenz' protest to the UN Security Council, declaring that it was not a case of international aggression but of 'internal civil war'. Arbenz, who had the backing of the labour movement but was deserted by many officers, then resigned, but Peurifoy refused to accept his nominated successors and flew Castillo Armas into Guatemala City in his own plane on 3 July. Bereft of leadership, the popular resistance to the invasion crumbled and the new regime began to dismantle the reforms of 1944–54 in a repressive campaign that included the taking of over 9,000 political prisoners. Protests took place throughout Latin America but they did little to shake the first major post-war salvage operation of the US in the hemisphere. Late in July, *Time* published a horrendous little sextet from the pen of Betty Jane Peurifoy that captured all the triumphalism of the period:

> Sing a song of quetzals, pockets full of peace!
> The Junta's in the palace, they've taken out a lease.
> The Commies are in hiding, just across the street;
> To the Embassy of Mexico they beat a quick retreat.
> And pistol-packing Peurifoy looks mighty optimistic
> For the land of Guatemala is no longer communistic![10]

The overthrow of reform in Guatemala has often been treated as an intrinsic part of the Cold War, but the organisation of the invasion, the political motives behind it, and the language in which it was pesented were to change little in subsequent US operations in Central America and the Caribbean. The Guatemalan operation did indeed take place under the shadow of Korea and McCarthy, and it was certainly given added impetus by the direct involvement of a large multinational corporation with powerful friends ready to lobby on its behalf, but it also provided the blueprint for US actions in Cuba (1961), the Dominican Republic (1965), Nicaragua (1979–) and El Salvador (1979–). Ten years after its influence had undermined the absolutist regimes of the 1930s 'our democratic neighbour in the north' had mutated in the popular vision into *imperialismo yanqui*.

The Osorio regime supported and provided some minor assistance to the invasion, having previously purged those officers who evidenced an admiration for Arbenz and a desire to deepen the 'revolution' of 1948. Benefiting from rising coffee prices, the PRUD held its own without major problem, and at the end of his term in 1956 Osorio obtained the election of his Minister of Interior, Colonel José María Lemus, without difficulty, that is, with 93 per cent of all votes cast. The challenge to Lemus in the poll was restricted to a handful of rightist parties formed specially for the election and easily outmanoeuvred by the combination of open tampering with ballot papers, annulments of 'incorrectly completed documents', and shifts of local military commanders – a combination that was to characterise every subsequent election. Nevertheless, Lemus needed to distinguish himself from his patron, and attempted to liberalise his regime by inviting the opposition to join the cabinet (without success), allowing exiles to return, discouraging excessive corruption and dropping the old dictatorial stand-by, the *Ley de Defensa del Orden Democrático*.[11] In the relatively secure economic and political climate of the mid-1950s, Lemus felt able to loosen the ties of control somewhat, permitting urban trade unions to exist provided they avoided strike action. The new president, who like Martinez was of humble origins and prided himself on his dabblings in poetry and study, became an accomplished demagogue and comported himself in the manner of a Latin American military caudillo, dispensing minor favours to the poor with all the authority of a concerned and benevolent *patrón*. John Martz, writing in the *Miami Herald* in September 1956, captured a scene that could be found in many a presidential palace, both then and now:

> José Maria Lemus, the genial handshaker who has just become Salvador's president [has his] door open to the unwashed public . . . to reach him I had to penetrate through seven antechambers of patiently waiting people, all eager to wring his hand and whisper in his ear . . . His favourite way of talking to men – I watched him handling dozens – is to place his left hand on their shoulder, hold their right hand tightly clamped in his, and listen to every word they say while staring into their eyes with the solicitude of a psychiatrist. When he breaks out of this double grip, the supplicant instantly knows the interview is over.[12]

Any expectations that this *dictablanda* ('soft dictatorship') might somehow evolve into an open liberal regime were rudely dispelled when, from 1958, the price of coffee began to fall. Although the market did not hit its lowest until the end of 1960, this cyclical crisis came on top of an appreciable decline in US coffee consumption from 20.1 pounds per capita per year in 1946 to 15.7 pounds in 1960. By 1959 conditions had reached the point where Lemus was trying to cut production, wages were being sharply reduced, unemployment rocketing and credit virtually unobtainable. Moreover, the formation (in 1958) of the *Confederación General de Trabajadores de El Salvador* (CGTS) was giving the working class an organisational focus significantly more independent than any of its predecessors since 1932, registering the presence of the PCS, itself substantially recovered from the trough of the 1930s and 1940s. This in itself was sufficient reason for Lemus to revert to the full repressive measures of his own predecessors, but the political impact of the growing crisis was qualitatively increased with the entry of Fidel Castro and the guerrillas of the Cuban Sierra Maestra into Havana in January 1959: US hegemony in Latin America had been breached and was before long to face a permanent challenge.

The effects of the defeat of Batista and the capture of power by the guerrillas were, not surprisingly, most strongly evident amongst the youth and students of El Salvador. Since the university had regained its autonomous government in 1950 it had fortified its independence under liberal rectors, the most recent of whom, Napoleón Rodríguez Ruíz, was a highly popular figure who made little effort to restrain the left-wing tendencies of the students. However, when the students took to the streets to demonstrate their support for the Cuban rebels, Lemus responded with an immediate crack-down, taking scores of prisoners. But this was not an adequate warning, and later in the year, celebrations of the eleventh anniversary of the 'Revolution of 1948' developed into a major riot in the centre of San Salvador. Significantly harking back to 1944 rather than 1948, the students and reformist sectors of the urban middle class formed the *Partido Revolucionario de Abril y Mayo* (PRAM), which constituted the left wing of a loose opposition coalition formed to challenge the regime in the 1960 congressional and municipal elections. This alliance, the *Frente Nacional de Orientación Cívica* (FNOC), contained only one legal party and was continually denounced by the government as being 'communist' and 'Cuban-backed', charges that were to recur over the ensuing two decades with monotonous and baseless regularity. The FNOC, which had no real common platform beyond demanding the right to participate in the elections, was duly declared a 'threat to democracy' and suffered a large number of arrests, but it fought the poll and managed to win six mayoralties – including that of San Salvador – from the PRUD, despite the employment of standard voting procedures. It was plain that the opposition had amassed considerable popular support, not least because of the prominence some of its members gave to anti-imperialist slogans.

In July 1960, Lemus tried to change tack by announcing a programme of half-hearted reforms. But it was too late. On 17 August, a student march in the capital led to the arrest of the university authorities as well as hundreds of demonstrators, the military occupation of the campus, and the introduction of martial law. Late in September the public relations office of the presidency declared to an incredulous nation that,

> The Salvadorean people ought to know that some foreign elements have been expressly contracted by the leaders of AGEUS [the students' union], the CGTS and the communists to massacre those people [the cabinet] who

honoured the Patria before the Statue of Liberty.[13]

The use of such a time-honoured ploy to justify a new round of repression and removal of constitutional guarantees indicated that Lemus was in a cul-de-sac. A month later, on 26 October, a group of officers responded with what *Newsweek* described as, 'one of the neatest, most peaceful coups d'etat in Latin American history'.[14] The only shooting was the victory salute.

As with many Salvadorean coups, that of October 1960 was not the work of one coherent group but a coalition of different military factions, in this case the backers of Osorio, who had become thoroughly disenchanted with his heir, and a smaller group of junior officers who sought a real *apertura* precisely to avert what had happened in Cuba before it was too late. This latter group gained the initial advantage and used it without delay to dissolve the legislature and supreme court, lift the state of siege, release political prisoners, and appoint three young civilian professionals to join their new junta, which was greeted by a crowd of 80,000 on the first night of its existence. The strongest figure in the new government was the US-trained pharmacologist Fabio Castillo Figueroa, who was also the most anti-American and, by virtue of this alone, the most popular. Accordingly, the US did not deign to bless the junta with its recognition although it was highly heterogeneous in its composition and scarcely jacobin in its resolve. Paul Kennedy, who was in San Salvador for the *New York Times*, recalled

> One of the strangest interviews in my experience. I had submitted a list of ten questions in writing and at the appointed time sat with the full junta, repeating each question. As the question was asked, the six members would whisper together before one took the responsibility of answering. Either that, or one of the six would answer immediately, at which the others would glare at him as if he had been speaking out of turn.[15]

Such interviews brought no concrete promises of reform from the civilian technocrats, who had only a tenuous relationship with the military and were both unwilling and unable to take any independent initiative. Their only clear intention was to hold free elections in which the left could participate. Although the PCS was not legalised, it was tacitly allowed to operate and take a leading part in the activity of the PRAM. When this became clear, the majority of the officer corps lost no time in preparing a counter-coup. On 25 January 1961, after three confused and frenetic months, the 'democratic junta' was overthrown, its military members refusing to hand out arms to the crowds which collected outside their barracks and clamoured for the means to defend a regime which was the closest they had had to a civilian government for 30 years and was to be the only break in right-wing military rule for 50 years. The hardened news-hound Kennedy, who had the ear of the US Embassy, noted that the junta 'never had a chance'. Indeed; its liberal democratic aspirations prevented it from providing itself with the mass armed support it needed if it was to survive the outright opposition of the oligarchy and all but a score of maverick army officers. Its ephemeral existence registered the first impact of Cuba, which was not going to fade away, but left no mark upon Salvadorean history other than to herald the revival of the military–oligarchic mandate. The junta closed what we may call the pre-history of the struggle for political power, which 20 years later was to reach civil war.

4
THE FAILURE TO MODERNISE

O.A.S.

The President of my country
is today called Colonel Fidel Sánchez Hernández.
But General Somoza, President of Nicaragua,
is also President of my country.
And General Stroessner, President of Paraguay,
is also a little the President of my country
although less
than the President of Honduras, who is
General López Arellano, and more than the
President of Haiti, Monsieur Duvalier.
And the President of the United States is more
the President of my country
than the President of my country
who, as I said, is today
called Colonel Fidel Sánchez Hernández.

Roque Dalton

Fidel Castro declared himself a Marxist on 1 December 1961. By that time diplomatic relations between Cuba and the US had been severed for eleven months. In April 1959, Castro had proclaimed that the new revolutionary government's ideology would be one of 'humanism', by which he understood, 'government by the people, without dictatorship and without oligarchy; liberty with bread and without terror'.[1] Such a pronouncement – generous, idealist, egalitarian but eminently unprogrammatic – befitted the radical liberalism of the guerrilla leadership, the bulk of which was of bourgeois or petty bourgeois origin. There was nothing unduly remarkable about such radical and populist sentiments; they had frequently been voiced before by politicians of widely differing positions. Yet the Eisenhower administration, perceiving unmistakable indications of radicalisation amongst the Cuban masses, stuck to its dullard policy of 'containment'. Encouraged by the example of Guatemala, the US government moved rapidly towards confrontation with the new regime which, after all, presided over a country in which US investment was higher than in any other Latin American state.

Diplomatic offensives and economic pressure were escalated so fast that by March 1960 the CIA was 'authorised' to organise an invasion of the island. During this period the Cubans continued to adhere to what might now be termed a 'non-aligned position': they would stand midway between the US and the USSR but, as Castro enthusiastically warned, if the US invaded, '200,000 *gringos* would die'. With extensive collectivisation in agriculture and nationalisation of US capital interests, for which the compensation originally offered was a fraction of the sums demanded, relations were broken in January 1961. The Soviet Union, already supplying oil, had committed herself to buying the sugar now boycotted by the US, and Czechoslovakian arms were beginning to arrive in Havana. Within two years of their triumphant entry into the capital, the guerrilla forces from the Sierra Maestra were shifting rapidly into the orbit of the Soviet bloc and had established a still uncertain but deepening alliance with the Communist Party (PSP). This alliance was sealed by the catastrophic Bay of Pigs invasion attempt of April 1961. The nationalisation of property relations was speeded up and the basis of a workers' state established. Of course, the process was far more complex than can be outlined here, but its consequences were all too readily apparent throughout the Americas: a 'communist' revolution been made by people who had not started off as 'communists' and the US was now faced with a close ally of the Soviet Union that was a mere 90 miles from the coast of Florida and had strong ties with the rest of Latin America, particularly Central America and the Caribbean, to which it was freely threatening to 'export' its revolution.

The fact that Kennedy had consolidated and expanded Eisenhower's policy towards Cuba and was responsible for the Bay of Pigs, gave the lie to claims that with the election of his administration a wave of liberalism would sweep southwards from Washington. With respect to Latin America, Kennedy's priorities were clear: to organise a counter-revolution in Cuba – a task as alive today as it was 20 years ago – and to halt the spread of 'subversion' to the rest of the hemisphere. What was new about the Kennedy policy was not its supposed abhorrence of interventionism, which in fact increased dramatically, but its style and form; application of the traditional stick would be modernised and 'professionalised' but, in addition, a carrot would be offered.

The stick was the programme of strengthening the region's armed forces by providing them with modern equipment and – more importantly – training them in 'counter-insurgency warfare', which, under the aegis of figures such as General Maxwell Taylor, rapidly evolved from a tactical necessity into a complete politico-military ideology. No less important but certainly more novel was its corollary, the project for the rapid 'modernisation' of the Latin American economies. This was the centre-piece of the Alliance for Progress, which Kennedy launched within a month of the Bay of Pigs in 1961 with unrestrained rhetoric:

> Our hemispheric mission is not yet completed. For our unfulfilled task is to demonstrate to the entire world that man's unsatisfied aspiration for economic progress and social justice can best be achieved by free men working within a framework of democratic institutions. If we can do this in our own hemisphere, and for our own people, we may yet realize the prophecy of the great Mexican patriot, Benito Juarez, that 'democracy is the destiny of future humanity'.[2]

Of course, the great majority of the world's population that has access to the grandiose pronouncements of US presidents has generated a healthy scepticism about their avowed ends, and nowhere is this more true than in Latin America; but even those, such as Pablo González Casanova, who have comprehensively demolished the liberal myth behind the Alliance and laid bare its enormous advantages for US capital, rightly concede that Kennedy's initiative 'constituted the most ambitious social project of imperialism'.[3] It was precisely the depth of the Cuban Revolution that required that the scope of the Alliance be unprecedentedly broad. The overbearing need for social change in Latin America had not advanced one inch, it was just as great as before; but it had now become a central issue in the maintenance of US hegemony. The miracle by which the Latin American countries would become autonomous, industrialised states – the only possible basis upon which to build a liberal democratic society – was to be achieved through a substantial increase in capital loans and direct economic aid, starting at $1,500 million, to fund major infrastructural projects. Economic integration would rationalise market systems, facilitate free trade and stabilise export prices; a concomitant expansion of incentives for foreign and domestic investment would be necessary, along with agrarian and fiscal reforms to redistribute income and expand the domestic market. For Central America, the Central American Common Market (CACM), established in 1961 after a series of tariff reform agreements over the previous years, was set up to optimise the region's market structure and overcome the disastrous economic effects of political balkanisation. If the CACM did anything, it at least recognised that these economies were too small to sustain a range of competitive producers in the same sector fighting over a very restricted regional market. But recognition never led to practical planning.

The projected scope and espoused ideals of the Alliance present us with an unparalleled opportunity to assess the potential for reforming a backward country like El Salvador within the context of monopoly capital as opposed to the model adopted in Cuba. This is, moreover, no academic enterprise; in the 1960s El Salvador became the country that is recognisable in the early 1980s. From this it is clear that no major transformation took place; the pattern of ownership and power within the oligarchy was shifted somewhat, and in a manner that was to generate a number of discernable effects in the political field, but the outcome for the vast bulk of the population was a restructuring and acceleration of impoverishment.

The coup of January 1961 bore the mark of the Alliance. The new 'Directorate' led by Colonel Julio Rivera did not attempt a counter-revolution in the fullest sense of the term. There was, of course, no revolution to be overthrown, only the threat of popular mobilisation to be stemmed. But it is notable that the regime did not seek to emulate Martinez, and repression returned to 'normal' rather than escalating into a pogrom. Many of the officers around Rivera perceived the need not only to restore Osorio's system of dictatorship gilded with populist motifs but also to substantiate some of its reformist gestures with strictly controlled but real changes in Salvadorean society. The experience of three months' 'anarchy' had sharpened the lessons of Cuba sufficiently for the simple reimposition of repression to be understood as inadequate. Thus, Rivera pronounced the regime anti-communist, anti-Castro and anti-Cuba, but 'not reactionary'.[4] Talking to the press beneath the pictures of Lincoln and Kennedy that adorned his office, the new *hombre fuerte* stated bluntly that, 'if we do not make reforms the communists will make them for us'.[5]

Although nobody was paying any attention to Rivera's pronouncement that in El Salvador, 'the exploitation of man by man has ended',[6] it seemed that some steps might be taken when urban rents

were decreased, one rest day per week made obligatory in the
countryside, an income tax law announced and eventually made law
(1963), exchange controls imposed, and, after considerable debate,
rural minimum wages established (1965). In the Directorate's first 270
days it passed 325 degrees. The oligarchy showed itself to be distinctly
upset by this activity; one coffee planter complained,

> I awake in the morning and immediately help myself to a couple of aspirin.
> When these begin working, I take a peek at the paper to see what new decrees
> have been issued and how much more broke I am that morning than I was
> the night before.[7]

Kennedy himself, identified as the 'intellectual author' of these
aberrations, was marked down as a 'bolshevik', and during 1961 the
flight of capital reached $30 million. The regime was insulted and
threatened but, after the initial furore, never actively destabilised, for
the majority of the rural bourgeoisie recognised that, as one of their
number put it, 'if Rivera goes down we all go down'.[8]

This grudging acquiescence was made possible by the fact that none
of the new reforms harmed the principal interests of the oligarchy and,
indeed, very few of them were finally realised. There was – most
importantly – no agrarian reform at all; the coffee sector was exempted
from the income tax law; the nationalisation of the fiscal banks was
accepted as an overdue rationalisation and made no impact on the
structure of credit: between 1961 and 1975 between 80 and 90 per cent
of agricultural credit was channelled to export enterprises, and in 1971
87 per cent went to farms of over ten hectares.[9] Obligatory rest days and
minimum wage levels were evaded with comparative ease or the costs
passed on to the labour force by altering non-wage conditions of work.
The rural bourgeoisie was the nominal butt of the various reforms, but
it remained the only possible intermediary for US interests and
continued to retain a high degree of economic autonomy which clearly
determined the limits within which the military could exercise political
power.

Industrialisation

One of the main effects of the Alliance was the expansion of El
Salvador's industrial sector so that, along with Guatemala, advances in
this sector were more rapid than in the other Central American states.
Between 1959 and 1969, industrial production more than doubled, its

share of GDP rising from 14 per cent to 19.6 per cent, with an average annual growth rate of around 10 per cent.[10] For a large part of the decade manufacturing was the dynamic sector of the Salvadorean economy although, as can be seen from Tables 1 and 2,[11] it never came to dominate it and by the early 1970s had reached its limits.

Table 1: GDP 1960 – 75 (per cent, at 1962 prices)

	1960	1964	1968	1972	1975
Agriculture	30	30	25	25	25
Manufacturing	15	16	19	18	19
Commerce	24	25	26	23	23
Construction	3	3	3	4	4
Government	8	7	7	8	8
Services	7	7	8	8	8
Others	13	12	12	14	13
Total (¢ millions)	1,383	1,827	2,246	2,646	3,115
Per capita (¢)	552.2	645.5	689.2	721.4	764.0

Source: Downing, p.34

Table 2: Growth Rates 1960–75 (annual average, per cent)

	1960-3	1964-7	1968-71	1972-5
Agriculture	7.1	1.2	4.7	6.1
Manufacturing	9.4	10.8	3.9	5.8
Commerce	5.7	6.9	-0.3	4.8
Government	5.5	7.1	7.8	15.7
Construction	6.8	8.0	7.5	4.6
GDP	6.6	6.0	3.7	5.6
Per capita GDP		2.7	0.2	1.9

Source: As Table 1

Grand though it was in name, the Alliance was a distinctly one-sided affair designed to give maximum advantage to US business interests. The 1961 Foreign Assistance Act stipulated that loans should be used for the purchase of US goods and services, and over a third of the initial loans made under the Alliance by the Export–Import Bank were to this end. In 1968. President Johnson assured Congress that 90 per cent of the following year's foreign loans would return directly to the domestic economy through the purchases of the client states. This made good sense from the US point of view but it fortified the dependence of the underdeveloped economies on that of their metropolitan partner. Moreover, it limited the expansionary effect of the new cash on the local economy: in the 1960s $179 million was loaned by USAID to El Salvador and over 20 per cent of this was spent on building roads, but in the majority of these construction projects the loans were largely used up in subcontracting foreign firms which imported heavy machinery and employed relatively few local workers.

This pattern was even clearer in the role played by foreign capital in El Salvador's manufacturing sector. The establishment of free trade zones and other direct incentives, such as a liberal tax regime and low labour costs, succeeded in their aim of attracting foreign investment in quite spectacular manner. In 1959 foreign investment in the country was $43 million with only $0.7 million, 1.6 per cent, in the manufacturing sector. By 1969 the total stood at $114.6 million, with $43.7 million, 38.1 per cent, in manufacturing.[12] Some of the world's leading multinationals set up plants in the country, the US firms unsurprisingly taking the lead with over 60 per cent of foreign capital investments. Yet, in a manner similar to the banana enclaves in Honduras, Costa Rica and Guatemala, these firms operated in a virtual enclave. They maximised the benefits proffered by El Salvador by importing the vast bulk of their raw materials and manufactured components, assembled the final commodity and then re-exported it, paying minimal export duties. Since multinational enterprises set a high store upon business secrecy, it is hard to break down their costs with great accuracy, but one serious estimate puts the level of imported components in Central American manufactured products as high as 85 per cent in 1970.[13] Another source indicates that while in 1951 the level of Salvadorean raw materials used in industry was 63 per cent of the total, by 1968 this had dropped to 39 per cent.[14] If we take the value added to products by the labour process as measured by wage costs, the figure for El Salvador in 1953 was the lowest in the continent at 17.3 per cent, rising to only 20 per cent in 1969.[15] Lea and Perrins, for example, imported large quantities of ready-made Worcestershire sauce into the country and simply transferred it into smaller bottles which carried the words 'Made in El Salvador'; Kimberly Clark, the paper manufacturers, operated in a similar manner by reducing large stocks of lavatory paper to small rolls. Another company imported screws, added grooves and then re-exported them.[16] Not all foreign firms went to such extremes but the practice of limiting local inputs and costs was generalised. This was not unusual in Central America as a whole: the multinational pharmaceutical firms in Guatemala, the majority of which employed less than 50 workers, imported all their raw materials bar air and water. In Nicaragua 86 per cent of the commodities used in this industry were imported.[17] This tendency became even more acute from the mid-1970s, after the acknowledged failure of the CACM and 'import substitution', when the remaining state measures to defend local industry were dropped and the economy fully opened up with the establishment of free trade zones, in which there was no pretence whatsoever of placing conditions upon the activity of foreign firms. In El Salvador, the San Bartolo zone has for years been a law unto itself.

The new industries, therefore, established relatively few links with the local market and did little to generate domestic production that could feed into them. El Salvador's production of consumer goods remained low and lagged well behind imports which, combined with the repayment of loans made under the Alliance, further damaged the balance of payments. Foreign capital utilised the advantages offered by the client state but did not initiate the 'take off' of an independent local industrial sector. Domestic demand continued to be tied to the traditional exporting sector and when this suffered a recession in the late 1960s so, too, did the economy as a whole. Private fixed capital formation fell from 14 per cent of GDP 1964 to 10.8 per cent in 1968; direct foreign investment itself dropped from 1.1 per cent of GDP (1962–4) to 0.3 per cent in 1970.[18] As Table 2 shows, by the end of the 1960s manufacturing industry was growing more slowly than agriculture. Yet the profitability of foreign capital remained high throughout the decade and the generous terms used to lure investment in also permitted the repatriation of profits to be undertaken without external constraint. Of the ¢177.9 million of foreign investment made between 1959 and 1969, ¢120 million was repatriated within the same period.[19]

The very partial integration of the new industrial sector (pulp, petroleum-based goods, glass, paper, chemicals, pig-iron) into the domestic economy and the increasing reliance upon imports of capital and consumer goods meant that the substantial increase in the volume of production did not, in fact, signify a corresponding shift in the structure of production. If we disaggregate the figures we find that the traditional products (foodstuffs, textiles, clothing) show a remarkable resilience despite the fact that a large proportion of them were produced in artisanal workshops. In 1958 these goods accounted for 88.4 per cent of industrial production, in 1968 they still represented 75 per cent.[20] In 1974, when El Salvador was acknowledged to be the second most industrialised state in the region, 26 per cent of manufacturing GDP was derived from food products, 12 per cent from textiles, and 8 per cent from footwear. Petroleum and chemical manufacture accounted for 8 and 5 per cent respectively, but the other new products were of marginal importance.[21] There had been some modernisation but no miracle.

None the less, in terms of the Central American market Salvadorean industry had attained a strong position by the end of the 1960s to the extent that some perceived the rise of a new, modernising industrial bourgeoisie that might challenge the hegemony of the landlords with an independent project for the development of the country. This was never the case. The simple reason was that the majority of domestic industrial capital either came directly from or was closely allied to the landed oligarchy. While some of the leading coffee planters expanded into processing and exporting or sugar and cotton production, others transferred capital into light manufacturing. In 1971, 38 per cent of El Salvador's top 1,429 firms were controlled by the 36 largest landowners, who owned 66 per cent of their total capital.[22]

This control was further tightened by the landed bourgeoisie's stranglehold over the local finance market. Of the country's four leading banks, the Banco Salvadoreño was controlled by the Guirola family (farming 19,882 hectares), the Banco de Comercio by the Dueñas, Regalado and Alvarez clans (40,273 hectares), the Banco Agrícola Comercial by the Escalante-Arce and Sol-Millet families (12,629 hectares), and the Banco Capitalizador by the Alvarez, Borja Natán and Alfaro clans (16,648 hectares). Of the top 30 families, none was engaged in coffee production alone and some, such as the Regalados and De Solas, were operating in processing, exporting, finance and manufacturing as well as having interests in sugar and cotton.

Industrialisation did, however, tend to highlight some of the secondary contradictions that existed within the oligarchy as a result of both the natural competition between capitals and their sectoral division. It is to be expected that there would be some divergence of emphasis in terms of economic strategy between, for example, the De

Solas, who were the leading coffee exporters but only the 25th largest producers, and the Regalados, who were the largest producers but only the 21st largest exporters. Such differences were somewhat more pronounced between these clans at the very apex of the bourgeoisie and the smaller enterprises, whose profits derived principally from cultivation. By the early 1970s, the De Solas and the Miraflor group had adopted a discernable strategy of encouraging a controlled expansion of the domestic market which entailed increased demand and, therefore, some redistribution of income. The inescapable consequence of this was some form of agrarian reform to match increased industrial output.

Yet the bulk of the landed bourgeoisie, if it appeared less perspicacious, maintained a resolute stance upon the traditional power-base of land, and refused to countenance significant alteration in the terms of its dominance. This 'ultramontane' sector comprised not only the families that had the bulk of their capital invested directly in cultivation but also the biggest enterprises, such as the Hills, Regalados and Dueñas, which were content to maximise their advantages in the world coffee market and the regional market for industrial goods. As a result, despite a number of brushes within the oligarchy, no major shift to Alliance-type industrial and agrarian reforms was ever permitted and there existed no faction of the capitalist class that was strong enough to push it through. Industrialisation neither stemmed from nor produced a 'national bourgeoisie' with its own economic project or political independence.

However, the growth of the industrial sector did have a lasting effect in the expansion of the working class. Although this was emphatic, it still did not match the increase in investment and output precisely because of the capital-intensive nature of the new manufacturing concerns. As a result, the proportion of the economically active population engaged in this sector actually fell slightly, from 12.9 per cent in 1961 to 11.2 per cent in 1971. Over the decade, production rose by 7.9 per cent, employment by only 2.6 per cent.[23] Quite obviously, the precise accuracy of the figures in Table 3 is open to question, but even if they are taken as a conservative presentation they still show both the small size of the manufacturing sector and the fact that over the 1960s it was the traditional sectors that accounted for much of the growth of the workforce. All the same, it would be misleading to identify the proletariat simply with workers in 'pure' manufacturing. With the inclusion of construction, transport and communication workers, the figure rises to about 120,000 in 1971 and, with major increases in government expenditure in these sectors in the early 1970s, to 152,000 in 1975.[24] This is certainly a far more substantial figure. In Central American terms it made the Salvadorean proletariat a force to be reckoned with, but it should also be seen in the context of an increase of all non-agricultural wage-earners from 246,000 to 361,000 between 1961 and 1975. Hence, by the early 1970s, when the Alliance for Progress was well and truly dead and El Salvador's surge of industrialisation palpably on the wane, the industrial working class comprised 42 per cent of all urban wage-earners and 27 per cent of all those economically active in the urban sector; even in the towns it was not a majority.[25]

Table 3: Size of the Industrial Labour Force 1960 and 1969

Sector	1960	1969
Foodstuffs	15,137	28,306
Drinks	868	756
Tobacco	135	155
Textiles	3,036	7,983
Footwear and clothing	698	2,249
Furniture	111	1,422
Paper	13	559
Printing	–	1,103
Leather	368	458
Rubber	31	400
Chemicals	442	1,281
Petroleum	–	61
Non-metallic minerals	650	1,232
Basic metals	–	612
Metallic products	169	690
Machinery	–	350
Electrical machinery	–	498
Transport equipment	–	784
Various	–	1,379
Total	21,268	50,278

Source: Bravo, p.131

The failure of the industrial sector to absorb the escalating population of El Salvador's few large towns was to have important social and political effects, for this influx was by no means a minor phenomenon. Between 1950 and 1980 the proportion of the population living in centres of over 20,000 rose from 18 to 44 per cent.[26] In 1946 the population of San Salvador was 116,000, 20 years later it stood at 732,000. By the mid-1970s the department of San Salvador contained over 20 per cent of the country's population, with a density of 843 people per square kilometre against a national average of 170 people, itself five times the Central American average.[27] Workers poured into the city in particularly large numbers on specific occasions, such as after the 1965 earthquake, but the principal reason for the inflow was to escape the worsening conditions in the countryside, where the concentration of land ownership was increasing and the potential for subsistence farming greatly reduced. The illegal but tacitly permitted squats established by these migrants mushroomed into a ring of ramshackle ghettos, *tugurios,* enveloping the city. The new settlements of Cuscatancingo, Mejicanos, Ayutustepeque, Villa Delgado and others were populated mostly but by no means exclusively by newer, poorer workers, many of whom lacked a regular wage. Many were self-employed in small-scale commerce or worked in the service sector, that pellucid category that covers a welter of menial jobs from housemaids to street cleaners and in 1974 comprised the bulk of the 40 per cent of wage-earners who were receiving pay that was less than the legal minimum wage of ¢28.7 (approximately £5) per week.[28]

The rapid growth of this sector of the population may be gauged from the fact that between 1971 and 1975 the number of self-employed in commerce grew from 47,000 to 131,000, only a very small proportion of which constituted successful entrepreneurs; by 1975 126,000 urban wage-earners worked in the service sector. Many thousands more escaped the official statistics, the majority in all probability being women. This impoverished urban mass greatly outnumbers the working class, but it would be a mistake to see them as two totally distinct forces. The *tugurios* contain factory workers and those that have moved out of the city centre as well as the new migrants. Moreover, since the Salvadorean proletariat is relatively young there is no deeply ingrained set of working-class traditions to act as a critical barrier to the absorption of wider groups; both broad groups hail overwhelmingly from the countryside, with which there is still a strong symbiosis.

For many years the threat of dispossession by rentiers, vulnerability to the municipal authorities, and the lack of a trade union organisation as a result of the atomisation of much of the *tugurio* workforce ensured an internally divided and relatively quiescent slum-dwelling population. These are characteristics often noted in studies of 'marginalised' urban sectors in the 1960s and 1970s.[29] But in San Salvador, as for many other Latin American cities, they do not amount to an every-present, determinate state of affairs, being constantly open to rapid changes and upsurges in radical political action spurred on not simply by poor working conditions but also common exasperation at the lack of such basic facilities as water, paved roads, transport, schools, etc. Such protests are often highly volatile and lack concerted organisation, but they can frequently acquire a militancy and radicalism that goes beyond the actions of bureaucratised industrial trade unions. In El Salvador this occurred on a number of occasions in the late 1960s and early 1970s, making it tempting to identify in these oppressed plebeian layers an inherent radicalism that, because of their generally more precarious economic position, goes beyond that of the relatively privileged proletariat. Such a perspective often interchanges with that which congregates all these groups under a blanket term such as the 'masses' or the 'oppressed', which correctly evokes shared poverty and backwardness in a manner that does not obtain in the metropolitan states but on its own takes no account of the very specific form of exploitation that exists in the wage relation and, more concretely, in the industrial labour process. The importance of this distinctiveness with regard to the peasantry is that the worker possesses nothing to sell beyond his or her labour power. With respect to other wage-earners the key difference is in experience of the factory or workshop which forges a strong sense of class, strengthens unity and consolidates rank and file organisation. Thus, however backward and imbalanced the growth of industrial capital in El Salvador in the 1960s, it conformed to type in fortifying its natural antagonist in the working class.

By 1965 the PCS was talking openly of the 'changed economic conditions', which were increasing the standard of living of factory workers and placed a premium on strengthened trade union work. The party, which had been producing statements about a 'popular uprising' in 1961, when membership was rising quickly under the influence of Cuba, now interpreted the temporary upturn in the economic climate and the reflux in radicalism as the opening of a new period in which legal and peaceful agitation would be paramount.[30]

Whatever the correctness of this analysis, it had at least some basis in fact. As Table 4 demonstrates, the growth of GDP in the industrial sector was sufficiently great in the late 1960s to allow modest increases in real wages until the dramatic and constant decline experienced after 1971.

Table 4: Real Wages in San Salvador, 1966–74

	1966	1967	1968	1969	1970	1971	1972	1973	1974
Cost of living	100	100.3	104.5	105.4	106.9	106.3	112.1	121.0	146.3
Growth in real wage		1.6	3.3	0.5	1.8	2.0	-5.5	-1.5	-8.5
Manufacturing wage	100	104.6	109.5	110.9	114.4	116.1	116.0	123.4	138.7

Source: Downing, p.51

Thus, in the 1960s the PCS-backed CGTS avoided militant action, being stalled by small wage increases and the party's line that it was necessary to back the 'industrial bourgeoisie' against the agro-exporting oligarchy. In line with its policy of co-opting urban labour, the governing *Partido de Conciliación Nacional* (PCN) continued to support and develop the pliant *Confederación General de Sindicatos* (CGS), set up by Lemus in 1958. With its strong anti-communist line and tight network of pro-government bureaucrats, some of whom actually represented the PCN in Congress, the CGS was a perfect tool for the implementation of the Alliance's labour policy. It received funds from the American Institute for Free Labor Development (AIFLD), itself partly funded by US corporations, and was affiliated to the US-controlled *Organización Regional Interamericana de Trabajadores* (ORIT). By 1966 more than 100 CGS leaders had travelled to Puerto Rico and the US for training in 'democratic' and 'apolitical' trade unionism. Although, as a result of this, no more than 30 stayed in union affairs, the CGS remained a loyal ally of all the military regimes, eventually obliging its expulsion, in October 1979, from the International Confederation of Free Trade Unions (ICFTU), of which ORIT was the discredited Latin American wing.

Throughout most of the 1960s the CGS was able to stem the growth of the CGTS and the small Christian democratic union, the *Unión de Obreros Católicos* (UNOC), without great difficulty. But its control at the level of national confederations did not reflect developments at rank and file level, where growing militancy ensured that certain unions (railway, soft drinks, beer and water workers) remained independent and pushed for a single confederation, setting up the *Federación Unitaria Sindical Salvadoreña* (FUSS), which allied with the CGTS in 1965 as a first step towards this aim. Later these two organisations joined with important dissident sections of the food and textile workers (FESTIAVECES) and a larger federation, FENASTRAS, that contained workers from a number of industries but was led by the powerful power workers' union STECEL. By the mid-1970s the combination of these forces numbered some 26,000 workers and, as the newly-formed *Confederación Unificada de Trabajadores Salvadoreños* (CUTS), posed a major threat to the CGS. The 'yellow' confederation was itself disintegrating, suffering a serious blow with the loss in 1968 of the transport and construction workers' federation, FESINCONTRANS, which numbered 20,000 members. Although FESINCONTRANS refused to break its *oficialista* ties completely and rejected the overtures of CUTS, the regime's hold over organised labour continued to weaken; by 1976 the CGS contained only 19 per cent of unionised workers against 42 per cent in 1971.[31]

By the mid-1970s the workers' movement had, therefore, made important steps in freeing itself from government control but it still remained divided, bureaucratically hampered and lacking in direction beyond a basic economism. The following five years were to witness substantial changes in this picture with working-class organisation breaking through the traditional limits of trade union structures.

Agriculture

Despite the expansion of the industrial sector and the migration to the towns, El Salvador remains a predominantly rural society. In 1982, as in 1932, the agrarian question lies at the heart of social conflict and the battle for control of the state.

The degree of industrialisation and poor market conditions in the early 1960s did reduce the absolute importance of coffee in the economy as a whole. But this decline was only relative, and it continued to be the country's single most important export by a long margin. In

1959, coffee represented 12.7 per cent of total GDP, 37.1 per cent of agricultural production and 62.9 per cent of total exports. In 1969, it accounted for 9.1 per cent of GDP, 35.8 per cent of agricultural production and 44.2 per cent of all exports.[32] The prime cause of this backsliding was the slump in the world market, but this did not result in any decrease of production: between 1961 and 1971 the area sown with coffee increased from 8.8 per cent to 10.1 per cent of all agricultural land and export volume increased by 3.6 per cent. The fact that this increase in tonnages shipped represented an increase of only 2.5 per cent in export value demonstrates the importance of shifts in the world coffee price for the Salvadorean economy as a whole.

For a period this drop was offset to a degree by a rapid expansion in cotton production which took over much land previously dedicated to cattle ranching on the coastal plain. In 1959/60, 43,000 *manzanas* (1 *manzana* = 1.73 acres or 0.7 hectares) of cotton were sown, in 1964/5 this area had risen to 122,200 *manzanas*.[33] Supported by a more advanced productive infrastructure and benefiting from a comparatively high degree of mechanisation in the early stages, cotton promised for a while to challenge coffee, but the failure to employ sufficient quantities of fertiliser on land noted for its high level of erosion, and a disinclination to use rotation methods in favour of extracting short-term market advantages, led to a steep drop in production. Cotton exports dropped from $37.8 million in 1964/5 to $14.5 million in 1967/8; thereafter they experienced only a gradual rise in generally adverse market conditions.

The third major crop is sugar, originally bolstered by the blockade of Cuba. But although prices remained stable, sugar cultivation expanded slowly, never accounting for more than 1 per cent of GDP or 6 per cent of exports. It was a crop that, unlike coffee and cotton, was undercapitalised and largely cultivated on small- or medium-sized farms, with only a few large plantations in the west of the country. Once coffee prices had returned to their previous high levels from the mid-1970s both sugar and cotton were relegated to the status of secondary crops.

Salvadorean agriculture did not, therefore, 'take-off' under the Alliance. The discrete introduction of modern techniques, attempts to diversify and accelerate production and efforts to capitalise small rural concerns resulted only in very sluggish growth rates and a gradual diminution in the proportion of exports emanating from the agricultural sector.

Table 5: Agricultural Contribution to GDP 1962-74 (per cent, 1962 prices)

	1962	1964	1968	1972	1974
Coffee	11.2	11.1	8.9	8.7	8.5
Cotton	5.4	4.9	1.8	2.8	2.8
Basic grains	4.7	3.4	3.8	2.8	3.1
Sugar	0.5	0.6	0.7	0.8	0.9
Other crops/ forestry	3.3	2.8	4.1	3.7	3.5
Total crops	25.1	22.8	19.3	18.8	18.8
Livestock	8.5	6.8	6.0	6.3	6.8

Source: Downing, p.38

Table 6: Traditional Exports 1962-76 (per cent at current prices FOB)

	1962	1964	1968	1972	1976
Coffee	54.7	53.2	44.2	43.1	53.3
Cotton	23.2	21.2	6.9	12.8	8.9
Sugar	1.8	1.6	4.3	5.9	5.6
Prawns	4.0	2.4	2.0	2.3	1.6
Total	83.7	78.4	57.4	64.1	69.4

Source: Downing, p.36

Emphatic though it was, this stagnation should not be allowed to obscure a number of important developments in social relations in the countryside. These centred upon an appreciable increase in the already gross concentration of land ownership and an acceleration in the removal of subsistence farmers from their plots. The number of landless labourers grew dramatically and dependence upon seasonal wages became increasingly acute. The result was a progressive pauperisation of the rural masses and a marked deepening of class polarisation.

These changes were underpinned by the shift to capitalist labour relations in the *campo*. Traditionally, large landlords had leased out portions of their lands either on the basis of sharecropping, whereby workers farmed the land and handed a part of their harvest or its proceeds over to the owner, or by the *colonato* system, a form of labour rent whereby peasants were granted the use of subsistence plots in exchange for a number of days' work on the main estate. This essentially feudal system of labour relations was already being partly revised by the 1950s as landlords sought to maximise revenues from export crops, which meant reducing the area sown for the peasants' subsistence crops. This led to a gradual introduction of money rent as opposed to rent in labour or kind (goods, crops). As land prices and rents rose, small farmers and peasants were progressively forced onto marginal land, illegal squats, smaller plots, to the cities or across the border to Honduras. During this period this same tendency was evident in many parts of Latin America, but in El Salvador it took a particularly acute form because of the narrow ecological limits to productive relations; money rent and wages progressively eclipsed labour rent because there was simply not enough land available to sustain commercial farming on the basis of *colonato* or sharecropping.

With its encouragement of capitalist agriculture, the Alliance accelerated this process. Increased funds were fed into the banks of the rural bourgeoisie, which monopolised the credit necessary for expansion.[34] Accordingly, lands dedicated to the main cash crops progressively took over those previously used for subsistence agriculture and grew by 43,000 hectares between 1960 and 1972.[35] This expansion is reflected in the changing structure of land tenure between 1961 and 1971: total land farmed in *colonato* dropped by 3.8 per cent while lands held by tenants paying money rent rose by 2.3 per cent.[36]

The resulting concentration of ownership is not immediately apparent from the precise size of holdings since the greater capitalisation of farming, allied with the oligarchy's residual fear of agrarian reform, had encouraged the management of commercial enterprises in smaller units. Nevertheless, the disparities in property and wealth in the countryside are overwhelming. By 1966 3,000 families controlled 43 per cent of all cultivated land, 33 per cent of the national territory. A mere 463 properties accounted for 29 per cent of cultivated land and 23 per cent of the total land area.[37] At the other end of the scale, the number of plots less than one hectare in size rose from 70,400 in 1961 to 132,900 in 1971 as the pressure on land forced subdivision of subsistence holdings.[38] Table 7 presents the structure of power in the Salvadorean countryside in colder style, but the picture is no different. These figures, like many others cited here, are used because 1961 and 1971 were agrarian census years. More recent statistics are often estimates and therefore less reliable. There was no census in 1981.

Table 7: Land Tenure by Size of Unit, 1961 and 1971

Size (hectares)	1961			1971		
	Farms	*Area (has.)*	*Area (%)*	*Farms*	*Area (has.)*	*Area (%)*
Less than 1	107,000	61,000	4	132,000	70,000	4
1–9.9	100,000	285,000	18	188,000	324,000	21
10–199.9	19,000	639,000	40	19,000	649,000	41
More than 200	1,000	596,000	38	1,000	538,000	34

Source: Downing, p.46

When we turn to the number of people affected by this concentration in ownership its social impact becomes much more vivid. Between 1961 and 1971 the number of families possessing less than two hectares grew by 37,194 and those with no land at all rose by 81,657.[39] The proportion of the rural population that was landless grew massively, from 12 per cent in 1961 to 29 per cent in 1971 and 41 per cent in 1975.[40] Table 8 confirms this phenomenon, showing that while the total temporary wage labour force fell in relative terms between 1961 and 1971, the number of landless workers grew enormously. The Salvadorean rural proletariat was created by dispossession, forcing large numbers of workers to rely exclusively on their seasonal wages when previously they had used them to bolster the produce and petty income from their plots. The impact of this dispossession was made all the greater by the landlords' corresponding capacity to keep wages low and even reduce them: in 1961 the average monthly wage income of a landless labourer was ¢464; in 1975 it had fallen to ¢429.[41]

The other notable aspect of these figures is the rise in permanent tenants, which may be explained by the complement of dispossession – the subdivision of plots, which was made necessary not only by the pressure on land but also by the fact that during the 1960s the labour force was, according to government statistics, growing by around 30,000 a year. The result was a rise not just in unemployment but also underemployment. The first was largely transferred to the urban sector, where between 1965 and 1968 it rose by nearly 30 per cent as a result of migration from the *campo*.[42] Underemployment, however, remains a structural blight on the countryside, with paid work only available on a meaningful scale during planting (April to June) and harvest (November to January). An estimate that post-dates Table 8 gives the number of those with permanent work as 16 per cent of the economically active population.[43]

Table 8: Changes in the Rural Labour Force, 1961–71

	1961 Number	%	1971 Number	%	Growth %
Temporary landed wage labour	197,597	42.3	122,121	20.5	- 4.9
Temporary landless wage labour	23,837	6.2	102,906	17.2	13.6
Total temporary wage labour	221,434	(48.5)	225,027	(37.7)	- 0.06
Permanent wage labour	76,576	16.4	87,033	14.6	1.3
Total wage labour	303,010	(64.9)	312,060	(52.3)	0.3
Permanent tenants	164,083	35.1	284,869	47.7	5.7
Total	467,093	100.0	596,927	100.0	2.5

Source: Downing, p.40

The dangers of all this were recognised by certain members of the landed bourgeoisie, such as the De Solas, as well as many members of the urban middle class, which sought in the mid-1970s to bring about a modest agrarian reform and break the process of concentration and polarisation whilst at the same time offering little threat to the structure as a whole. The prospects of such a reform were not good: late in 1970 the government of Colonel Sánchez Hernández had, under pressure from the US and the Christian Democrats, tabled an 'Irrigation and Drainage Law' *(Ley de Riego y Arenamiento)*, designed to improve irrigation and yields on the lands of small and medium owners. Claiming that such a measure, which involved a very limited amount of expropriation, infringed basic property rights, the oligarchy steadfastly blocked the proposal despite the fact that it offered them generous compensation. However, the landed bourgeoisie was neither so omnipotent nor sufficiently perspicacious to forestall all further efforts at reform. The demands of the US and the reformist parties for change in the mid-1970s were emphatic enough to push Sánchez Hernández' successor Molina into partial opposition to the most entrenched elements of the oligarchy; in June 1976, the regime tabled a reform law that established the *Instituto Salvadoreño de Transformación Agraria* (ISTA) and sought to provide itself with broader support and a populist image with discrete redistribution.

The scope of the Molina reform proposals was never great, being limited to expropriating 56,000 hectares of cattle and cotton land belonging to 250 owners in Usulután and San Miguel and distributing it to some 12,000 peasant families. The concentration of ownership in these areas was particularly severe with five landlords possessing 12,000 hectares between them. But although the new law affected only 4 per cent of the country's land area and provided generous compensation, full rights of appeal and strenuous guarantees against further measures, resistance was quick to develop. It was orchestrated by the vanguard organisation of the oligarchy, the *Asociación Nacional de Empresas Privadas* (ANEP), and the newly-established *Frente de Agricultores de la Región Oriental* (FARO), which was formed by landlords from the east of the country to fight the reform law. FARO not only lobbied publicly against Molina but also organised opposition within the officer corps and set up independent vigilante groups in an unprecedented show of defiance. At the same time so much capital was being taken out of the country that the exchange rate of the *colón* against the Guatemalan *quetzal* fell from 2.5 to 3.0. In the end such precautions proved unnecessary; so vociferous was the press campaign against the regime that after four months of brinkmanship Molina ditched his plans and not an inch of soil changed hands.[44] This failure to bring about a modicum of social change in the countryside, even when such a project had the backing of the military government, had a discernable effect upon political developments, especially amongst the reformist parties, which had set great store by the reform. However, before we consider this in more detail we should take stock of some of the major features of the society that the economic changes of the last 20 years have produced.

The Quality of Life

In a country of only 20,000 square kilometres and five million people the impact of such structures of industry and agriculture could only be all-encompassing. In 1961 the poorest 61 per cent of the population earnt 21 per cent of the national income while the richest 5 per cent received 32 per cent, the top 1 per cent alone accounting for 18 per cent of earnings.[45] When the Alliance quietly faded away in the early 1970s this enormous imbalance of wealth had in no sense been rectified: the top 8 per cent of the population received 50 per cent of national income, 92 per cent of Salvadorean citizens having to make do with the remaining 50 per cent. Nearly one third of the population lived on $5 per month per head and 58 per cent existed on less than $10.[46]

Such a distribution of wealth and power has led to a situation in housing, for instance, where less than a sixth of all homes have three rooms or more and nearly a third possess only one room for an average of five people.[47] The consequences of this in terms of crowding, lack of privacy and absence of basic hygiene are only too obvious. Only 15 per cent of the population live in houses with potable water, 36 per cent have ready access to it, and 42 per cent do not have a readily accessible source. In the countryside 80 per cent of the population lack a close source of drinking water and there is no plumbed system whatsoever.[48] The statistics for sanitary facilities are equally bad: a mere 24 per cent of housing units are provided with latrines (internal or external). Some 70 per cent of homes possess only an earthen floor and 66 per cent lack electricity.

There is an almost mathematical relation between this state of affairs and the disastrous condition of the nation's health. Life expectancy at birth is 58.5 years, a figure which, if considered alone, occludes the high levels of both births and infant mortality, which in 1975 stood at 58.3 per thousand live births (the corresponding figure in the US was 16.1). Yet, in the 1960s the population grew by 3.7 per cent a year, and between 1972 and 1977 it rose a full 15 per cent. This is certainly in part due to a gradual diminution over the last 40 years of the overall death rate, but it is clear that the birth rate, one of the highest in Latin America, is the main factor.

The progressive aggravation of El Salvador's acute population problem has been only marginally affected by official family planning schemes which formally encompassed a meagre 4,000 women in 1971/2, although many middle-class women acquire contraception privately and a much greater number of peasant women come into contact with the state birth control system through rural clinics. As demonstrated most acutely in the case of India, but evident in the majority of neo-colonial countries, population control programmes are almost invariably authoritarian, frequently embody substantial deceit, and are designed to facilitate state control rather than that of women over their own bodies. There is ample evidence to suggest that this is the case in El Salvador, where sterilisation is frequently practised – with or without a woman's consent – with clinics being allocated quotas for sterilisations which they must meet to ensure continued funding. In the Salvadorean *campo*, contraception comes into conflict less with the Church than with the ideology of fertility, which is sustained by the need to maintain labour power in the household, the expectation of high mortality amongst infants, and the requirement of *machismo* that a wife bear many children. Thus, women find themselves in conflict both with men and and with the state in their need to retain autonomy over their fertility.[49] This is commonplace in Latin America and many peasant societies, but El Salvador is somewhat distinct in that it has one of the lowest marriage rates in the hemisphere, in 1976 at 4.4 per thousand people (9.9 in the US). This undoubtedly reflects the weakness of the institution as an economic mechanism (inheritance) in a very poor country as well as its dislocation with a labour system that depends upon migration – both internal and external – but by no means signifies any relief from the exigencies of male expectations of female fertility, no less overbearing within 'free unions' than legally sanctioned relationships. The testimony of a woman doctor working near Santa Ana suggests that in addition to the manifest importance of women's labour outside the strictly domestic domain, the division of labour in the countryside of an unambiguously *machista* society embodies appreciable inter-sexual conflict:

> I worked 26 kilometres from Santa Ana and came across many cases of little girls of two or three months who were suffering from very serious vaginal infections. At first I thought that it must be a parasite but I soon realised that it wasn't. I began to question the mothers, but it is very difficult because the peasant women are very withdrawn and it takes a lot to win their confidence. At last, after a couple of months, one of them explained it to me. She told me that in the countryside it was customary to take the 'virtue' of recently-born girls.
> 'And what do they do to take their "virtue"?', I asked.
> 'They make a cross there with a razor blade', she told me.
> 'Why?'
> 'Because that way they become better workers and last longer without needing a man.'[50]

Activity of this sort should be understood in the context of male conduct that has compelled the contemporary guerrilla movement to adopt the slogan 'A real revolutionary is a man who doesn't beat his wife.'

Normally this doctor would be principally concerned with treating gastroenteritis and other diarrhoeal diseases as well as a plethora of parasitic ailments which, taken together, accounted for 22 per cent of all deaths in 1973 (0.8 per cent in the US). These complaints are caused by lack of hygiene rather than poor nutrition, although when they take hold they damage the body's capacity for nutritional intake and lead to wasting. The most rational form of prevention would be less directly medical than a massive sanitary and housing programme, but even in the absence of this the Salvadorean countryside lacks all but the most minimal facilities for medical care. The country possesses 1,100 doctors, one for every 3,592 people, by far the lowest ratio in Central America. This is bad enough in itself, but with 725 doctors (67 per cent) working in the capital, the real position in the *campo* is very much worse. In 1973, when 100 Salvadorean doctors were living abroad, the entire country bar San Salvador and Santa Ana relied on the services of 159 physicians (16 per cent of the official total); only five doctors were working in the departments of Morazán and Chalatenango, which possess 10 per cent of the population and can boast one doctor for every 90,000 inhabitants. In the city there are 1.4 hospital beds for every 10,000 people — the lowest provision in all Latin America – and in the provinces the figure is 0.1 bed per 10,000.[51] With notable and often heroic exceptions, the medical profession has a long tradition of conservatism and a marked proclivity for the rewards of private practice: 245 work exclusively outside the state system. But this of course, is as much a function as a cause of the miserable number of doctors. The root problem is once again economic; not only do a mere 15 per cent of medical students graduate (largely because of lack of funds) but the country possesses only 1,000 nurses, 400 dentists, a dozen sanitary engineers, ten trained nutritionists and half a dozen health education workers.[52] The corollary of this is a widespread reliance upon the stock of amateur 'paramedics' bred in chemist's shops, schoolrooms and churches, as well as the more traditional remedies of indigenous medicine which are by no means ineffective in certain respects but scarcely compensate for, and still less justify, the bankruptcy of the state health system.

The other major item of state social expenditure – education – is in an equally bad condition. The costs of El Salvador's backwardness are borne intellectually as well as physically by its people, only 55 per cent of whom can read and write (39 per cent in the countryside and 45 per cent of all women). Consistent with the internal balance of power, schools are more plentiful and generally better in the towns than in the *campo*, where absenteeism is very high because of the reliance upon the labour power of children from the earliest possible age. At the start of the 1970s only 65 per cent of all eight-year-olds were registered in schools; the number that actually attended must have been much less. In 1974, only 18 per cent of the population had completed primary education, 3.6 per cent had finished secondary schooling and 0.8 per cent had acquired a university degree.[53] Such figures scarcely require embellishment; if one source reports that 14-year-olds were having to memorise the names of Mohammed's 15 wives as part of the history syllabus, this would seem to be a marginal impediment when set against the capital gains of mastering literacy and elementary mathematics.[54] However, the question of the orientation of the curriculum combined with the problems of attendance and finance to fuel a major crisis in education in the late 1960s and early 1970s.

This crisis had a great political impact, one central reason being simply the very youthfulness of Salvadorean society, 46 per cent of which is less than 14 years old and only 14 per cent older than 45.[55] This places a premium on both educational facilities and the influence of teachers at all levels but particularly in the rural areas where they have a status akin to that of the parish priest deriving from their literacy and position as 'broker' with the authorities. The poor pay and bad conditions of the teaching profession in Latin America has produced a deep-seated radicalism, particularly in the countryside; perhaps the most acute case is the Maoist-dominated teachers' union in Peru (SUTEP), but the malaise and its effects are general. In El Salvador discontent with conditions – frequent instances of sexual molestation by inspectors as well as more obvious factors such as low pay and the cutback of training colleges – broke into the open in 1968, when a major rebellion against the *oficialista* union's attempts to impose various government 'reforms' (cuts in a broad range of facilities in the name of rationalisation) led to a national strike by the left-wing *Asociación Nacional de Educadores Salvadoreños* (ANDES). Although the Sánchez Hernández regime broke the strike, it was unable to destroy the union, which struck again for two months in 1971, for which it received extensive popular backing. By this time ANDES had become established as one of the principal foci of opposition in the countryside, with many of its members supporting the new revolutionary groups. It is no coincidence that over the last decade, and particularly during the civil war, teachers have been a principal target of government persecution, several hundred losing their lives in the repression.

These developments were not unnaturally mirrored in higher education, especially at the National University, which underwent major expansion in the 1960s with the student population doubling in size and the budget rising fourfold between 1962 and 1969. Although prone to what might be termed the natural deviations of youth – adventurism, tendencies towards gangsterism and an aversion to patient organisational work in the mass movement – Latin American students have demonstrated a much more consistent radicalism than their European counterparts. Defence of university autonomy and, in many cases, staff–student co-administration combined with the need to work in another job have contributed towards a political commitment that flies in the face of archaic teaching methods, the often dropsy-like effect of career-orientated subjects, and the suffocative esotericism central to many aspects of the hispanic intellectual inheritance. So strong was the rebellion against this conception of the university in the 1960s that even certain elements of the European Trotskyist movement, bedazzled by the events of May 1968 in their backyard, elevated the Latin American student movement into the revolutionary vanguard and embraced the essentially elitist strategy of guerrilla *foquismo* practised by Che Guevara and systematised by Regis Debray. These points will be taken up in more detail later on; here we should just note that the Salvadorean university was no exception to this general tendency. The liberalisation and standardisation of admissions in 1963 under the new rector, ex-junta member Fabio Castillo, and the introduction of courses, such as *Areas Comunales*, that directly addressed the social problems of the nation contributed to the upsurge in radical debate and a deepening hostility between the university and the military regimes. While law and engineering courses continued to be popular for obvious reasons, by 1974 nearly half the 30,000 students were enrolled in the 'subversive' faculties of Humanities and Social Sciences. Yet, as one astute reactionary journalist noted, this process was still constrained by the limits of the liberal academy:

> the communists succumb better to money than to bullets. In Guatemala the
> anti-guerrilla struggle costs us approximately $50,000 a day, or an annual

cost of more than $18 million, plus the blood. The University of El Salvador costs approximately $6 million and there are the communists fighting amongst themselves . . . When a communist earns $400 a month he no longer thinks of Sierra Maestras . . .[56]

All the same, a great many students were not prepared to emulate the armchair Marxists who were their professors, and by the end of the decade social democrats like Castillo were themselves under fire from their pupils. The traditional student march *(bufonada)*, in which political leaders were lampooned and subjected to sexual satire, had been transformed into a major political demonstration of the left with an impact well beyond the confines of the campus. Although the prolonged university strike of 1969/70 failed to destabilise the regime or have a profound effect on the reformist opposition parties, it was no ephemeral outburst and registered its impact less obviously in strengthening the dissident wing of the PCS, which by virtue of its adherence to a parliamentary strategy was in the midst of a profound internal crisis.

The progressive pauperisation of the rural working class and peasantry and the radicalisation of the petty bourgeoisie (students, teachers, certain professional and small commercial circles) conform to long-term tendencies in Salvadorean society but the charges wrought by the Alliance for Progress speeded them up and gave them an edge that had been lacking in previous decades. In the towns this process was uneven largely because of the limited expansion in industry and the partial recomposition of the working class which, though still extremely poor, experienced a temporary increase in its earning power. Yet even this factor was contradictory and unstable, for not only did there emerge a small kernel of industrialists who sought to refine the terms of the landed bourgeoisie's mandate, but the urban proletariat itself also began to acquire greater cohesion. The resolution of the interests of these groups was impossible in the context of existing Salvadorean society, but until the early 1970s these antagonisms were prevented from reaching a political crisis-point by the military regime, which engaged in a series of partial concessions and manoeuvres while maintaining an omnipotent veto in the shape of its capacity for unrestrained repression.

5

'REPRESSION WITH REFORMS'

The Salvadorean people are noble; they have trusted and they continue to trust their leaders. But they have now reached their limit. At this moment, the reforms under consideration are like a rock teetering on the edge of a precipice that no one and nothing can prevent from falling.

President Fidel Sánchez Hernández, September 1970

The *Partido de Conciliación Nacional* (PCN) ruled El Salvador for 18 years, from its foundation in September 1961 until the coup of October 1979. In establishing the party, Colonel Julio Rivera aimed to provide a durable vehicle with which the military might maintain power and yet avoid the pitfalls of a purely institutionalist rule, retaining space for negotiation and a degree of flexibility. Aside from the avalanche of grandiose pronouncements which the party's functionaries rained down on the Salvadorean people, its principal claim to being democratic lay in the commitment to hold elections every five years. These, through a combination of fraud and open coercion, it unfailingly won, never courting the risks of proving that it was not really the party of officialism. Hence, Rivera converted his provisional presidency into one that was 'constitutional' in March 1962, opposed only by a donkey nominated by the students as 'the only candidate worthy of competing with officialism'.[1] The party's founder arranged to be succeeded, with few problems, by Minister of the Interior Colonel Fidel Sánchez Hernández in 1965, and Sánchez Hernández in turn secured the election of his secretary, Colonel Arturo Molina, in 1972, albeit with much greater difficulty.

By conceding formal democratic liberties with a modicum of consistency but refusing with equal regularity to countenance their implementation, the PCN avoided being tarnished as an outright dictatorship in most of the chancelleries of the world. At the same time, it bolstered its control by holding out the promise to occupy the 'middle ground' to the bourgeois and liberal opposition parties, which, despite a number of tactical boycotts, continued to fight elections up until 1977. This gave the PCN regimes a veneer of legitimacy, even if it was at the expense of periodic mobilisation followed by denunciations of foul play. Moreover, it enabled the military to fire an occasional salvo across the bows of the oligarchy, which invariably put up its own candidate, usually under the banner of the *Partido Popular Salvadoreño* (PPS), less in the expectation of defeating the PCN than with the aim of exerting pressure on it and reaffirming the interests of the coffee clans in their rawest form. At no stage did the PPS or any other oligarchic political initiative make serious inroads into the PCN's authority: the family elders of ANEP and FARO were fully aware that the PCN's candidate enjoyed the support, albeit often grudging, of the bulk of the officer corps. As we have seen, the fundamental unity of interest between the landed bourgeoisie and the military did not deter the colonels from brushing with the oligarchy. In September 1970, for example, Sánchez Hernández did not hesitate to rebut suggestions that he was leading the country down the path taken by Chile following the election of the *Unidad Popular* government, and he employed forceful language, warning the 'fierce opponents of evolution' that if they did not accept 'peaceful and orderly change' they could expect 'terror and violence'.[2] The president even acquiesced for a while in a bureaucratic coup by the parliamentary opposition, which rearranged the composition of congressional committees so as to give it effective power to halt legislation. Molina likewise courted full oligarchic opprobrium before he backtracked on the 1976 agrarian reform. These, though, were extreme instances at times of difficulty. Although the PCN was not simply a compliant extension of the oligarchy, it was none the less the leading party of reaction, umbilically tied to dictatorship, popular in so far as it dispensed favours, and atrophied in the sense that its staff of landlords, ambitious colonels and time-serving bureaucrats was palpably incapable of delivering to El Salvador even the smallest part of what it promised.

The enhanced capacity of the military for this role, and its reorientation towards counter-insurgency warfare was a major preoccupation of the PCN regimes. In this they were directly encouraged by the US, which had from the start conceived of this as an integral feature of the Alliance for Progress. In the words of General Enemark,

The role of Latin American security forces . . . is of basic importance. In order for the Alliance for Progress to have any chance of success, the governments must have enough power to control subversion, prevent terrorism and eliminate flows of violence which may reach unmanageable proportions.[3]

Since Cuba was the principal cause of the extensive US programme of revitalising the military apparatuses of the hemisphere, it is not surprising that Central America received special attention, but within the region the main beneficiaries were Guatemala and Nicaragua, which had the most powerful armies. The Salvadoreans, with an army of only 6,500 men and paramilitary forces *(Guardia Nacional; Policía Nacional; Policía de Hacienda)* of 5,500, continued to be regarded as a subsidiary power. Nevertheless, the Military Aid, Civic Action, Counter-Insurgency Warfare, Office of Public Safety and Basic Officer Training programmes were all instituted. Together with a new round of arms sales they served to strengthen both the military and the regime, locking them more tightly into the US military network centred on Southern Command HQ in the Canal Zone. Between 1950 and 1975, 1,682 officers underwent US training, nearly 400 of them at Fort Gulick in the Canal Zone.[4] The Military Assistance programme yielded $4.3 million between 1950 and 1960, rising to $2.8 million for 1970–5, while military sales agreements over the period 1955 to 1975 were valued at $2.3 million.[5] From 1963, the Office of Public Safety transferred its attentions from the National Police to the National Guard, eventually training 450 men at a cost of $2.1 million.

In comparative terms the US military programme in El Salvador was, therefore, quite modest: the military's arsenals were replenished, but until 1975 mostly from ex-Second World War stock, and force levels were not greatly expanded, the missions concentrating on the professionalisation of the existing apparatus. However, within El Salvador itself the impact was not negligible; if the aid poured into the country in the 1980s was to make these amounts seem paltry, the framework for its use was laid in the 1960s. US officers in the country nurtured contacts and built up a network of friends, a practice that beyond doubt was undertaken in close liaison with the CIA and in a number of instances involved control of lucrative contracts and political favours beyond the institutional domain. In the euphemistic prose of the Pentagon,

our security assistance program facilitates our overall relations with the government of El Salvador and fosters useful professional contacts with key members of the Salvadorean armed forces.[6]

El Salvador fitted unremarkably into the pattern of US military policy in the region as outlined in 1966 by Defense Secretary Robert McNamara: the US preferred to build up efficient and co-operative local armies rather than rely upon periodic invasion by the Marine Corps, not just because of the attendant difficulties in foreign relations but also because the local forces possessed a far greater knowledge of 'geographical and psychological conditions'. Local armies were also more likely to attract local support and to have a stronger motivation 'to defend the country'. Last, but not least, they were cheap: Central American soldiers could be trained at a cost of $540 per man per year against $4,500 for each US soldier.[7]

In order to strengthen this strategy, in 1964 the US sponsored the foundation of CONDECA (the Central American Defense Council), in which all regional states except Costa Rica and Panama originally participated. The delay in establishing CONDECA was largely due to nationalist rivalries, but it soon proved to be a successful form of co-ordination. A number of joint manoeuvres were held in the mid-1960s and the level of co-operation and exchange of information between defence ministries increased markedly. This enlarged military community, explicitly designed to thwart internal subversion and to act as the penultimate guarantor of the dictatorships of Central America, served as a critical prop for the PCN although it was not until the 1970s that it played an open role in defending the Salvadorean dominant bloc.[8]

There are very few Salvadorean peasants or workers who have even heard of CONDECA but almost all have experience (and a deep-seated fear) of the paramilitary force that imposed PCN rule in the countryside, provided essential support for the official repressive apparatus, and in itself gave the lie to the pseudo-democratic facade carefully tended by the colonels. Officially dubbed *Organización Democrática Nacionalista*, this organisation was known to all by its unmistakable acronym ORDEN (order). The origins of ORDEN are far from clear, which is consistent with its semi-clandestine character. Some versions have it being founded in 1968, others suggest an earlier date, 1964 or 1965. Nobody, however, disputes that its founder and driving-force was and is General José Alberto ('Chele') Medrano, chief of the National Guard until late 1970. ORDEN has always occupied an ambiguous position with respect to the formal state apparatus since no secret was made of the fact that its 'ex-officio' head was the president and that daily control rested with the Ministry of Defence; yet there was no formal budget, no published statutes and certainly no public accountability. In practice ORDEN continues to be not just the shock-force but the organised constituency of the right in the *campo*. Comprising somewhere between 50,000 and 100,000 members, it is no elite but a species of political party. Some of its members are former conscripts from the army or National Guard but many more are recruited through the promise of land, cheap credit and supplies, permanent work and medical facilities, joining as the only means of avoiding abject poverty and repression; an ORDEN *carnet* is the best passport to safety from the 'security forces'. Recruited through a system of petty favours and working as spies, vigilantes and executioners in their home *pueblos*, these men constitute a vast auxiliary force, the principal strength of which is its immersion in the peasantry. The real military kernel of ORDEN, perhaps 10,000 strong, operates openly in the more formal *patrullas cantonales*, the part-time police force of the villages.

The existence of ORDEN and its sheer size meant that political conflict in the countryside could never be a simple case of whole *pueblos* opposing the military; the battle would also take place within the communities, with every village becoming a microcosm of the wider civil war. The particular pattern of violence and terrible atrocities of the Salvadorean war owe much to this fact. Moreover, one group on the left – FARN – identified in ORDEN a key element in the rise of a fascist tendency within certain military and oligarchic circles. The term 'fascist' is freely used in the propaganda of the left, but in this case it was applied with greater precision and clear reference to the European movements of the 1920s and 1930s, being understood to be not simply synonymous with military dictatorship but also to incorporate a mass movement pledged to the destruction of independent working-class organisation and the establishment of a corporativist state. Significantly, the first serious analysis of ORDEN, written at the end of the 1960s by Roque Dalton, the effective founder of the FARN, suggested but did not develop this interpretation, which, despite being open to question at a number of levels, was very much a product of political developments in the mid-1970s.[9]

In the 1960s ORDEN was far from quiescent, but neither was it overworked for there was only intermittent need for a militia 'to counteract communist subversion'. The main political opposition to the PCN was neither communist nor subversive; it espoused a variety of reforms but always within the orbit of capitalism and with a remarkably consistent conviction that charge could be obtained inside the existing political structures. The party that led this opposition was the *Partido Demócrata Cristiano* (PDC), set up in the Hotel International in November 1960 as a 'moderate' and 'Christian' alternative to the 'communist threat' its founders perceived during the heady days of the civilian junta. In its early years Salvadorean Christian Democracy differed little from its sister parties in the rest of Latin America, and evidenced the same influences and orientation that made the movement one of the leading political phenomena of the decade. The Christian Democrats strove to elevate the social doctrine of the Roman Catholic Church over its tradition as the eager bible-bearer of the *conquistadores*, the sanctifier of centuries of temporal oppression, and a huge commercial concern no less exploitative than the lay elite through the extensive lands of the orders and the insistent demands for tithes from the parish priests.

In the 1960s the reformist strain of catholicism evidenced in the papal bulls of Leo XIII (*Rerum Novarum*, 1891, supporting the social obligations of private property) and Pius XI (*Quadraggesimo Anno*, 1931, attacking the effects of *laissez-faire* capitalism and defending workers' rights to organise) was revived in John XXIII's *Master et Magister* (1961), Paul VI's *Populorum Progressi* (1967) and the writings of Jacques Maritain, Teilhard de Chardin, Hans Kung and others. In addressing the social implications of established liturgical practice, the Second Vatican Council, established in 1962, was to provide the doctrinal basis for the Latin American Church's tentative adoption of the hazy causes of 'development', 'integration' and 'basic reforms'. This movement gained greater momentum and coherence following the conferences of the Latin American Bishops' Council (CELAM) at Mar del Plata, Argentina, in 1967 and, much more strongly, at Medellin, Colombia, the following year. The fundamental contradictions bound up in this movement were not long in gestation. By the 1970s a powerful current inside the lower orders of the Church was adhering to the radical postulates of the 'Theology of Liberation', challenging the religious hierarchy in terms of its ecclesiastical power, political alliances and biblical exegesis, embracing liberation struggles as legitimate incarnations of the revindications of the oppressed and defending political activism as an integral part of pastoral work among the poor.

Camilo Torres was the first and most celebrated martyr of this cause, but there were many more like him.

Christian Democracy has always been fervently opposed to this movement, and never posed a real threat to either the religious or lay status quo. In affirming the viability of a reformed capitalist system, Christian Democracy manifests a 'moment' in the erratic and crisis-ridden course followed by the Latin American Church over the last two decades. In the 1960s, the era of the Alliance for Progress, the parties of Christian Democracy represented a 'safe option' both as manageable sparring partners in opposition and as capable, if occasionally unreliable, allies in government. The obvious high-point of Latin American Christian Democracy is the 'Revolution in Liberty' introduced in Chile by the government of Eduardo Frei (1964–70) that prepared much of the ground for the reforms of *Unidad Popular*. The Salvadoreans learnt and benefited a great deal from the example of their Chilean colleagues and many of them were sent to Santiago for training, but they retained tighter links with the closer and more cautious Venezuelan party, COPEI, which was to support them consistently, regardless of the consequences.

Of the eight-man committee that founded the party late in November 1960, one soon emerged as an obvious political leader: José Napoleón Duarte. Born in 1926 to a father who was a minor confectionary entrepreneur, Duarte had in his youth supported the PUD of Arturo Romero and even suffered a spell of imprisonment under Colonel Aguirre. After obtaining a degree in civil engineering from the premier Catholic university in the US, Notre Dame, he married the daughter of an owner of a large construction firm, shortly afterwards entering into partnership with his father-in-law. Such a background was common to the leaders of the PDC, but Duarte set himself apart with his populist touch, presenting himself as a man of the people on the grounds that his mother, a seamstress, was of humble stock and that he had worked his way to the top by dint of his own efforts. Duarte's craggy features, his knack of using popular argot and his preparedness to address the concrete problems of the people lent an appeal to the PDC's rambling and ill-defined programme that it would otherwise never have generated. In stressing that its 'revolution' would not be destructive but scientifically planned and implemented by a technically efficient state, that property was a natural right and that by investing savings the working class could as a whole ameliorate its position and achieve a classless society, the PDC was in fact ideologically very close to the PCN. In 1961 agrarian reform was placed fifth on its list of seven priorities for the peasantry; by 1967 it had been given more emphasis but was still not a leading demand. The party's strength lay primarily in its demand for free elections, and its base was in the urban petty bourgeoisie, particularly the market-sellers *(comerciantes)*, for whom its attacks on co-habitation outside marriage and exaltation of the family and woman-as-mother provided a comfortable complement to more immediate economic initiatives.[10]

In 1964, the PDC was allowed to win 14 seats in Congress against 32 held by the PCN. That year it also won control of 37 municipalities, including San Salvador where considerable resources had been poured in to obtain Duarte's victory in the election for mayor, a post he held until 1969 and which the party controlled until 1976. The relative lack of fraud in the 1964 and 1966 local elections and the consolidation of the PDC's power-base in the capital persuaded the party that its strategy was correct and encouraged Mayor Duarte to make pronouncements on US foreign policy that ten years later were to look distinctly hollow:

> [the US] maintains the Iberoamerican countries in a condition of direct dependence upon the international political decisions most beneficial to the US . . . Thus the North Americans preach to us democracy while everwhere they support dictatorships.[11]

Such statements helped to buoy up support for the PDC to the extent that even the PCS viewed it as the most influential popular party and its leading competitor.[12] None the less, besides the still illegal PCS, the PDC had to contend with the unstable, marginal but ever vocal and at times threatening presence of the social democrats.

The social democratic lineage, such as it was, can be traced back through the *Partido de Acción Renovadora* (PAR) that had sustained a tenuous existence since the late 1940s posing as a liberal alternative to the incumbent colonel. In 1965 sectors of the PAR's constituency that had been radicalised by the experience of 1960–1 and had rejected the soft line of the PDC forced a split in the party's heterogeneous membership with the right moving out to form the PPS while the PAR–*Nueva Linea*, led by Fabio Castillo, built its strategy around the demand for an immediate agrarian reform. This prompted the Archbishop of San Vicente to warn all who associated themselves with the party that they faced excommunication. Yet, despite a major campaign from the right, Rivera refused to ban the PAR immediately, preferring to draw it out into the open and increase police harassment until after the 1967 elections, when the party won 29 per cent of the vote and was promptly outlawed.

The PAR was quickly succeeded by a similar anti-communist 'party of the centre', the *Movimiento Nacional Revolucionario* (MNR), which had originally been formed in 1964 as a small group around the lawyer and university professor Guillermo Ungo. The MNR only came to prominence in 1968 following the proscription of the PAR, with which it had much in common, especially the critique of the PDC and insistence upon agrarian reform. But after a modest success in the 1968 congressional elections it lost all its seats in 1970. Since then the MNR has been unable to grow beyond a redoubt of intellectuals attached to 'democratic socialism' along the lines of the British Labour Party, with which it shares membership of the Second International. Yet, the MNR leadership has proved remarkably resilient in producing many of the major political initiatives of the liberal opposition. It might be said that in the 1960s and for most of the 1970s social democracy in El Salvador offered an alternative to Christian Democracy that dispensed with its religious precepts and put resolve into the PDC's electoralist and gradualist reformism, but it never broke with it, remaining an articulate but isolated left wing within the besieged bourgeois alternative caucus to the PCN.

The need of the PCN to resort to widespread ballot-rigging in the presidential poll of 1967 and the elections to the legislature in 1968 suggests that the military regime would have run into deep water earlier than it finally did had it not been for the 1969 war with Honduras. In reality, the 'Football War' had very little to do with soccer: although it was skilfully managed by the military and the PCN, it was no simple distraction but an event that sprang logically from the escalating domestic social crisis and increased regional tension.

For decades the emigration of large numbers of *campesinos* to Honduras had provided the Salvadorean oligarchy with a cheap and convenient safety valve. Not only was Honduras underpopulated but since the 1920s the fruit companies had provided a constant demand for labour that offset the regional variations at home. By 1968 there were perhaps 300,000 Salvadoreans living in Honduras. This in itself had generated deep discontent on the part of the Honduran ruling class with the Salvadoreans' discreet policy of *lebensraum*, but by the mid-1960s the position was worsened by a number of other factors. First, the fruit companies' major reduction of their labour force from the late 1950s had thrown many immigrant workers onto the land;

since the Salvadoreans comprised nearly a third of the companies' workers the numbers involved were substantial, leading to occasional friction with Honduran *campesinos*, especially in the broder area.[13] Secondly, Honduras had done badly out of the CACM; this was most evident in its commercial relations with El Salvador. Of the regional total of value added in the manufacturing sector in 1968, Guatemala contributed 34 per cent, El Salvador 24 per cent and Honduras only 7.7 per cent. Between 1960 and 1968, Salvadorean exports to Honduras had increased five-fold, whereas Honduran sales to El Salvador had only doubled.[14] In the first six months of 1969, the Honduran trade deficit with El Salvador alone was $5 million. Thus, the CACM's encouragement of free trade without any consideration of regional planning had engendered within the Honduran dominant bloc a deep resentment and the fear that Salvadorean capital would monopolise Honduras' weak internal market.

In addition to these economic factors, there was a political motive for building a campaign against the Salvadorean settlers. Colonel López Arellano, who had come to power through a coup in 1963 and had himself elected president in 1965, was coming to the end of his term and wished to prolong his rule. A substantial part of the Honduran military, its parasitic following of civil servants, small traders and landlords, as well as the fruit companies, backed this scheme in view of the growing mobilisation of the peasantry and working class, which had threatened the precarious stability of the ruling bloc with a general strike in September 1968. One obvious means of channelling discontent away from the ruling class and at the same time ministering to the country's accelerating economic crisis was to escalate the tension with El Salvador that had been rising since May 1967 with the harassment of immigrants and a number of border incidents.

The first move was, like many that followed it, made in highly demagogic fashion. Following the July 1968 agrarian reform law, letters were sent to Salvadorean settlers at the end of April 1969 giving them 30 days to 'return' their lands to the Honduran state for redistribution to its own citizens. The letters had barely arrived before expulsions began. It was, however, football that provided the happy pretext for a full onslaught. On 8 June the two countries played in Tegucigalpa in the first leg of a match to decide who would challenge Haiti to represent the Caribbean region in the 1970 World Cup; the Hondurans won 1:0. The first refugees crossed the border the same day, as reports arrived in San Salvador explaining the country's defeat in terms of a possible poisoning of the team's food and the fact that it had been unable to sleep the night before the match because of the continuous demonstrations outside its hotel. A week later El Salvador won the second leg 3:0 at home, with incensed Salvadoreans bombarding the visiting Honduran fans with fireworks. In Honduras it was rumoured that the fans had been stoned and women had been raped. In reply the Sánchez Hernández regime alleged that its Honduran counterpart's vigilante group *Mancha Brava* was terrorising immigrants in Tegucigalpa, and on 25 June filed a complaint of 'genocide' with the Inter-American Human Rights Commission. By this time some 10,000 refugees had returned and nobody paid much attention to the final play-off of the football match in neutral Mexico City. The Salvadorean regime was under great pressure to adopt a belligerent position – not just from the military, convinced of its overriding superiority, but also from the PDC and MNR. Stung by oligarchic accusations of cowardice and agreeably surprised (with good cause) at the legal opposition's capitulation to jingoism, the Sánchez Hernández government rejected all efforts of the CACM to mediate and formed a bloc with the parliamentary opposition in the Front for National Unity (FUN). There was little opposition to this belligerence largely because of popular antipathy towards the Honduran expulsions; even the PCS backed the regime's position to the extent that it encouraged its student militants to present themselves as volunteers at the San Carlos barracks. On 24 June the PDC called for military action, and Duarte made use of his control over the municipality of San Salvador to provide logistical support for the military in organising civilian patrols of the city while the army was away fighting.

The army invaded Honduras on 14 July and remained for four days. Two Salvadorean columns captured the roads to Santa Rosa de Copán and Choluteca, encountering little resistance from the poorly-prepared Honduran forces. The relative absence of fighting did not mean, however, that there were no casualties. Some 4,000 Hondurans died in the invasion, the majority being civilians killed in militarily pointless but typically enthusiastic 'mopping-up operations'. The Salvadorean high command later proudly drew parallels with the Arab–Israeli Six-Day War; even commentators such as Alastair White, who should have known better, made this analogy. In fact, although the Salvadoreans had opened the roads to San Pedro Sula and Tegucigalpa, they were operating with overextended lines, lacked ammunition and had not destroyed enough of the surprisingly efficient Honduran airforce to stop it bombing their oil-storage tanks at Acajutla, causing a severe shortage of fuel. Guatemala, alarmed at the prospect of a long-term occupation and an upset in the regional balance of power, moved quickly to condemn any possible boundary changes, while the US, equally seriously concerned at the idea of collapse of the CACM and CONDECA, organised an OAS-controlled ceasefire agreement which both sides eagerly accepted.

The immediate damage was bad enough: both countries lost the market of the other, for El Salvador this amounted to $23 million's worth of trade. In addition to this, the country had spent about $20 million on the war and had to disburse a further $11 million over the next two years to replenish its depleted arms stocks. Moreover, the regime had to cope with tens of thousands of refugees, for whom it had neither immediate resources nor a long-term solution, contenting itself with the remedy of ordering those who flooded into the cities to return to their home regions. But worse still than this was the fact that the oligarchy had lost its highly important demographic safety valve, compounding the social crisis in the countryside which was soon to see the emergence of radical peasant unions, an important contingent of which were refugees. With the withdrawal of Honduras from both the CACM and CONDECA, the regional ruling class as a whole also suffered a setback which would not readily be mended. All this occurred in the same year that Nixon formally recognised the failure of the Alliance for Progress, a step that could barely be construed as positive since it did not presage any positive change in policy, which now shifted back in a nondescript fashion to the basic task of overseeing and encouraging the military domination of Central America in the context of free market capitalism. The reformist ideals of yore were accounted ambitious and costly mistakes.

The war with Honduras did not lead to the political relaxation the opposition had hoped for. The steady rise in coffee prices restored oligarchic self-confidence and stiffened its resolve in opposing the regime's tentative agrarian reform measures of 1970. Badly shaken by the students' and teachers' strikes, Sánchez Hernández did, however, attempt the ambitious step of offering an alliance to the PDC. This was rejected in favour of fighting the 1972 elections in a more logical coalition of the legal parties in opposition: the MNR, the PDC and the *Unión Democrática Nacionalista* (UDN). The UDN, formed in 1969, stood to the left of the other two parties, and while it incorporated several leaders of the old PAR, was to all intents and purposes a front for the PCS, securing legal status by limiting itself to minimal democratic demands. The UDN's modest following of urban workers and artisans as well as the influence of the PCS provided the new alliance, the *Unión Nacional Opositora* (UNO, the acronym meaning 'one' in Spanish), with sufficient internal balance and breadth of popular appeal to raise expectations of an easy victory in the elections of March 1972. The reasoning of the PCS was that rising popular mobilisation meant that the UDN was obliged to contest the poll:

> [the] campaign revealed a favourable realignment of forces . . . it demonstrated the vitality of the broad front policy . . . it made for the people's political awakening and helped them to realise their potential . . . [15]

Duarte refused to countenance the participation of the PCS in the campaign and demanded the presidential candidature for himself with Ungo as his running-mate. These were conditions that the rest of UNO was obliged to accept, given the PDC's continuing popularity and Duarte's particularly high standing. Moreover, because of the very broad nature of the alliance, the personalities who headed its campaign were not expected to be in agreement with anything more than the common denominator of UNO's necessarily vague programme, encapsulated in the slogan 'Democratic Government, Reform and Progress'.

The formation of UNO was obligatory; the liberal and reformist opposition could no longer afford the luxury of fighting amongst itself if it was to keep the electoralist strategy alive and retain the initiative against the option of armed struggle which was now emerging, albeit sporadically, in a number of guerrilla raids and kidnappings. The judgement of the PCS was at least partially correct: the establishment of a united opposition bloc made the 1972 poll qualitatively different to those which had preceded it. Popular imagination was fired and expectations were high.

Recognition of this and disgust at the PCN's confused meanderings led an important faction of the oligarchy based around the Salaverría family of Ahuachapán to sponsor the strong ultra-right campaign of the *Frente Unido Democrático Independiente* (FUDI), led by General Medrano. Medrano's challenge to the PCN is at least partially explained by the fact that he had been removed as commander of the National Guard in December 1970 for 'disciplinary reasons' – the planning of a coup as a result of discontent with Sánchez Hernández' irrigation law. In

February 1971 Medrano had been arrested for shooting a policeman in what appeared to be a vendetta between the Salaverría and Regalado families, but although the boisterous general admitted the killing, his explanation that it had been done in self-defence sufficed for the charges to be dropped. This was largely because Medrano had not been removed from his position as head of ORDEN, which threw the regime momentarily onto the defensive and enabled Medrano to press home his attacks on the PCN without moderation: 'If the government party wins the elections there will be a coup d'etat. The government party is corrupt and the armed forces do not like corruption.'[16]

Threatened from both sides, Sánchez Hernández lost no time in protecting the candidacy of Molina in traditional style. Duarte's increasingly exuberant campaign tour was attacked and an aide shot dead, UNO broadcasts were sabotaged and control of the voting booths secured by government supporters. But even this was too little too late; the first returns of the presidential poll gave UNO an overwhelming 62,000-vote lead in the capital, with national returns at 54 per cent. On the day after the vote there was a complete radio black-out on the election followed by an announcement from the electoral commission that Molina had won by 9,844 votes, a mere 1.3 per cent of the total number cast. The president-elect, aware that the scale and openness of the fraud could not be brazened out as before, generously offered a recount, but Duarte and Ungo insisted upon completely fresh elections and threatened a general strike if they were not forthcoming. Caught off-balance once again, the PCN quickly convened the National Assembly and had Molina ratified ten days early in a ceremony boycotted by all other parties and badly attended by the regime's own deputies, many of whom could not be ferried to the capital in time. Two weeks later the PCN romped home in the congressional and municipal elections, in which UNO campaigned for defaced ballot papers which, if they outnumbered valid votes, would invalidate the poll. This tactic failed although in San Salvador 75,000 papers were found to be spoilt against 70,000 cast for non-UNO candidates. After over a month of electioneering and two instances of blatant thwarting of popular will, tension in the country was high. A number of armed clashes occurred and several UNO members were killed by ·the National Guard, which was in turn attacked by an anonymous guerrilla group. Troops were stationed throughout San Salvador in expectation of the strike, but UNO appeared to be bereft of any initiative. The only cogent response to the regime's legal coup were the guerrilla attacks.

This stalemate was broken early on the morning of 25 March, when the commander of the Zapote barracks, Colonel Benjamín Mejía, launched a coup in liaison with Major Pedro Guardado and Colonel Manuel Antonio Nuñez, head of the strategically important San Carlos barracks. The rebels drew their support from junior field officers, had no links with UNO and at first tried to establish a military junta without it. However, they openly supported UNO's claims of foul play and when, after eight hours, it was plain that acting alone they would not amass popular support, they urged the alliance to join them. Once he was persuaded that the rebellion was not of Medrano's making, Duarte gave it his support and went on the radio to call for popular resistance to the counter-offensive being prepared by the regime. This was not long in coming, for the coup had gained no military support outside the capital, and the National Guard was mobilising rapidly in Sonsonate and San Miguel under the direction of its commander, Colonel Oscar Gutiérrez. Throughout the afternoon the airforce bombed the rebel barracks while CONDECA, readied for eight years for such an eventuality, went into action with Guatemalan and Nicaraguan planes flying arms and supplies into San Miguel. This action enabled the attack to be pushed home with such speed that the *golpistas* surrendered at 4 p.m. Over 100 people had died and several hundred were wounded; the entire country was put under martial law and large numbers of political prisoners taken. Duarte was unceremoniously dragged out of his asylum in the house of the first secretary of the Venezuelan Embassy, viciously beaten up and dumped on a plane which eventually conveyed him to his spiritual home, Caracas. Molina, who had confidently left on a tour to Taiwan a few days previously, was immediately flown home by the USAF. With a good deal of help from its friends in CONDECA, the PCN had survived, but the experience of the 1972 elections meant that the already very tightly circumscribed rules of the game had changed for good.

Despite the categorical defeat they had suffered, the parties of the legal opposition failed to recognise this until at least 1977, and even thereafter they proved incapable of independently recomposing their strategies in a coherent form. In the interim they were progressively challenged by the forces of the radical left, itself far from unified in organisation or programme but distinguishable from the polished and besuited *politicos* of the PDC and MNR in its commitment to mass organisation and armed struggle.

6

THE RISE OF THE LEFT

In this country there have been good people prepared to
die for the revolution.
But the revolution here and everywhere needs people
who are prepared not only to die
but also to kill for it.

Roque Dalton

The origins of the contemporary left and guerrilla groups in El Salvador
lie in the severe internal crisis faced by both the PDC and the PCS at the
end of the 1960s. Neither party was able to justify its conduct and
policies in a convincing manner to the new generation of radicalised
youth that populated their rank and file. Both, as a consequence, lost
substantial numbers of these militants who, from very different
positions, through distinct routes and with differing results, moved
towards the armed struggle. The crisis in the PCS was the most severe
and of the greatest consequence for the left since it was extended and
expressed through a debate over Leninist strategy rather than simple
frustration and voluntarism.

Ever since 1932 the PCS had formally adhered to the policy of armed
struggle as 'the most probable means of attaining victory', in the words
of the party general secretary, Shafik Jorge Handal, speaking in 1980.
But even Handal is forced to admit that this was scarcely the case in
practice.[1] The PCS intermittently attempted a guerrilla in the wake
of Cuba, 1961-3, without preparation or consideration of the logistical
and social distinctiveness of El Salvador. As a result, it was easily
suppressed by the military, and the party once more set itself firmly
against the armed struggle. As late as 1980 Handal claimed that the
popularity of UNO in the 1972 elections vindicated the electoralist
strategy of the PCS. Furthermore, although the party leader asserted

that this policy was replaced with one of armed struggle in February 1977, with VIIth Congress of the PCS produced a resolution in May 1979 that reiterated its support for UNO, which 'voiced the democratic aspirations and structural changes required by the great majority of people, grouped them behind it, and forced a polarization in the electoral confrontation'. The basis for such a line was spelled out unequivocally elsewhere in the resolution: 'the bourgeois democratic path to solving the political crisis has today to be an inseparable part of substantial socio-economic reforms'.[2] Significantly, the popular version of the resolutions passed by this Congress and published by the PCS mentioned 1932 in only two lines in reference to 'the defeat'.[3] The PCS did not finally embark on guerrilla warfare until the spring of 1980, after three months of a political purgatory in which it found itself, as a logical consequence of its belief in the 'bourgeois democratic path', allied with the military against the left. The fact that matters had to reach such a point a full decade after the party's initial division on the question of the armed struggle demonstrates the strength with which the PCS held to its position. This, in turn, accounts for much of the antipathy shown towards it on the left.

The rebellion against the 'bourgeois democratic path' came at the IVth Congress of the PCS, early in 1970 and before the establishment of UNO. This revolt had been brewing for some time but was finally sparked off by the party's support for the war with Honduras. Consistent with its belief that there existed an industrially-based national bourgeoisie which would challenge the power of the landed oligarchy, the party leadership surmised that this faction would head the campaign against Honduras on the basis of defending national independence. The oligarchy, on the other hand, which was distinguished by its close links with imperialism and secondary interest in inter-state feuds, would seek to avoid a conflict which would only disrupt the rhythm of production in the *campo*. The major flaw in this interpretation was, as argued by the opposition inside the PCS, the absence of any 'national bourgeoisie', which the PCS apparently identified in the De Sola faction of the oligarchy. This might have been of purely academic interest were it not for the fact that it was precisely the De Solas that opposed the war and the most reactionary and entrenched elements of the landed bourgeoisie that supported it, not least to gain more land and relieve the manifest dangers of overcrowding. Already committed to its line, the PCS found itself backing both the 'wrong' faction of the oligarchy and its *lebensraum* policy, not to mention a campaign based on spurious nationalist interests in which both Salvadorean and Honduran workers and peasants were slaughtered. PCS student militants were instructed by *La Opinion Estudiantil* to 'close ranks around the army to defend national sovereignty', and members of the still outlawed party joined the PDC in patrolling the streets of San Salvador to enable more troops to be sent to the front. (The Honduran CP, far from incidentally, gave exactly the same support to the other side, praising the 'genuine patriotism of the armed forces' as an expression of the anti-imperialist struggle.)

The policy of the PCS in the war was the last straw for that current inside the party which had opposed not only the bourgeois democratic line, the belief in the efficacy of a broad electoral front and an alliance with a reformist constituency within the military, but also the conception that these would fuse into a mass movement that would take power after a short insurrectionary period. Identifying most of these policies as little more than adaptations of the line laid down by Moscow, this group attempted to reverse the hegemony of the CPSU inside the PCS in a vehement rejection of the 1968 invasion of Czechoslovakia. At the same time, while it did not develop fully along the lines of Maoism or Trotskyism – the currents that have historically derived most strength from dissidence with post-war Stalinism – the opposition studied the experience of Vietnam and the writings of Giap with keen interest. The principal strategic lesson that the dissidents derived from this – that the 'people's war' was of necessity extended and had to derive from the return to the masses – stood in stark contradiction to the tenets of that other school of thought on rural guerrilla warfare, *foquismo*.

Foquismo had acquired enormous popularity amongst the Latin American left in the 1960s, largely as a result of its identification with the victory in Cuba. Its central tenet, as expressed by its leading propagandist Regis Debray, was that the insertion of a small nucleus (*foco*) of revolutionary fighters into the countryside would act as a spark for mass peasant rebellion. The experience of the campaign would proletarianise the revolutionary vanguard and the peasantry, with the guerrilla acting as a substitute for the Leninist party.[4] Although Debray was responsible for taking many of the features of the Cuban experience to the extremes of Parisian intellectualism, it was precisely these aspects that many of the new generation of the left found most attractive. In its critique of the reformism and stale backwardness of the Latin American communist parties and their concentration upon patient organisational work with the urban masses, and its insistence – also contrary to Leninist tradition – that the peasantry was the new revolutionary class and could be brought to a dazzling awakening through discrete acts of revolutionary violence, *foquismo* touched the nerve of a generation. It combined the prestige of Cuba with an invigorating alternative to the CPs that had its essence in immediacy and individual voluntarism, features of special importance to the angry and confused youth of the Latin American middle class.

This Sorelian hodge-podge was sufficiently novel to mesmerise not only many members of the CPs themselves but also the majority of the Latin American Trotskyist parties, for whom the one-sidedness of its critique of Stalinism proved to be a disaster that cost a great many lives and led to years of isolation even greater than they had previously experienced. Remarkably, the Trotskyist self-criticism and rejection of *foquismo* postdated by a number of years the Maoist and Stalinist invectives against it.[5] However, none of these critiques was as eloquent or chastening for the Salvadorean left as the succession of defeats suffered by guerrilla foci in the mid- and late-1960s. Of these, the comparatively easy annihilation of Guevara's Ñancahuazú guerrilla in eastern Bolivia by a notoriously disorganised and corrupt army in the autumn of 1967 was the most renowned but not the most relevant; in the same period the Guatemalan guerrilla of several years' standing was destroyed, the Venezuelan movement decisively stalled and reduced to a handful of isolated fighters, and the Pancasán offensive of the Nicaraguan FSLN defeated by Somoza's National Guard.[6] Moreover, the 1965 US invasion of the Dominican Republic was effected with a rapidity and ease that had a considerable impact on the Central American left. It was taken by the dissidents of the PCS as a clear indication that imperialism could eradicate without difficulty any assault on state power that did not result from a prolonged struggle and guerrilla war in which the pro-imperialist forces were progressively debilitated and the mass movement slowly strengthened and radicalised to the point where it could resist an all-out offensive. In this way the lessons learnt from Vietnam were combined with a rejection of *foquismo* and the distant insurrectionary orientation of the PCS to form a Maoist-influenced strategy known as the *guerra popular prolongada* (prolonged people's war) that the dissidents warned might last for ten of fifteen years – an estimate that, in the event, was surprisingly accurate.

The final split took place in April 1970 after a bitter factional fight that hardened the opposition's denunciations of the lack of democratic centralism inside the PCS. The party lost its general secretary, the veteran trade union leader Salvador Cayetano Carpio (later known as 'Marcial' and dubbed with telling flattery as 'the Ho Chi-Minh of Latin America'), the general secretary of FUSS, José Dimas Alas, and the secretary of its youth wing, Ernesto Morales. This represented a considerable blow to its industrial work in addition to the loss of many student militants. The new group spent two years in absolute clandestinity before it announced its existence in September 1972 after the death of a number of its members in combat. The establishment of the *Fuerzas Populares de Liberación-Farabundo Marti* (FPL) was, therefore, a rather belated but none the less important landmark in the development of the Salvadorean revolutionary left. It was to remain the largest, most consistently radical and influential force on the left over the ensuing decade.

From its very beginnings the FPL counterposed itself to the politics of the PCS and saw itself as 'acquiring the political personality of a Revolutionary vanguard Party, with a Marxist–Leninist character'.[7] It explained the failure to achieve such a party and the previous defeats of the revolutionary movement in the lack of genuine Marxist analysis of Salvadorean society, the consequences of 'elitist and immediatist conceptions of petty bourgeois origin', the subjective and militarist deviations of much of the left, the dogmatic application of the lessons of Cuba, and a false belief 'based on populism' that a rapid victory was possible.[8] El Salvador was characterised as a dependent capitalist society dominated by

> the creole bourgeoisie, allied to the imperialist bourgeoisie. This bourgeoisie is dependent and subordinated to the imperialist bourgeoisie. It is NOT a NATIONAL bourgeoisie, because it does not have the capacity to advance a national project independently of the imperialist bourgeoisie. (emphasis in original)[9]

The fundamental opposition to this ruling class lay in the working class, both urban and rural, which held the leadership of all the exploited classes, including the rich, middle and poor peasants, the petty bourgeoisie and middle class. The character of the revolution was identified as anti-oligarchic and anti-imperialist, in which the exploited bloc led by the working class sought to establish a 'popular revolutionary government' on the basis of the destruction of the bourgeois state.[10] This government would not be fully socialist but a 'popular revolutionary dictatorship under the hegemony of the working class; it would take radical measures to ameliorate the condition of the masses, dismantle the remaining vestiges of capitalist organisation, oversee their replacement by organs of popular power, and create the conditions for the establishment of 'full socialist construction'.[11] This anti-oligarchic and anti-imperialist revolution could, therefore, only be anti-capitalist and socialist and could only be completed by a proletarian leadership.[12] Moreover, it could only be achieved through the strategy of *guerra popular prolongada*,

> in which the people join the struggle, strengthening their forces, winning space, wearing down the enemy's forces, gradually altering the balance of forces, creating the political and organisational instruments needed for the final defeat of the enemy, with mass armed struggle maintained as the final element.[13]

The precise nature of these positions was to be very important in the years that followed, but until 1976/7 the FPL's activities and programme remained the property of the limited circles of the left. A highly disciplined cell-based organisation protected it against major setbacks but it did not grow rapidly and restricted its operations first to selected bombings and then, increasingly, to executions of leading rightists. This tactic was employed with spectacular success in the summer of 1977, when, within a matter of weeks, the FPL executed Mauricio Borgonovo, the Foreign Minister, ex-president Colonel Osmin Aguirre, the two senior military commanders in Chalatenango, and Dr Carlos Alfaro Castillo, the large landowner who had been appointed rector of the university. This policy of *ajusticiamiento* of reactionaries was also practised at local level and was preferred by the FPL to kidnapping although it did not altogether avoid this tactic, on one occasion successfully abducting a senior member of the powerful Sol Meza family.

The foundation and development of El Salvador's other leading guerrilla, the *Ejército Revolucionario del Pueblo* (ERP), was far less consistent and fraught with problems that were to do it major damage. The ERP was set up in 1972 by radicalised Christian Democrats who, in line with the PDC's natural constituency, came overwhelmingly from middle-class, professional and petty bourgeois backgrounds. Without experience of work in the mass movement and with a largely academic knowledge of Marxism, this group unhesitatingly accepted into its ranks and elevated to its leadership Roque Dalton García, the country's most famous poet, essayist and historian, and perhaps the most celebrated member of the PCS. Dalton's incorporation into the ERP still remains something of an enigma because by rights he should have joined the FPL, with whose members he shared a common background and, as it transpired, certain central ideas. However, in 1969/70 Dalton was in Cuba not El Salvador, absent from the internal struggle of the PCS and somewhat distanced from his ex-comrades.

The first three years of the ERP's history witnessed an erratic and vociferous engagement with the unrefined *foquismo* of its initial leadership, headed by Sebastián Urquilla and Mario Vladimir Rogel, with a slowly developing alternative wing led by Dalton which rejected pure militarism in favour of a 'mass line'. It is, in retrospect, difficult to capture the precise movement of this debate because the opposition has subsequently monopolised its presentation, while the remnants of the original leadership disown the line of the early years. Nevertheless, it seems clear that the conflict took the form of a challenge to the purely military orientation of the leadership, its petty bourgeois composition and conception of the struggle – which was reduced to the successful execution of individual operations (normally bombings) without consideration of their political effect on the working class – and its absolute control over the organisation.[14] In reaction to this challenge, the *foquistas* made an abrupt turn towards Maoism, heavily criticised the Cuban revolution, characterised the Soviet Union as 'social imperialism', and attacked the opposition as 'workerists'.[15] Given their background and political formation, such a response was not perhaps the aberration it appears. In any event, the result was the establishment of federalism inside the organisation, with each sector setting up its own paper and popular organisation. Although this was not alien to a certain interpretation of Mao's writings, it was soon reversed by a reimposition of direct control from the top at the end of 1974. Returning to its insurrectionist line, the leadership remained unable to extricate itself from what had become an impasse with Dalton, who now headed a substantial sector of the ERP that held that the way forward was through an unequivocal rejection of the *foco* and an open commitment to organisational work in the masses around a strategy of 'national resistance' which would be fundamentally defensive and anti-fascist in orientation.

On 13 April 1975 a dissident ERP militant named 'Pancho' was arrested by the leadership and accused of 'military rebellion'. Within two hours Dalton himself was captured and charged with inciting 'Pancho' to rebellion. Three days later these facts were announced in an internal bulletin, and on 17 April the national leadership met to discuss the issue, only to break up without having reached agreement. The opposition called for an emergency national congress to discuss 'the majority line' and the accusation that Dalton was a 'right-wing revisionist' and a Cuban agent. The leadership rejected this demand, labelled Dalton an agent of the CIA, and announced that the 'army' had taken control of the organisation through its 'general staff' in order to save the party. On 8 May attempts were made on the lives of three dissidents; on the following day all members of the opposition were sentenced to death or exile. Both 'Pancho' and Roque Dalton were shot on the 10th. Such was the outrage in response to news of the event that only the emphatic intervention and mediation of the FPL stopped a complete bloodbath and the mutual destruction of both groups.[16]

The assassination of Dalton, whose prestige was paralleled only by that of Cayetano Carpio, was enormously damaging to the ERP. It is something of a political miracle that it was able to survive the event. Not only did the opposition take with it a substantial part of the organisation to set up the *Fuerzas Armadas de Resistencia Nacional* (FARN, often known simply as *Resistencia Nacional*) but the remnants of the ERP found themselves isolated within the left and devoid of links and credibility with the mass movement. As late as 1977 Fidel Castro denounced the ERP as 'another arm of the imperialist police',[17] while the kidnap and execution of Roberto Poma, a leading landlord and president of the National Tourist Board, three weeks before the 1977 elections gave rise to rumours that the ERP was in fact an extreme right-wing organisation set up to destabilise the elections by Colonel José Francisco Chacón and General Fidel Torres.[18] Outside of the country it was not uncommon to hear the ERP referred to as in league with the CIA.

In reality, between 1975 and 1977 the ERP put itself through a process of self-criticism and purged the hardliners from the leadership, but even thereafter its brand of politico-military activity was highly adventurist. This it styled 'people's revolutionary war' to the end of establishing a 'popular democratic government' that would 'lead to socialism'.[19] While the ERP set up a political party, the *Partido Revolucionario Salvadoreño* (PRS), which argued unequivocally for a broad front comprising all democratic forces opposed to fascism,[20] the *erpistas* continued to be the ultras of the guerrilla movement, rejecting the *guerra prolongada* in favour of *insurrección popular armada*, and dismissing any possibility of a democratic stage in the revolution, as held by the PCS.[21] The ERP argued that the left had submerged itself in a mechanistic exchange between the electoral path, the *foco* and the Vietnamese road, without attempting to combine these elements and failing to concentrate on the question of taking power; what the rest of the left was seeking in the medium or long term it considered possible in the near future.[22] In the sense that it challenged reformist reluctance to engage with the question of power and to move to the offensive, the ERP's orientation was particularly sharp, but it lacked any conception of how to reach the point of insurrection or how, in practice, to build a mass movement. In this respect it remained 'maximalist' in the extreme.

The ERP's response to these difficulties was largely pragmatic. Now led by young men such as Joaquín Villalobos and Jorge Antonio Meléndez, it decided to concentrate its organisational work in the isolated and underpopulated eastern department of Morazán, where it built up an apparatus that was to bring the first major victories in the civil war, late in 1980. However, the ERP's influence was largely restricted to Morazán and the neighbouring department of La Unión, and the guerrilla found it difficult to expand its activities. For most of the 1970s its work was limited to perfecting its impressive military capabilities (operations in the cities being primarily bombing raids), in which it far outstripped the other groups.

As might be expected, the FARN or RN, followed a very different line. On one point RN was in accord with the FPL: it rejected the *foco*, both from its own experience and as a clear lesson of the failure of the Guatemalan guerrilla.[23] Moreover, as guerrilla operations moved towards civil war and presented new problems of fighting in larger formation and on a wider scale, RN reconsidered Dalton's writings on Vietnam and had them published, but without coming to the conclusion that the *guerra prolongada* was the answer.[24] The line taken by RN was that of 'national resistence', built around an anti-fascist front in which the guerrilla would act as the military vanguard less for insurrection than for halting the rise of the right while the organisation of the masses was improved and a united movement of the left built. This was the polar opposite of the ERP's insurrectionism and one of its military consequences, identified by both the ERP and the FPL, was to limit the FARN's manoeuvrability and its capacity for a broad offensive, both central features of all guerrilla warfare.

The concept of *resistencia nacional* was founded on an unambiguous political stance on the nature of the class struggle in El Salvador; but there are to be found in RN's positions more elisions and contradictions than in those of the other two groups. This can be explained to some degree by the group's origins. In inheriting much of the ERP's membership, RN remained in the orbit of the ex-PDC middle-class activists for whom the experience of *foquismo* constituted a severe political and psychological shock necessitating radical reappraisal. This revision bore many or the hallmarks of simple reaction, of a fundamental 'trial and error' approach that although steadfastly defended and exhaustively argued, was as exaggerated in its emphasis as was the ERP's militarism.

In its early years RN spoke of the task of 'unification of the party of communists', of the necessity of proletarian hegemony, the absence of a national bourgeoisie and, therefore, the impossibility of a national democratic, anti-feudal and anti-imperialist revolution led by such a class.[25] It attacked the PCS as a 'hegemonic tendency in which right-wing opportunism predominates',[26] and insisted upon its opposition to any type of alliance with bourgeois groups (but not individuals) on the grounds that the struggle was not for bourgeois democracy in itself but as a first stage in the construction of socialism.[27] On this basis it attacked UNO and the electoralist strategy for their bourgeois aspirations and failure to recognise the threat of fascism, pointing out that in the 1972 elections, 'the people defeated the bourgeoisie in its own camp, but at the same time the bourgeoisie ended up defeating the electoral aspirations of revisionism'.[28] Yet, RN also attacked the FPL as 'terrorist', 'divisionist', overly emphatic in its 'proletarian purity' and dangerously averse to unity.[29] At the same time as it enveighed against the illusions of the PCS, RN argued that there would be a 'democratic stage' in the revolution, in which the 'popular democratic revolution' would give rise to a 'popular revolutionary government', exactly the same formulation as the FPL.[30] The precise distinction between these aims and those of the FPL and the PCS were not greatly clarified when, two years later, the leaders of RN, Ernesto Jovel and Ferman Cienfuegos, were asked to elaborate upon the question. They resorted to an admirable but obfuscating depiction: 'It will be the instrument for the construction of the new society; without misery, illiteracy or lack of hygiene. A society with peace and justice, for all Salvadoreans.'[31] These words might well have been spoken by Castro in 1959.

In practice, despite all its invectives against the PCS, RN was moving consistently towards an anti-fascist stance in which the forming of alliances with the bourgeois reformist parties and elements of the military became increasingly important; the communist language employed to argue the necessity of socialism against the intrinsic betrayals of reformism acquired a progressively formalistic character. The FPL was attacked as following an 'all or nothing' strategy; the contesting of elections in 1972 was, in fact, correct because there was 'no political alternative'; emphasis was placed less on establishing socialism than upon removing the fascists from government. RN came to occupy the middle ground between, on the one hand, UNO and the PCS and, on the other, the FPL and, at some distance, the ERP. This was to be a source of considerable friction in the years to come.

Despite this less radical line, it was RN that attracted most international publicity in the late 1970s with its policy of kidnapping. This was extended beyond leading members of the oligarchy, such as Carlos Emilio Alvarez, to foreign businessmen. In 1978 the group made the headlines by capturing and killing the Israeli consul, Ernesto Liebes, and then sequestering a string of managers of transnational corporations: Fuji o Matsumoto and Takaku Suzuki (the Insinca textile company); Fritz Schuitema (Philips); Kjell Bjork (Ericcson); Ian Massie and Michael Chatterton (Banco de Londres y Sudamerica, a subsidiary of Lloyds International). These actions brought valuable propaganda victories and ample funds, but they established little contact with the working population, a contact that – after the initial phase of consolidating their organisations and beginning operations – became the central issue for the left.

None of the guerrilla groups considered themselves to have developed into a political party and, with the exception of the ERP's largely artificial PRS, none had any ties with any party. Both the FPL and RN saw themselves as the party in embryo but this scarcely addressed the considerable problem of how to situate themselves in the masses and make their campaigns popular in the sense that they were of the people and not just supported by the people from a distance. In this respect until at least 1975 all the groups, regardless of their strategies, shared the consequences of the guerrilla being an extreme form of vanguard. The organisational resolution to this historical problem was eventually found, ironically, in developing the method used by the PCS to circumvent its illegality: a mass front or 'popular organisation' linked through the programme to the politico-military vanguard but dedicated to popular organisation rather than guerrilla activity. In the case of the UDN this activity was structured primarily around fighting elections, but it proved even more viable in grouping unions, neighbourhood committees, peasant groups, students and professional organisations to fight for concrete economic and democratic demands. Since the affiliated organisations maintained their identities and specific roles – and it was these bodies rather than individuals that comprised the rank and file – the organisation took on the character less of political parties than of fronts, blocs or leagues. Their composition and the nature of their activities made them authentic organs of plebeian radicalism. The popular organisations are a peculiarity of the Salvadorean revolutionary movement, even compared to that in Nicaragua, where the FSLN was a predominantly military organisation until it came to power. Nevertheless, the manner in which the normal divisions between guerrilla, party and union have been constantly traversed and increasingly blurred has not of itself led to a subordination of the political to the purely organisational. Rather it has resulted in a remarkably efficacious fusion of the two. This, it should be stressed, is unlikely to remain the case over a long period of time, especially after the taking of power, because of the absence of full internal democracy that is a characteristic of these organisations under conditions of severe repression. But, all the same, it is through them that the Salvadorean guerrillas were able to make a qualitative breakthrough and take a leading role in the mass movement.

One of the central features in the emergence of the plebeian fronts was the upturn in peasant mobilisation. Rural unions had been illegal since 1932 although a number of carefully vetted and ideologically 'safe' bodies had been allowed to exist in the 1960s. One of these, the *Unión Comunal Salvadoreña* (UCS), was the creation of the AIFLD, which, together with the Israeli union organisation Histadrut, poured in over $1.6 million to develop a network of co-operatives that would be 'responsive to change' but led by 'moderates' who were decidedly anti-communist.[32] In the event, for all their money and influence, AIFLD, the US Embassy and the CIA operatives who collaborated with the two in overseeing the affairs of the UCS were unable to avoid friction with the regime; they found themselves lumbered with leaders who were corrupt beyond the call of compliance, an ORDEN-inspired coup, and the progressive influence of radical currents which entered and subverted the union with increasing success. The UCS remained the site of US operations in the Salvadorean countryside, but it never developed into the large and influential 'yellow union' that the AIFLD, USAID and the CIA sought to create.

Older and more powerful than the UCS was FECCAS, the Christian Federation of Salvadorean Peasants, set up by the church in 1964 less as a union than as a self-help organisation with a strong emphasis on communal and pastoral work. By the end of the decade FECCAS was breaking these limits not solely because of the emergence of a radical current in its rank and file but also because many rural priests saw the necessity of a more combative role. By 1972/3 this resulted in an alliance with the PCS-led peasant union ATACES, but the experience proved to be an unhappy one, with a high turnover in the leadership and the eventual rejection by FECCAS of the PCS line as reformist.

A parallel process of temporary alliance with and then rejection of the PCS was taking place within the urban unions, with the party losing much influence, albeit over a longer period. It lost control first of FUSS and then FENASTRAS, the union federation set up in 1972 and rapidly expanded under the leadership of the power workers' STECEL to include 20,000 members, over a third of the unionised workers in the towns, by the end of the 1970s. Workers from these two currents of the urban and rural labour movement combined to form the backbone of the first popular organisation independent of both the state and the PCS: the *Frente de Acción Popular Unificada* (FAPU), set up in June 1974. However, the real initiative came from ANDES, which by this stage had become an independent political force of considerable standing in the country.[33] The foundation of FAPU occurred at the time of the crisis inside the ERP and it did not first establish close links with any guerrilla, but by mid-1975 it aligned itself with RN. This allegiance was not openly proclaimed by either side for some while but it soon became manifest in the positions taken by FAPU.

Identifying the Molina regime as fascist, FAPU argued that the key political issue was the formation of a broad front on a minimal programme that would secure basic economic objectives and democratic freedoms, and halt the rise of fascism. This front would include all democratic and revolutionary forces, it would combine parliamentary and extra-parliamentary action and fight for a 'representative revolutionary government'.[34] FAPU adhered to the RN line that the electoral path was now exhausted, and also denied the existence of both a national bourgeoisie and a bourgeois democratic phase in the revolution. However, its differentiation of two sectors within the landed bourgeoisie, its high estimation of the importance of the middle sectors, and its concentration above all else on building the anti-fascist movement, led it to place greater importance upon securing partial reforms and tactical victories than on the question of class power.

In this it found itself rapidly outstripped by the radicalisation of the rural labour force. After only a year's existence, FAPU lost the forces of FECCAS and then ANDES. This restricted its influence to a portion of the urban working class (FUSS and FENASTRAS) and the petty bourgeoisie, and led it to launch a vociferous attack on the 'sectarians, divisionists and hegemonists' who had left it to cause 'enormous damage to the popular struggle' as a result of the 'manifest immaturity of some political tendencies'.[35]

The break was led by FECCAS, which in the course of 1975 allied itself with an independent peasant union based in San Vicente, the *Unión de Trabajadores del Campo* (UTC). The combination of these two forces gave a powerful impulse to peasant unionisation, which doubled between 1972 and 1977, and formed the basis of the *Bloque Popular Revolucionario* (BPR), which soon entered into alliance with the FPL and became the largest and most radical of the mass organisations. Although the BPR frequently proclaimed the leadership of FECCAS–UTC, it also drew much strength from the slum-dwellers, organised in the *Unión de Pobladores de Tugurios* (UPT), from ANDES, and from the student organisation UR–19 *(Universitarios Revolucionarios – 19 de Julio)*. The students had been under almost constant attack from the Molina regime since 1972, when the president declared the university to have 'fallen into the hands of the communists', closed it for a year, revoked its autonomy and appointed a new rector in Carlos Castillo, later executed by the FPL. In July 1975, a peaceful student demonstration in Santa Ana against the holding of the 'Miss Universe' contest in San Salvador led to further police crack-downs. When the students of the capital came out in solidarity, the campus was invaded by troops, 40 students killed and 20 'disappeared'.[36] A five-day occupation of the university and a 50,000-strong protest march evidenced the strength of opposition to the regime but their failure to have any impact also led to a discernable shift in student activism towards the guerrillas and the mass organisations. This movement was also felt in the secondary schools where the students set up their own organisation, the MERS *(Movimiento Estudiantil Revolucionario de Secundario)*, which also joined the BPR and gave it the unmistakable stamp of youthfulness that is a major characteristic of the Salvadorean revolution.

The BPR was quick to distinguish itself from the other opposition forces. It considered that UNO was attempting to 'orientate the masses towards bourgeois objectives' with its demands for the 'retrieval of constitutionalism', condemned by the *Bloque* as the 'legalized system of capitalist exploitation'.[37] UNO was fighting for a 'democratic government' that would be led by the opposition bourgeoisie not the workers or peasants, thereby halting the mobilisation of the masses towards their own interests. FAPU, on the other hand, was a 'vacillating petty bourgeois current, the political objectives of which (broad anti-fascist unity, stopping the fascist offensive, etc.) have led it to revisionist positions . . . and alliance with the electoralist parties'.[38] Although FAPU characterised the Molina regime as 'fascist-like' *(fascistoide)*, BPR argued that FAPU failed to understand that in a backward capitalist country fascist tendencies were integral to imperialist and oligarchic counter-revolutionary movements and not a simple aberration within the bourgeoisie. As a consequence, FAPU was organising workers in a front that could only be of a tactical nature, ignoring the question of the political leadership of that front, and failing to fight for proletarian hegemony within it. This, despite all FAPU's phraseology, was a great impediment to the forging of a genuine revolutionary alternative and contrary to the interests of the working class.[39]

Against the type of front supported by FAPU, the *Bloque* counterposed a worker–peasant alliance forged over a long period through the *guerra prolongada*. While this alliance must attract sectors of the petty bourgeoisie and middle class, it would be distinguished by its proletarian leadership and the 'driving force' of the worker–peasant alliance.[40] By placing emphasis on revolutionary unity against democratic unity and by insisting upon the primacy of class, the BPR came closer to orthodox Leninism than all the other groups. It also grew very fast, gaining 60,000 members within two years, which made it twice as large as FAPU.

This process of conflict and realignment on the left was not completed with the establishment of the *Bloque*. In 1977, the ERP turned away from unadulterated *foquismo* and, as part of this process, established unity with the *Ligas Populares 28 de Febrero* (LP–28), named after the day of that year when the armed forces killed over 100 people demonstrating against the fraudulent election of Molina's successor, General Romero. The LP–28's small membership was heavily influenced by its student militants, which accounted for a pronounced erraticism in the direction of its tactics. Yet its strategic line remained faithful to that of the ERP: insurrection rather than extended war, rejection of a bourgeois democratic phase, and strong criticism of the PCS/UDN and FAPU for their policy of broad alliances.[41]

Finally, although it did not make its existence public until late 1979, we should note the *Partido Revolucionario de Trabajadores Centroamericanos* (PRTC), which was set up late in 1975 in Costa Rica and possessed an important Salvadorean contingent. This group numbered some who, like Fabio Castillo, had worked with the PCS until the Honduran war and then found no natural place with the existing guerrillas; some Salvadorean exiles in Costa Rica and Honduras; and a number of early opponents to RN's line on fascism. Following an early setback resulting from the assumption that the same political line could be applied in all the states of Central America, the PRTC was slow in developing. During four years of clandestine preparation it undertook few operations. Distinguished by its regionalist orientation, the PRTC's military strategy was closest to that of the FPL while, in arguing for a more sensitive approach to the question of forming fronts, its politics were less hardline than those of the BPR. Late in 1979 the PRTC established the *Movimiento de Liberación Popular* (MLP), the smallest of the popular organisations and formed too late to impose its individual stamp before the country slid into civil war. By that stage the left had come together on a unified programme that attained unprecedented co-operation between the forces that had hitherto been engaged in often bitter conflict:

    PCS (1930) – UDN (1969)
    FPL (1970) – BPR (1975)
    ERP (1972) – LP–28 (1977)
    RN (1975) – FAPU (1974)
    PRTC (1975) – MPL (1979)

On the ground, in the day-to-day struggle of their militants, the differences between the forces of the left were less obvious; all were involved in the defence of basic democratic rights and the fight for economic gains. All were also persecuted with equal vigour by the military and uniformly attacked as 'subversive' and 'communist' by a regime that understandably had no interest and little capacity for identifying esoteric points of disagreement between people who were equally intent upon destroying it.

7
THE MODEL IN CRISIS: FROM MOLINA TO ROMERO

The new government . . . ought to promote intensive and extensive campaigns, using all the means of social communication, so that the people become more aware of the gravity of the situation and turn their backs on the false apostles of dissolution and organised crime. It would also be necessary to apply severe penalties to those implicated in subversive acts, and to treat campaigns of agitation just as if they were terrorist actions.

Professor Héctor Andino, *El Diario Latino*, 5 October 1977

You know, I believe some people are going to be surprised at the measures that my government will take.

General Carlos Humberto Romero, June 1977

Dubbed either fascist or *fascistoide* by the left, the Molina regime was the first in El Salvador since 1932 to face armed resistance; it responded in kind. Repression in the countryside escalated rapidly from 1974, with ORDEN taking a much higher profile in the offensive against the peasant unions. As in the towns, arrests and killings were not made on a general scale but were confined to selected activist leaders. 'Disappearances' became increasingly frequent and owed much to the right's appreciation of the methods used by the Chilean military after the coup of September 1973. When the guerrillas began to respond, ANEP and FARO, judging the activities of the official repressive apparatus insufficient, combined to establish and fund independent right-wing terror squads. The first of these, set up in 1975, was the FALANGE *(Fuerzas Armadas de Liberación Nacional – Guerra de Exterminación)*, which promised the extermination of 'all communists and their collaborators' and openly accepted responsibility for its killings, which in one week of October 1975 numbered 38. In 1976

FALANGE changed its name to the *Unión Guerrera Blanca* (UGB, White Warriors' Union), but it remained the main perpetrator of 'dirty operations', in which off-duty members of the military and vigilantes undertook specific assassinations that could not be sanctioned formally by the armed forces' hierarchy. Even more than in the case of ORDEN, this division of repressive labour enabled the regime to disown and condemn such actions. In this the Salvadoreans followed the example of their Guatemalan colleagues who for years professed a determination to halt the activity of their death squads, *Ojo por Ojo* (Eye for an Eye) and *Mano Blanca* (White Hand), when their operational centre backed onto the presidential palace.

To preserve an ephemeral sense of legitimacy – and to halt the slide of proponents of the 'middle way' and parliamentarianism into the camp of the armed struggle – Molina preserved the PCN's veneer of constitutionalism. UNO was granted its legal rights and encouraged to participate in the congressional elections of 1974 and 1976. In 1974, true to form, the opposition 'won the count but lost the election'. As a result, UNO took the dangerous course of calling for a boycott in 1976. This did not bode well for UNO's central belief in the efficacy of electoralism; with the growing capacity of the guerrillas, the emergence of the popular organisations dedicated to extra-parliamentary activism, and the increase in repression, UNO seemed set for extinction as a viable political force in the presidential poll of February 1977.

This turned out to be the case, but it did not occur without a major crisis and a significant alteration in the political direction of both the right and the centre. Within the PCN and the power bloc as a whole this was determined by the considerable discontent of the landed bourgeoisie with Molina's agrarian reform effort. The 1976 campaign had greatly increased the standing of ANEP and FARO, which sought a replacement who was clearly set against further tinkering, however anodyne, with the system. They found their candidate in the architect of the new repression, Minister of Defence General Carlos Humberto Romero, whom Molina was obliged to support as his successor.

Romero was, like his predecessors, of a humble background, using the army as a means of social advancement, but he had established very good relations with the oligarchy. This appears to be connected less with his capacity as a soldier than with the result of having spent six strenuous years on 'special courses in horsemanship' in Mexico, which made him one of the country's premier jockeys and gave him a special entrée into the circles of the elite. Romero lacked both political skill and professional expertise; his dismal action in a key command during the war with Honduras had weakened support for him amongst junior officers. But, acknowledged as utterly 'safe', he trudged up the institutional ladder to become president of CONDECA in 1973, establishing close friendships with President Laugerud of Guatemala and Somoza, both of whom appeared in San Salvador during his campaign.

Even inside the army Romero's candidature was perceived as a swing to the right. Chele Medrano, who in 1972 had labelled the PCN 'a corrupt band infiltrated by communists', now happily backed its candidate. But many younger officers, organised in the semi-clandestine Military Youth Movement (MJM), opposed him. Some members of the MJM had backed the 1972 coup but few espoused leftist ideas; it was more a case of retaining faith in the original PCN project while the PCN itself had dropped it and was moving steadily towards an open and unrefined dictatorship. The MJM believed in the guided constitutionalism ditched by its superiors and, therefore, came out in support of UNO within the military, although it made no pronouncement outside its ranks.

The appearance of the MJM, combined with UNO's disastrous experience in 1972 and the knowledge that the BPR's call for a boycott would lose it many votes seems to have turned the minds of UNO's leaders to the possibility of a coup.[1] The original candidates, Duarte and Ungo, were replaced by a respected retired army officer, Colonel Ernesto Claramount Rozeville (whose father, General Antonio Claramount, had contested the polls of 1931 and 1944), and a right-wing Christian Democrat, Dr Antonio Morales Erlich. These two were considered more amenable to military reformists and the *aperturista* sector of the oligarchy; their less populist character scarcely threatened to undermine the UNO vote when the *Bloque* was already boycotting and there was no other serious opposition slate. Rafael Menjívar argues persuasively that UNO was also placing considerable importance on backing from the new US administration of Jimmy Carter, which, with its pronouncements in favour of human rights and 'viable' democracy, was expected to go further than its predecessors in pushing for the decision of the poll to be respected.[2]

The regime took these threats seriously. In response to Claramount's declaration that he was sure that there were honest and uncorruptible men in the army, 200 officers were retired in January and a vituperative campaign launched against UNO's two most visible military supporters, Colonels Mariano Murguía and Mariano Castro Morán.[3]. A threatened strike by port workers just before the election was crushed by the police, and the regime encouraged lock-outs in the construction and steel industries where workers were demanding substantial wage rises. This tactically-timed bout of union activity was still more economic than political in motive and sought to use the election as an extra lever for bargaining. However, it occurred after a long series of strikes and marked a high-point in working-class mobilisation that made the period of the poll unprecedentedly tense, providing the regime with reason and excuse to flood the city with troops. Not content with this, the regime had also revised the electoral registers with an excess of efficiency for, as UNO pointed out when demanding another revision of the lists, whereas El Salvador's population was growing at a rate of only 3.2 per cent, registered voters had risen by 11 per cent since 1972.[4] Over 150,000 of the new voters were 'phantoms', either dead, duplicated or simply dreamed up by PCN officials.

In order to capitalise on these moves, the government broke with established practice and placed all San Salvador's 400 voting booths in an industrial fairground five miles outside the city centre, far from the *barrios* inhabited by the working class. UNO was again denied observer's rights, the boxes were stuffed with PCN votes, paramilitary forces and troops were used to intimidate, assault and eject voters of a contrary frame of mind, and a radio network was set up to co-ordinate the PCN's 'campaign'. The official result was that Romero beat Claramount by 812,281 votes to 394,661. At those voting stations where opposition observers had managed to maintain a presence, the vote ran 157,574 to 120,972 in Claramount's favour.[5]

Romero rejected claims by employees of the electoral commission that its president had ordered them to destroy UNO votes, ignored the six hours of tape-recordings of PCN radio messages organising the fixing of the poll produced by UNO, and claimed outright victory. For his part, the smiling Molina told the press, 'Only God is perfect.'[6] On 24 February, four days after the poll, the official result was confirmed. Claramount, declaring that the legal path was now exhausted, led a march of some 40,000 UNO supporters into the capital's main plaza and refused to move until the elections were annulled. This action followed several days of spontaneous demonstrations against the regime and strikes by students, teachers, construction, factory and transport workers.[7] The city was paralysed.

The occupation of the plaza lasted over three days but failed to lead either to a general strike or the expected coup d'etat. As in 1972, UNO was waiting for 'something to happen' while the workers were waiting for UNO to give a lead; it never did. Early on the morning of 28 February, large numbers of troops cordoned off the plaza, where some 6,000 demonstrators were left. They were given ten minutes in which to disperse and many left; after the stipulated time, the soldiers opened fire. Claramount and a group estimated at between 1,500 and 2,000 took refuge in the Church of El Rosario, only to have tear gas canisters thrown in after them. Alarmed at the prospect of a massacre, the US Embassy sent along senior members of its staff to mediate, but they were denied access to the square. Eventually, at 4 p.m., the auxiliary bishop of San Salvador and the Red Cross organised a truce and guaranteed the evacuation of the plaza. Claramount went into exile while Morales Erlich took refuge in the Costa Rican Embassy. Most UNO officials had already gone into hiding, been arrested or 'disappeared'.

At daybreak demonstrators returned to the city centre, burning cars and attacking government buildings. The troops fired with intent to kill. Some 200 people died, many of them workers responding to radio bulletins urging them to return to work. Similar riots took place in Santa Ana. In the evening Molina announced a state of siege, banned assemblies and suspended all constitutional guarantees, blaming the violence on 'agents of communist subversion'.[8]

Resistencia Nacional considered the events of February constituted a 'pre-revolutionary situation'.[9] The ERP likewise pinpointed them as a critical moment in the development of the revolutionary movement, and the PCS – in retrospect – located its adoption of the armed struggle in the failure of the election and the strength of the popular response.[10] Yet, if UNO continued to have a tenuous existence for two more years it was largely the result of the continued backing from the UDN; the MNR and PDC had effectively given it up as a viable option.[11] UNO had been created for elections and elections were quite patently useless as a means of voicing opposition or obtaining change. This was as true for the bourgeois opposition as it was for the workers' parties. February 1977 marked the end of a political era.

It also marked the opening of a period of sustained attacks by the right on the Church. This was the turning-point for the majority of the country's faithful, lay and religious alike. The campaign, initiated personally by Molina, went beyond the persecution of proponents of liberation theology to attack all who protested the increasing violation of human and democratic rights as supporters of 'subversion'. In this way the first steps towards the implementation of a 'national security' campaign against communism took the form of an offensive against religious groups. It was, of course, unacceptable that this be a secular offensive; it was expressed in terms of the black tradition of redemption and inquisition, drawing on the historical affinity between catholicism and absolutism. In this it had a multitude of local antecedents, such as the 1927 pastoral letter of Monseñor Belloso y Sánchez on socialism which affirmed that 'a Catholic who pledges himself to any of the systems of socialism runs the grave risk of heresy . . .'[12] In this vein, the Bishop of San Miguel and Vicar General of the Armed Forces Monseñor and Colonel José Eduardo Alvarez refused in November 1977 to denounce the torture of one of his priests on the grounds that it was as a man and not as a priest that he had been tortured.[13] Alvarez and a cluster of religious dignitaries never wavered in their support for the regime, whatever excesses it inflicted on their peers and parishioners. Significantly, they received constant backing in this from the papal nuncio, Monseñor Gerada. Throughout the entire bloody calvary of the Salvadorean Church the papacy steadfastly desisted from any act beyond gratuitous and ingenuous exhortations to understanding, which, under the circumstances, constituted an abdication of the defence of persecuted Christians and a passive compliance in that persecution.

From the viewpoint of the right, the campaign was not without justification. Many of the sectors of the Church were directly involved in radical activity; in some rural areas they were the source of that activity. They were identified, principally through their work in FECCAS, as responsible for mobilising support for the 1976 agrarian reform. They were perceived as overseeing the intellectual preparation of a new generation of communist youth in the Jesuit-run Catholic University, which was the target of a bombing campaign in December 1976. The fact that over the last two years all bar seven of the country's bishops had either collectively or individually signed pastoral letters condemning the violation of human rights was taken as an indication of the scale of the corrosion.

The campaign began shortly after the election with a series of arrests and expulsions of foreign priests who belonged to the orders, mostly Jesuit, Maryknoll and Benedictine. By May this attention was extended to Salvadoreans. Between February and May 17 priests were expelled or exiled, four were jailed and tortured and six killed 'by unknown hand'. Repression in the countryside was directed towards Christian groups, the most outstanding example being the full-scale military occupation of the town of Aguilares on 20 May. The 'unknown hand' responsible for the death of the priests can be confidently identified as that of the UGB, which by June was issuing the slogan 'Be Patriotic– Kill a Priest'.[14] On 21 June the UGB presented to the press its 'War Bulletin No.6', in which it accused 46 Jesuits of 'terrorism' and gave them until 20 July to leave the country; after that date their execution would be 'immediate and systematic'.[15]

This caused the new Archbishop of San Salvador, Oscar Arnulfo Romero, and all his fellow bishops to boycott the inauguration of President Romero (no relation) on 1 July. It also attracted considerable attention abroad, particularly in the US. Aware of the dangers of this exceedingly bad publicity, Romero took a soft line. He ordered a diminution in the activity of the armed forces, placed guards around the residences of the Jesuits, made ostentatious visits to them and pledged full guarantees for their safety. The word went out to the UGB that they had gone too far; El Salvador was getting a (deserved) reputation for killing priests that ill became the only country in the world named after Christ. The lull was short, but it was also emphatic, the principal reason being pressure from the Carter administration.

The 'discovery' of human rights by the US government has in retrospect attained a certain notoriety because of its novelty, the partiality of its application – amongst others, the Philippines, Korea and Iran were effectively excluded – and the speed with which it was jettisoned when it came into conflict with essential foreign policy needs.[16] The consideration of human rights in US policy-making had less to do with the ephemeral enlightenment supposedly introduced by a president who was a southern Baptist than with the trauma of Watergate. Moreover, recognition that the deepening US trade deficit required urgent treatment hastened the ditching of the defensive foreign policy of Kissinger and Nixon for a more pugnacious mercantilism combined with greater flexibility in political relations. This development was most clearly crystallised in the ascendence of the Trilateral Commission, the 'think tank' headed by David Rockefeller which incorporated representatives from Japan (ideologically if not geographically part of the 'west') and the EEC, as well as leading US figures.[17] Despite the diversity of views contained within it, trilateralism was the force behind the nominally 'low profile' and the more mobile defence of US interests evident in the SALT, Helsinki and Camp David agreements (all highly advantageous to the US), and the short 'relaxation' of relations with Cuba (January to November 1977).

The integration of human rights into this tactical shift was not in itself anomalous. As an ideological motif, human rights were important — the 'soul' of his foreign policy, according to Carter — but they were also hazardous. They simply could not express US interests in their most basic form. It was this contradictory aspect of form and substance that led to the speedy demise of the policy. It also made the demise all the more messy, for 'human rights' could only be acceptably jilted in terms of 'interests', making manifest the distance between the two. Yet, if Reagan was later to do this in an unequivocal manner, the process was already well under way during the Carter administration.

The human rights policy was applied with most vigour – and resisted with most resilience – in Latin America. US support for the overthrow of Allende, and the plethora of CIA 'dirty tricks' in the region revealed in the aftermath of Watergate, made action in this quarter necessary – partly to improve the badly tarnished US image. For Carter and Cyrus Vance this could best be achieved along the lines of the Alliance for Progress in voicing unhappiness about dictatorships, working for the establishment of 'viable' democracies, and expressing a willingness to tolerate the existence of progressive regimes – but only provided that they were 'democratic' and not 'communist', a distinction which, given Washington's record, was neither semantically enlightening nor politically reassuring.[18]

While it lasted, this policy created a number of tensions with the military dictatorships which, although highly dependent upon the US, also relied heavily on the notion of national independence and their self-proclaimed nationalism. This compelled them to reject as 'interventionist' the requirement that they cease violations of human rights in exchange for military aid, a requirement that was in any event totally unacceptable to them. While the more sophisticated regimes of the southern cone led the counter-offensive, the dictatorships of Central America did not lag far behind. Following congressional hearings and State Department reports on the condition of human rights in El Salvador, Guatemala and Nicaragua early in 1977, the first two states joined those of the southern cone in rejecting US military aid before it was withdrawn. The Somozas escaped US censure in this way by dint of their well-organised lobby on Capitol Hill. One contributory reason for this surprisingly defiant position was that the regimes were well aware that they would not as a consequence suffer a loss of military capacity: the Israelis were more than willing to act as alternative suppliers of arms; this they were soon doing, as well as acting, less openly, as advisers.

Salvadorean relations with Washington had not been good for some time. In May 1976, Chief of Staff Colonel Miguel Rodriguez was unfortunately arrested in New York for attempting to re-sell 10,000 machine-guns to the Mafia. The Rodriguez affair strengthened the hand of the US Ambassador in San Salvador, Ignacio Lozano, who from the summer of 1976 exercised considerable pressure on both Molina and Washington on the question of human rights. Molina's eventual expulsion of AIFLD and the conduct of the 1977 election widened the gap even further. The US responded by suspending a $90 million loan from the Inter-American Development Bank (IDB). Throughout the period between Romero's election and his inauguration, February to July, relations deteriorated even further, hitting rock-bottom with the UGB's campaign against the Jesuits. Romero had effectively been in charge of El Salvador during this period and showed every sign of encouraging the descent into dictatorship. However, the UGB's activities had had such a great impact, and had promised to isolate the country so completely at a time of crisis, that Romero was momentarily obliged to deny his instincts and make his assumption of power a 'turning point'.

In Washington events were following a similar path. The central State Department document, written by Richard Arellano, was for the most part unremarkable in its adhesion to Vance's view that 'social justice' was the best means of defeating 'terrorism'. In his report Arellano gave a potted history of military rule and the country's economic development, concluding that the prime cause of the violation of human rights lay in 'the unbalanced nature of [the] socio-economic structure'.[19] Yet, in open contradiction to this finding, Arellano also declared that Washington wished 'to work with the Salvadorean government to prevent the trend of an anomalous, unsettled period becoming a continuing part of normal Salvadorean life'.[20]

This change in emphasis from 'structural' to 'anomalous' is significant because it indicates the manner in which Washington had decided to present the easing off of the pressure placed on Molina. This coincided with Romero's own line: the violence and fraud of the election and the persecution of the Church occurred under Molina not Romero, whose government was 'new' and therefore deserved to be judged on its own record. For the State Department the reason for this shift was not simply the growing threat of the guerrilla movement, although this was certainly giving much cause for concern. In August 1977 the Carter government was presented with a number of problems in Central America: the calling of a plebiscite on the canal treaty by the Panamanian head of state, General Torrijos; elections in Guatemala in which it was believed – quite erroneously – that the social democratic forces might triumph, with unpredictable consequences; and a severe heart attack suffered by Somoza in July, which opened up the possibility of extreme instability in Nicaragua.[21] Under these circumstances, with control of two key client states uncertain and the new canal policy in the balance, further to destabilise the Salvadorean regime would only weaken the 'forces of stability' in the region at a particularly critical time.

Arellano had talks with Romero in July; Patricia Derian, the State Department's liberal adviser on human rights, visited him in August. He behaved himself impeccably on both occasions, no doubt encouraged by the remarks of Assistant Secretary of State for Inter-American Affairs Terence Todman, who publicly sympathised with the 'cruel dilemma between a government's responsibility to combat terrorism, anarchy and violence, and its obligation to avoid applying any means which violate human rights'.[22] In suspending martial law, Romero opened the way for a complete *rapprochement*. At the end of August, a US loan of $32 million was released; several days later Romero was invited to the signing of the canal treaty in Washington; in November the $90 million loan from the IDB was granted. Todman wrote to FARO's women's organisation, the Salvadorean Women's Front,

> Let me assure you that your government can continue to count on our active collaboration and support in promoting economic and social development while combating the cruel and unforgiveable challenge of terrorism within the framework of our shared standards for the protection of human rights.[23]

Over the following two years the precise nature of this 'framework' was to be tested many times over by events. Henceforth it would not be permitted to prejudice US support for the Salvadorean armed forces; as the violation of human rights became ever more frequent in incidence and horrible in method, US 'standards' became correspondingly more flexible. *Realpolitik* so manifestly underpinned protestations of political morality that even members of the US political establishment, celebrated for a hard-headedness that in certain quarters is accounted co-substantial with deceit, began to make public pronouncements about hypocrisy. It is, of course, not unseemly that policy which takes morality as its centre-piece is not only explained by political economy but also judged on moral grounds.

As far as the Salvadorean right was concerned, human rights were a dangerous distraction. According to *El Diario de Hoy*, suppressing terrorism had to mean violating human rights. It was impossible to treat a 'political offender' as a human being in terms of the UN Charter, which was a 'Russian salad . . . with every sort of aspiration [and] sophistry'.[24] For the bourgeois press,

> one of the objectives of the red conspiracy is . . . to weaken the collective morale. This is part of the psychological warfare by which they affect our labourers' capacity for work and, at the same time, cut back the rhythm of national production.[25]

ANEP, clearly concerned at Romero's back-peddling in relation to the Carter administration, launched a major press campaign centred around its 'Statement to the Government of the Republic', which was nothing less than an open threat. The 'tragic reality' through which El Salvador was living was ascribed to 'escalating communist violence' and the paralysis which affected 'the primary obligation of the government to maintain public order' and 'the free exercise of legal liberties'. The regime was paralysed because of its 'indifference', 'tolerance', 'fear' and 'incapacity'. Moreover, its tolerance amounted to 'an utter disrespect for those human rights they say they are defending'. The Statement closed with the slogan, 'Enough of the fears and hesitation!'[26]

The Salvadorean Association of Cultivators and Exporters of Coffee (ABECAFE) went further than this, stating that, 'it is time we realised that internal security against whatever may eventually prejudice the density of our homeland is the first priority'. In evoking the memory of Martinez, ABECAFE made no bones about how this should be done:

> many years ago one of our rulers understood this [fact] very well when he made the Republic's internal security, peace and order a primary and indispensable condition for the development and prosperity of our country.[27]

Others also remembered the halcyon days of the Central America of

Somoza, Ubico and Martinez, when such trifles as human rights were not even dreamed of, let alone allowed to interfere with the primary tasks of government. Today, in Central America, 'the armies are lacking the counter-revolutionary tradition and have suffered, like the rest of the population, from the mania for freedom'.[28] If all this was so much ideological chest-beating, ABECAFE did not hesitate to identify whence it derived when it expressed its 'particular concern' with,

> the problems presented by the *gathering of the harvest* in normal conditions, in accordance with the law, observing the scale of minimum wages . . . already approved . . . on the basis of technical and economic studies which take account of the cost of living, the cost of production, and the prices on the *world market*. (emphasis in the original)[29]

Thus, Romero was warned not to attempt an increase in wages and to return to an unqualified policy of repression if he was to retain the backing of the oligarchy, without which he could not hope to survive. To strengthen their campaign, ANEP, ABECAFE and FARO set up phantom organisations, such as the 'Committee for the Defence of the Fatherland', the 'Committee of Patriotic Salvadoreans' and the 'Salvadorean League for Human Rights', which bombarded the press with manifestos and paid advertisements calling for 'peace, security and order' and, if need be, the putting to death of the 'rabble' who would not accept the 'rule of law'.[30]

This concentrated campaign for the full restoration of dictatorial powers was made all the more vociferous by the upsurge in mass mobilisation. Between July and November 1977 the *Bloque* organised two important land invasions and a dozen demonstrations in the larger cities, demanding political freedoms and an end to repression. FAPU also increased its activity, and both organisations gave their backing to the strike movement of the early autumn, when there were major stoppages in the power, textile, food, clothing, mining and construction industries. In mid-October the major rural unions, FECCAS–UTC and ATACES, presented a demand for the minimum daily wage in the coffee, cotton and sugar harvests to be increased to ¢11 (in the 1976/7 season it had been ¢8.0, ¢6.0 and ¢5.0 for these crops). The demand was based on the government's own figures for the 1978–82 development plan, which identified a decrease in rural wages from an average of ¢530 a year in 1971 to ¢429, while the coffee planters' income in 1976 had replaced all their losses over the period

1971-5 and were expected to be three times higher in 1977 than they had been in 1976. It was further pointed out that while taxes were higher in Guatemala, wages there accounted for 41.5 per cent of the value of coffee, whereas in El Salvador the figure was only 12 per cent.[31]

The rural wage campaign reached its peak on 10 November, when the Ministry of Labour was occupied by rural workers not only seeking to gain negotiations but also in support of the striking textile workers. After two days, and an alarming increase in the number of demonstrators gathered outside the ministry, the regime accepted negotiations. But it had already decided to bow to oligarchic pressure and impose a severe crackdown. It could no longer rely upon the selective repression in the countryside with which it had replaced the full-scale operations, such as that at Aguilares, undertaken by Molina. The scale of repression necessary for control becomes evident when one considers that, in Chalatenango alone, the 'low profile' of mid-1977 led to 28 political arrests, seven municipality-wide joint searches with ORDEN, one three-day military occupation, several cases of smallowners' crops being fired, seven killings and three rapes by National Guardsmen in a period of six weeks.

On 24 November Romero announced the Law of the Defence and Guarantee of Public Order. Modelled on the national security codes of the dictatorships of the southern cone – most particularly Institutional Act No.5 of 1968 in Brazil – this measure declared a state of emergency and suspended the formal democratic liberties protected by the constitution.[32] Stiff penalties were laid down for those who disturbed public order in any one of 18 stipulated ways, from 'establishing relations with foreigners or foreign organisations in order to receive aid or instructions of any nature' to participating 'as members in any organisation that maintain doctrines which are anarchic or contrary to democracy'. The way was now clear for a full offensive against the guerrillas, popular organisations, unions and sectors of the Church without any need to adhere to the niceties of the constitution or consider the carping objections of human rights activists. Almost any attitude, affiliation or act could be interpreted as 'conducive to' terrorism under a law which scrupulously avoided the specific for terms such as 'in general' (article 1, no. 1), 'by any other means' (article 1, nos. 2, 7, and 13), 'in any form' (article 1, no. 5), and 'of any nature' (article 1, no. 8). The measure was manifestly designed to provide blanket legal cover or the complete annulment of democratic guarantees.

The law remained in force from December 1977 to March 1979, a period of constantly increasing repression which was met by continued guerrilla activity and worker and peasant resistance. 1978 was a year of bitter local conflict; Romero took no initiative other than to sanction extensive activity by the military and ORDEN. In an action typical of this period, ORDEN seized a number of FECCAS–UTC leaders in La Esperanza, near San Pedro Perulapán, on 22 March. The next day one was found decapitated. This led to a gun battle between ORDEN and peasant militants resulting in nine more deaths and a score of wounded. Four days later five ORDEN members were executed by the FPL, the viligantes responding by driving villagers out of four nearby *pueblos*, 2,000 of them taking refuge in San Pedro. Further clashes resulted in another 15 dead and 50 wounded. Five members of FECCAS were shot in a subsequent demonstration in the capital in which four embassies and the cathedral were occupied by union militants in protest at the repression.

The San Pedro events were particularly bloody but by no means extraordinary. In October Alma Guillermoprieto, a journalist working for the *Guardian*, visited the village of Cinquera to learn of the routine occupation by 300 members of the National Guard and 80 members of ORDEN. Her report was to be the first of many from the Salvadorean countryside that over the following three years froze into a static and general picture in which names and numbers progressively lost their significance. Guillermoprieto was told that there were in the area 2,000 members of FECCAS and 1,000 members of ORDEN. According to her informants from FECCAS,

> The army is afraid of our organisation because it makes people think . . . people realise that if we're poor it's not because we are lazy. If we're poor it's because we work from six in the morning until six at night to make the landowners rich. The peasants and workers create the wealth of this land. The Government doesn't want us to know that, and that's why it's trying to destroy our union organisation.

ORDEN was identified as the principal threat:

> The Government created ORDEN to control the peasants, because the army cannot be everywhere, watching what we are doing all the time. So the peasants in ORDEN watch us for them – and they're sent in to provoke us. Since we don't challenge the government militarily, it has to have an excuse for attacking us. If ORDEN provokes us and we react, then the army comes

in 'to pacify' the situation. Some join ORDEN because they see us as some kind of monster . . . They're convinced we're communists. Others join simply because they're afraid of what will happen to them if they don't . . . Fortunately, we have a vigilance system that lets us know when the Guard is coming, so we were all able to get away in time . . . They search house by house, looting and destroying everything we have. The young women . . . have to come with us – otherwise they will be raped . . . They shot one of us last year. They opened a flower in his chest. All over he was bullets. The ORDEN people had denounced him as a union organiser.[33]

In April 1979 Guillermoprieto returned to the village to find the Guard remaining in occupation and the women still smuggling out food to the men hiding since October in the surrounding countryside. Over the previous month eight men out of a population of 5,000 had been killed.[34] The very bad harvest of 1978/9 contributed to this state of high tension in the countryside.

By the autumn of 1978 guerrilla raids were occurring at the rate of at least one a week. In the first two weeks of November the FPL killed six policemen, attacked the US Embassy, destroyed the San Miguel plant of the Bayer pharmaceutical company and blew up an electricity plant; the ERP planted at least 40 bombs in San Salvador and destroyed PCN offices in three towns; RN made its presence known with four spectacular kidnappings early in December, capturing Japanese, Dutch and British businessmen, netting an immediate $1 million from Philips alone, and deriving considerable publicity from paid advertisements in 39 papers around the world. The guerrillas were recruiting well and the skill of their militants was shown to be high.

The Romero regime had acquired publicity of its own, all of it bad. At the beginning of the year the British Labour government cancelled the sale of 15 armoured cars, while the president faced increasing and well-publicised criticism from his namesake, the archbishop of San Salvador, who in February declared,

Soldiers are to be seen everywhere, people are arrested, people disappear. We've even had complaints of torture from the police . . . The root of all violence is institutionalized violence. Profound and urgent reforms are needed to create more just economic and social structures and to eliminate violence . . .[35]

In August two officials from the State Department visited San Pedro to investigate the events of the spring, and in December a British parliamentary commission published its report on human rights in El Salvador. At the press conference to present their findings, Labour MP Dennis Canavan declared, 'I think the government of El Salvador is the most extreme rightist dictatorship I have ever seen.'

The public order law had palpably failed to stem the left or reduce discontent. On the contrary, it had served to isolate the regime further in international circles and to consolidate internal opposition. The increased activity of the military had only encouraged a corresponding escalation of guerrilla operations. Romero appeared to be losing ground, and it is telling that in 1978 both the De Sola group and the State Department held discussions with the PDC with a view to a possible 'centrist' alternative to the regime. In March 1979 Romero finally accepted that the law was more trouble than it was worth since conflict had anyway reached a point where spurious legal sanction for repression was scarcely necessary. Its repeal was greeted by the Carter administration as a healthy sign of flexibility, but as the year progressed this view was shown to be completely false, and Washington became markedly concerned about the regime.

The single most important factor in the State Department's considerations was the overthrow of Somoza by the FSLN in July. The Nicaraguan Revolution, the first in Latin America for 20 years, completely transformed the terms of political conflict in Central America, sending shudders through its capitals and Washington. Nowhere was its impact more immediate and forceful than in El Salvador.

8
THE IMPACT OF NICARAGUA

The issue isn't Somoza but Nicaragua and the security interests of the US. This *Sandinista* uprising is a Cuban, Venezuelan, Panamanian, Costa Rican operation. It's another Vietnam and it's in this hemisphere.

US Congressman John Murphy

Somoza painted us as Marxists. We have some Marxists with us but the *Frente* is much wider. The concept of the prolonged people's war was not marxist. It is a military concept which will lead to taking the advantage of the favourable moment.

Comandante Tomás Borge, FSLN

The victory of the *Frente Sandinista de Liberación Nacional* was far more than an exhilarating example for the rest of the national liberation forces in Central America; it became their model. National differences were identified, as befits parties dedicated precisely to the task of national liberation. But given that the FSLN had taken power, that its politics were broadly similar to those of the other groups, and that Central America is a balkanised region marked by great similarities between its constituent nation states, the lessons of the FSLN's success were taken as applicable on a general scale. Nicaragua was seen as embodying the successful realisation in the specific conditions of Central America of the lessons learnt from anti-imperialist struggles elsewhere in the world since the Second World War.

July 1979 also marked a watershed in US strategy for the region. As Regis Debray puts it, 'the revolution revolutionizes the counter-revolution'. This is an old dialectic, as familiar to Machiavelli as to Hegel, but it should not be read as a cast-iron guarantee for the wholesale revision of errors, let alone a complete volte-face, which in this case was quite patently impossible. None the less, the Carter administration was forced to recognise that within its schema for Central America it had committed a series of serious political mistakes bred of confusion and lack of determination. It had failed to protect and support Somoza adequately – as he himself pointed out with increasing vehemence as the revolt progressed – yet it had proved equally incapable of finding an acceptable substitute, creating a dangerous vacuum. First it threatened to cut military supplies to the Nicaraguan regime early in 1978. Then, in face of the February 1978 general strike, it drew back from a complete boycott and released loans worth $150 million. In July Carter appeared to confirm this change in tack by sending Somoza a personal letter congratulating him on the regime's respect for human rights; this was six months after the National Guard had indiscriminately bombed the rebel township of Monimbó into submission with the loss of hundreds of lives. Yet, inconsistent in its policy of shoring up the dictatorship when it was faced with armed insurrection, Washington suspended all military aid in September 1978, just as the FSLN was opening its autumn offensive. At the beginning of 1979 new loans and aid were suspended, only to be released in May when the regime was already beyond repair.[1] In this way Washington found itself universally identified with a government for which it had no further use and which it had objectively undermined.

By June 1979 the State Department, under the direction of its roving ambassador, the taciturn William Bowdler, was expending much effort in attempting to persuade Somoza to resign. But in seeking to split the opposition alliance and ally the non-FSLN forces with large capitalist interests independent of Somoza and with supposed dissidents in the National Guard, Washington demonstrated that it had no conception of the popularity of the *sandinistas* and was striding up a cul-de-sac. Washington was not alone in believing that it was possible to have *somocismo* without Somoza, but it suffered the most severe consequences of such a belief. It compounded these errors when, taken aback by the rapidity of the FSLN advances in June 1979, it changed its tune and attempted to obtain a 'moderate' majority in the already undeniably moderate provisional junta set up by the *sandinistas* in Costa Rica. Failing in this, Vance went to the OAS to demand an 'Inter-American Peace Force' three weeks before Somoza's final collapse. While the civilian regimes identified this as nothing less than old-style yankee interventionism, the military dictatorships saw it as a blow against Somoza rather than against the FSLN and a dangerous

1. San Salvador, *c.* 1920.

2. Arturo Araujo, President 1931.

3. Maximiliano Hernández Martínez, President 1931-44.

4. Agustin Farabundo Marti (seated right) with Sandino (third from left) *(above)*.

15. Farabundo Marti, 1932 *(right)*.

6. President Fidel Sánchez Hernández (third from left) with Lyndon Johnson, 1968.

7. Arturo Molina, President 1972-77.

8. Carlos Humberto Romero, President 1977-79.

9. Refugees near Usulután. (*Mike Goldwater – Network*).

12. José Napoleón Duarte.

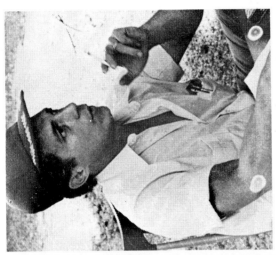

11. Major Roberto D'Aubuissón.

10. General José Guillermo García.

13. Cuscatancingo, 16 March 1982. *(Mike Goldwater – Network).*

14. San Salvador, February 1980.

15. FMLN checkpoint, Usulután, March 1982. *(Mike Goldwater – Network)*.

precedent that might some day be used against themselves. Moreover, only one day before, the US public had seen on their TV screens the cold-blooded execution of a CBS correspondent by the National Guard; the feeling at home was as antipathetic as it was in the rest of the Americas. For the first time in its history the OAS stood ready to reject a US request for intervention. Vance was obliged to have the plan withdrawn; two days later his delegate voted in favour of a motion tabled by the Andean Pact calling for the removal of both Somoza and the *somocista* apparatus. No amount of naval activity in the Caribbean at this late stage could alter the military situation.[2]

The attitude and actions of the US towards the Nicaraguan revolution were in part the result of the residual incompetence and lack of integration in a massive diplomatic and intelligence network. This is a factor that should always be taken into account and must qualify estimations of the impressive military capacity of the US. Because Central America was in the 'backyard' it had merited relatively little serious political analysis: the quality of the senior diplomatic personnel posted there was far from impressive. Before the summer of 1978 the US Embassy in Managua had never even made contact with the FSLN to assess its political positions. The *sandinista* victory changed all this. It revived the question of Cuba, underlined the strategic importance of the Panama canal, and highlighted the weaknesses of Washington's client regimes in the rest of the region. One response to this, voiced by the Brzezinski faction within the administration, was the revival of the domino theory and a distinct aversion to negotiations with the radical forces on the ground that Nicaragua now lay within the sphere of 'Soviet–Cuban military activism in the Third World'.[3] However, the fundamental lack of coherence inside the Carter administration was demonstrated by the fact that Vance and Assistant Secretary of State for Inter-American Affairs Viron Vaky opposed such a hardline approach. In December 1979 Vaky told Congress,

> I think the ball game is still on in Nicaragua . . . I think that we would have desired a different outcome to that which occurred, but given the situation, it is possible in my view for the United States to have a major and significant influence over what evolves there.[4]

These important differences remained inside the government until Vance's resignation, prompted by the effort to rescue the US hostages in Iran. Yet, neither current disputed the growing importance of

Central America or the necessity of ensuring the military defeat of the left. In February 1980 the State Department had three special working parties, one for Afghanistan, one for Poland and one for El Salvador. Central America had come to the forefront of US foreign policy, and El Salvador, by virtue of being seen as the 'next Nicaragua', came top of the list.

The victory of the FSLN was no less critical for the left in Central America. The key lessons drawn from it were the importance of unifying the guerrilla groups, the central role of a broad cross-class alliance based on agreement over a democratic programme, and the potential for stalling US momentum towards direct military intervention in establishing links with the European powers through the Second International and exploiting the growing fissure in the unity of the metropolitan states. These supposedly unique features of the Nicaraguan rebellion were seen as crucial to its success.

The formal unification of the three 'tendencies' of the FSLN only took place in March 1979, a mere four months before Somoza's defeat. The division of the original guerrilla front had taken place over the period 1975–7 with the splitting off first of the *Tendencia Proletaria*, which argued for a greater orientation to organisational work in the masses, particularly the working class, and a turn away from rural guerrilla warfare. The *proletarios* conceived of themselves as the orthodox Marxist wing of the FSLN and entered into a fierce polemic with the original group that stood by the strategy of *guerra popular prolongada*, which name it took as its own (GPP), and continued to wage a low-key rural campaign. The third group, known first as the *terceristas* and then as the *insurreccionales*, differed with both the others in arguing for a more rapid, insurrectionary campaign in which not only the workers and peasants but also the middle sectors and opposition capitalists would be drawn into a broad anti-dictatorial front.[5]

There was little love lost between these groups, all of which claimed the title of FSLN. In many respects their differences appear similar to those of the Salvadorean left but they were never so deep and neither did they run along exactly the same lines. The FSLN factions continued to be guerrilla groups rather than mass organisations until very near the end of the war; there were no bodies analogous to FAPU or the BPR, and the *sandinistas* had no real organised presence inside the working class. However great its popularity, the FSLN was essentially the military vanguard, and the political differences between its tendencies were largely subordinated to a function of military differences. This was in no small part due to the fact that although the FSLN had its origins in the PSN, the local CP, these were far less important than the experience of the PCS for the Salvadorean left. As a result, the predominantly petty bourgeois leadership of all the factions engaged in a debate that was noticeably less Marxist in tenor and direction than that of their Salvadorean comrades.[6] The *terceristas* embraced a military strategy close to that of the ERP but their politics may best be described as social democratic, insurrection being seen as the most effective means of removing the dictatorship and establishing a pluralist democracy rather than socialism, a term that was progressively marginalised in the *sandinista* vocabulary.[7] It is possible to see the FPL and BPR as possessing both the strategic line of the GPP and many of the political positions of the *proletarios* in Nicaragua, but the FPL was always much harder in its profile than either of the two 'orthodox' Nicaraguan groups.

From September 1977 onwards the *terceristas* took the leadership of the FSLN through a number of enterprising military actions, the most celebrated of which was the capture of the National Palace led by Edén Pastora and Dora Tellez in August 1978. Their military predominance led to a strategic and political *rapprochement* that incorporated elements of the other tendencies' lines but reflected overall *tercerista* hegemony; after March 1979 the question of the divisions inside the FSLN subsided very quickly. This ascendancy was marked by the rapid development of alliances with other oppositional groups, many of them far from left wing and some representing important sectors of the capitalist class.

Such broad fronts are, in fact, far from rare in anti-imperialist movements, but the polyclass bloc built around the FSLN was broader than many others because of the peculiar nature of the Somoza regime. The family dynasty is frequently understood to have exercised a virtual monopoly over the Nicaraguan economy. This was not, in fact, quite the case. Since 1934 the Somoza family had maintained absolute control over political power and the state but the family clan, while it guaranteed and provided the conditions for capitalist rule through the state, did not monopolise the market. At least until the 1972 earthquake, its dominance was expressed in relatively unproblematic competition with two other large industrial groups based around the Banco Nicaragüense (BANIC) and the Banco de América (BANAMERICA), which, in terms of total assets, were on a par with the Somoza clan.[8] These groups, and other important independent interests organised around the private enterprise confederation (COSEP), relied on the *somocista* state for the maintenance of the conditions for capitalist development but competed with the *somocista* economic interests for control of the market. After 1972 this fragile relationship began to erode as Anastasio Somoza, his family, and the National Guard used their control of the state to ameliorate their economic position, principally through the post-earthquake 'reconstruction' process, at the expense not only of the Nicaraguan masses but also of the rest of the capitalist class.

Thus, unlike its Salvadorean counterpart, the Nicaraguan capitalist class experienced major internal divisions at a time when it was under unprecedented pressure from its workers. BANIC and BANAMERICA were by no means the core of a national bourgeoisie since they were closely tied to the Chase Manhattan and Wells Fargo banks, but as their positions were challenged by Somoza they would no longer rally to the defence of the state. Other entrepreneurs, particularly a group formed around cooking oil millionaire Alfonso Robelo's *Movimiento Democrático Nicaragüense* (MDN), were in even sharper disagreement with the dictatorship.[9] This group, rather than simply standing aside from the conflict as did the bulk of the BANIC and BANAMERICA clans, enlisted in the active opposition to Somoza and were to the fore in his defeat. Thus, the *terceristas* were able to draw on support well beyond the ranks of the 'exploited masses' of workers, peasants and petty bourgeois and lead a movement that maximised anti-dictatorial sentiment and simultaneously subordinated class antagonisms.

The formation of this popular front was greatly assisted by the fact that the National Guard was not a normal national army subject to a number of distinct institutional conditions that can on occasions lead to splits with the incumbent regime or even the prevailing strategy of the ruling class. The Guard was loyal less to the state than to the *somocista* state; it had been created and was directly commanded by members of the family, upon which it depended for its numerous privileges. Without Somoza the Guard was nothing; for 40 years it had derived its *raison d'être* from *somocismo* and acted on the family's behalf against the masses, the left and the other capitalist interests.[10] Hence, the bulk of the opposition entertained few illusions about splitting it; a battle against Somoza was a battle against the Guard. This not only placed added importance upon the FSLN's armed capacity but also cut out much potential middle ground for compromise with the regime.

Nowhere else in Central America did similar conditions obtain. The Somoza dictatorship was an optimum target; it fused economic dominance and political reaction in such a complete manner that nothing appeared more natural than the forging of an alliance of all sectors against its rule.

This was evident from the very start of the last phase of the dynasty in January 1978 with the assassination of Somoza's leading liberal opponent, Pedro Joaquin Chamorro, the editor of the daily *La Prensa*.[11] Chamorro's death removed the last real possibility of an orderly transfer of power within the ruling bloc. When the opposition front that Chamorro had led – UDEL – responded to his death with a general strike, supported by employers and workers alike, the strength and radicalism of the mass movement shocked its leadership so deeply that it brought the stoppage to a halt as quickly as possible.[12] Yet, as Somoza refused to negotiate – the only real independent activity open to the bourgeois opposition – and the Guard continued its repression, the FSLN gradually gained the leadership of the mass movement with its unchallenged monopoly of the armed resistance and its policy of no negotiations and the complete destruction of the dictatorial apparatus. At times the *sandinistas* were themselves overtaken by the level of mobilisation; in February and September 1978 precipitate popular uprisings in Monimbó, Matagalpa and Managua found them logistically unprepared and unable to impose organisation on the rebellions or press their offensives home. However, by the spring of 1979 the FSLN had clearly captured the organisational as well as the political leadership of the anti-Somoza movement. This had not been a simple process; until the last days of the dictatorship the liberal leadership of the broad opposition front formed in July 1978 – FAO – attempted to eclipse the FSLN by holding out for some sort of compromise and close relations with the US.[13] This had necessitated a break after four months but by March 1979 it was apparent to the MDN that Carter's ambivalence, the necessarily uncompromising stance of Somoza and the Guard, and the popularity of the FSLN gave it no other option than to ally itself with the guerrillas. This option was made all the more plausible by the *sandinistas'* guarantees for private property within a state capitalist system run by a popular democratic government.

Under these terms the national liberation movement retained the allegiance of important business sectors and succeeded in neutralising others. Moreover, its broad programme of democratic liberties and economic reforms proved acceptable to international social democracy, for which extensive nationalisation, primarily of Somoza property, was compatible not only with the struggle for democracy and development but also the retention of capitalism, which was expected to benefit from improved infrastructural facilities and state planning. The contradictions and latent dangers of this scenario for both sides were not slow in emerging. Although some of these were anticipated by the FSLN, they were accounted an integral part of the cost of a victory that terminated 40 years of dictatorship, brought basic democratic freedoms to the Nicaraguan masses, and inflicted a major setback on the US.[14] Thus, while the FSLN was now obliged to address the problems of holding state power and the indeterminate nature of its social policy, its counterparts in El Salvador and the rest of Central America sought to capture power along the lines of the Nicaraguan model.

In El Salvador the *sandinista* victory had an immediate effect; slogans appeared in the streets of the capital declaring, 'Somoza today – Romero tomorrow'. However, the regime had been losing its grip long before July. As soon as it lifted the public order law in March, the Romero government was confronted by a wave of discontent. The first strikes had broken out in February, but after the removal of the statute they spread through most of the urban sector and set off a series of occupations and demonstrations. The centre of the spring strike movement in San Salvador lay at the *La Constancia* and *La Tropical* soft drinks plants where the majority of the workers supported the BPR and had occupied the factories in demand for better working conditions, including the right to go to the lavatory without asking permission and the provision of transport at 2 a.m. when the second shift stopped work.[15] On 10 March, *La Constancia's* owner, Alfonso Quinoñez, the former ambassador to Britain, called in the army, which surrounded and then attacked the plant, killing eight workers and wounding over twenty more. By 13 March 24 unions had declared strikes in solidarity with the soft drinks workers; a week later FAPU called out the power workers, bringing industry in the city to a halt. When the power workers of STECEL at the Rio Lempa station barricaded themselves in and wired up the plant for an explosion in the event of an army attack, Romero was forced to give way and leant on Quinoñez to make concessions to his workers.[16] Some 150,000 workers had been involved in this movement, the first major independent working-class action in the city for a decade. The victory was all the more significant in that it had been won in the face of extensive military mobilisation. Although the strike was neither general nor insurrectionary, it betokened a strengthening of the proletariat that was ominous for the regime, which was now deeply concerned by a flight of capital that had reached alarming proportions. The Japanese business community, responsible for the third largest share of foreign capital, had fallen from 2,400 two years previously to 200 by March; in 1979 private investment reached barely $5 million against $32 million in 1978, which was itself considered a bad year.[17]

Romero once again came under extreme pressure and reimposed martial law in May. The Carter administration resumed talks with the PDC and the De Solas, its proposed bloc of the centre taking on greater importance when ANEP, concerned at the lack of international business confidence in the country, momentarily lost its collective nerve and called for 'peace . . . to correct errors that have been committed'. This tendency towards a softer line had played an important part in the lifting of the security statute and had obliged Romero to fire the chief of the National Guard, General Ramón Alvarenga, widely identified as the leading figure in the right's terror campaign. But the president was not about to embark on a re-run of the events of the summer of 1977: the forces of reaction would not tolerate any major concessions. Alvarenga may have lost his position but he still had considerable influence, which was soon allied with that of Medrano, Colonel Eduardo 'Chivo' Iraheta (Deputy Defence Minister) and Major Roberto D'Aubuissón (Assistant Chief of Intelligence) to form impressive military backing for the alternative strategy of the right under the leadership of the Hill and Regalado families: complete annihilation of the left along the lines of 1932.

In order to stave off this threat and keep popular mobilisation at bay, Romero maintained a hard line. In March and April 130 people vanished without trace at the hands of the paramilitary, and at least 50 members of the *Bloque* were killed by ORDEN. When five *Bloque* leaders were arrested late in April El Salvador once again made the world headlines. On 8 May, the *Bloque* occupied the embassies of Costa Rica and France as well as the metropolitan cathedral, eight churches and five schools, demanding the release of its members. Romero's reply was unambiguous: troops fired on the demonstrators outside the cathedral, and some 25 people died in the mad scramble to reach the precarious safety of the church. The number of dead was much less than in February 1977 and the methods used were no different, with the plaza being sealed off and sharp-shooters carefully picking off defenceless demonstrators from the surrounding government buildings. But this time the world at large viewed the event through its TV screens; it was the first image of the residual violence of Salvadorean society to be piped into the living rooms of the metropolis. Two days later 10,000 people marched in funeral procession through the city chanting 'the fight is constant'; one man turned to a journalist from UPI and asked, 'What is President Carter saying about this? This is the same as Nicaragua and Idi Amin.'[18] The same question was being posed by others further afield.

The total death toll in May was 188. While the strikes had diminished, guerrilla attacks increased, together with direct action by the popular organisations; burning of buses, road blocks, occupations of embassies and radio stations were the principal methods used. The Romero regime had entered a crisis of the proportions suffered by Somoza in September 1978. By July, Japan, Switzerland, West Germany, Britain and Costa Rica had closed down their embassies, and the government was badly isolated. Clearly the US had to take speedy and emphatic action if it was to avoid the loss of two client states in the same region within a matter of weeks.

Although the Romero regime was similar to that of Somoza in terms of its extraordinarily narrow social base and repressive nature, it was a different type of dictatorship in that it drew its strength from a military institution amenable to the possibility of changing figureheads for its collective survival. However, the State Department was well informed about the threat from the ultra-right, knew that a new face alone would do little to improve the situation, and could not have forgotten that in 1977 Romero had proved pliant to its pressure for a softer line. Hence, Washington's first step towards reducing polarisation was to attempt to draw Romero towards the centre with the promise of reforms. Headed by Viron Vaky, the Vance strategy of linking military aid to guarantees of a reduction in violence held temporary sway. Over the summer of 1979 Vaky and William Bowdler made a series of secret visits to San Salvador to pile on the pressure. At first they appeared to have succeeded. Towards the end of August Romero stunned his colleagues by publicly contemplating on the possibility of an official civilian candidate for the 1982 elections, inviting the Red Cross to inspect the prisons, and readmitting exiles. But Vaky failed to persuade Romero to move the elections forward, a move that Washington considered essential for neutralising the popularity of the left. As one diplomatic observer commented, 'it's too late, too late for anything'.[19] Yet Washington was not yet prepared publicly to give up the pretence; the press was informed that Romero was prepared to make 'real and significant electoral reforms' for 1981.[20] He had no such intention. In the face of pressure from the US and its allies in the military, he had entered into a truce with the ultras and rejected any possibility of a democratic 'exit'.[21]

By early September popular mobilisation in the capital had surpassed the level it had reached in May. This time it took the form of demonstrations, occupations and attacks on public buildings, as well as the ritual burning of buses. It was clear that the crisis of the regime had come to a head. Romero's own brother was killed by the guerrillas and the independence celebrations had to be cancelled for fear of an urban insurrection after 100 people had lost their lives in street clashes in the space of three weeks. Nearly 800 had died in the course of the year. There was widespread recognition that El Salvador would be condemned for violation of human rights at the forthcoming meeting of the OAS in La Paz. Indeed, it was believed by some that the ultras under Alvarenga and Iraheta planned to launch a coup during the OAS meeting.[22] On 11 September Vaky went before the House Foreign Relations Committee and made the situation plain:

> A great part of Central America – especially the north – is subjected to strong pressures of change, terrorism and potential radicalization . . . Even without Nicaragua the situation would be explosive . . . The basic question is not whether this change is going to take place but whether it will be violent and radical or peaceful and evolutionary, preserving individual liberties and democratic values . . . The geographical proximity of Central America means that the US has a special interest in the fact that the region enjoys peace, prosperity and cooperation . . .[23]

This innocent declaration was, in effect, notice of a new initiative. Three days later a presidential spokesman, Hodding Carter, admitted to the press that in their trips to San Salvador both Vaky and Bowdler had urged Romero to resign, 'although perhaps a little dramatic, it would be a convincing demonstration of his commitment to democratize the country'.[24]

On 20 September the political picture became more complicated with the announcement of the formation of the *Foro Popular*, an alliance in many respects similar to UNO in which the PDC, MNR, LP–28 and FENASTRAS, the principal union affiliate of FAPU, as well as other unions and professional associations, came together to support a 'common platform' for free elections, political pluralism, respect for human rights and economic reforms. The BPR did not join, declaring 1980 'the year of liberation'. At the height of the crisis a new centrist formation had made an opportune appearance.[25]

Two weeks later, on 10 October, Carter anounced the establishment of a new 'Caribbean Contingency Task Force' to combat 'possible communist domination', declaring military mobilisation in the Caribbean because of the 'discovery' of 3,000 Soviet troops in Cuba. The administration promised full military aid to all regimes fighting communism in the region and instructed the Pentagon to treat such requests as a priority.[26] This move was the first major US response to the Nicaraguan revolution; the Cold War was returning. The issue of the Soviet troops in Cuba was a complete distraction since similar numbers had been stationed there for 17 years. The real need was to clear the way for a full offensive against the indigenous left and tie such an offensive into a wider context. The era of human rights was over.

If Washington had dawdled over the summer, nobody could reasonably accuse it of being dilatory with respect to El Salvador in the autumn. On 11 October, the day after Carter's declaration, Romero travelled to the US 'for a medical checkup'. He returned the next day. On 14 October his family left on a flight to Miami. At midnight that night the BBC World Service announced that there had been a coup d'etat in San Salvador. The situation remained confused until 4 p.m. of the 15th, when Romero recognised that all major units of the armed forces had withdrawn their support. He asked for guarantees for himself, his aides and the senior officers. These were given and the president was hurried away to a Guatemalan airliner that took him into exile.

The army occupied all the major towns. Later that day telex machines around the world tapped out the text of the 'Proclamation of the Armed Forces of El Salvador'. This document indicted the Romero regime for the violation of human rights, corruption, sowing 'economic and social disaster' and besmirching the name of the armed forces and the country. It identified the cause of all this in the 'inadequate economic, social and political structures which have traditionally prevailed in the country'. Electoral fraud and inadequate development programmes had resulted from the 'ancestral privileges of the dominant class'. The military would now adopt an emergency programme to halt violence and corruption, dissolve ORDEN, guarantee human rights and create the proper conditions for free elections with the participation of all ideological groups. A full amnesty was declared, trade unions were offered guarantees, and rights of assembly and free speech were permitted. There would be an agrarian reform, programmes to increase production and fulfil the right of all citizens to housing, food, education and health. Private property was recognised as inviolate provided it had a social function.[27]

The first successful coup since 1961 appeared to be of a determinedly reformist nature. It clearly had not been led by the likes of Alvarenga and Iraheta; the mark of US support was undeniable. Amidst all the confusion one thing was clear: El Salvador had reached another political watershed.

9
REVOLUTION AND REACTION

We're not talking about pragmatic Sandinistas. This is a Pol Pot Left.

El Salvador News Gazette, 27 April 1980

We believe that the reform programme of the Revolutionary Junta offers the best prospects for peaceful change to a more just society . . . The United States will not interfere in the internal affairs of El Salvador. Nevertheless, we are seriously concerned by the threat of civil war . . . which might endanger the security and welfare of all the Central American region.

Secretary of State Cyrus Vance to Archbishop Romero, 12 March 1980

We came last night. There, where I come from, things are ugly. It was a tough trip but here we are. They wanted to scare us off, but they haven't been able to . . . and I agree with all this . . . the bosses, they've got no problems . . . we have to fight now, like everybody says.

Carlos Vázquez, a *campesino*, 22 January 1980 at the march to mark the establishment of the *Coordinadora Revolucionaria de Masas*

Between October 1979 and April 1980 Salvadorean politics underwent a qualitative change; the country moved from widespread social conflict and a breakdown in the regime of the ruling class to a state of civil war. As in all revolutionary situations, the transition was both simple and highly complex. At one level the process of polarisation continued on its inexorable course, although far more rapidly than over the previous decade. At another, political life was shot through with confusion, stops and starts, and contradictions both real and apparent. It was, above all else, a period of politics, a melée of manoeuvres. The grim margin was, as before, a loss of life that accumulated with such steadiness that it soon matched and overtook anything the country had seen since 1932; eventually it was to outstrip even that historic toll. Neither description of the individual experience of terror nor narration of its aggregate cost do justice to this, the everyday reality of the revolution.

There were three main phases in this period. Of course, these overlapped and fused in a multitude of ways but each possessed a distinct political character and dynamic. By separating these phases it is much easier to see why events took the course they did, and how it was possible for Washington to insist for so long that the new government was one of centrist reformism, gallantly fending off the equidistant extremes of left and right. This is important less because it was untrue than because it contained at least an element of truth. For its part, the left counters that there are not three forces in play but two: the regime and the people. This is also true as far as it goes, but as propaganda it fails to take account of the fact that the various juntas that successively comprised the Salvadorean government from October 1979 had to stall the political ambitions of the extreme right in order to realise the most efficacious counter-revolutionary campaign. This, to be sure, made the regime no less repressive. Neither did it entail breaking the numerous ties it possessed with the oligarchy. But it did correspond to a shift of power within the dominant bloc, and it led to a number of secondary conflicts. From October 1979 El Salvador was ruled by what Nicos Poulantzas would describe as an 'exceptional regime', one bred of crisis and inherently unstable not just because it was under severe challenge from the left but because it had to meet this challenge by mediating the forces of the right.[1] Finally, the popular view on the left that it is the 'people' that confront the state and its armed apparatus is correct in so far as the vast majority of the population is opposed to the regime and a significant proportion of it makes an active practice of this opposition. However, the use of the term 'people' also obscures the fact that this opposition was not exclusive to the masses but also incorporated important bourgeois and petty bourgeois political forces in a broad front. The consequences of this, as we have already seen, go well beyond a shared democratic programme and a liability to persecution. In the last instance it is the resolution of the contradictions in this class alliance, in many respects as unstable as the regime it confronts, that will determine the course of the Salvadorean revolution.

The first of the three phases runs from October to the end of December 1979, the period of the 'first junta'. In these ten weeks the officers that led the coup against Romero ruled alongside representatives of the bourgeois and petty bourgeois opposition, drawn predominantly from the *Foro Popular*. In this period the aim was less to destroy the left physically than to contain it forcefully by military means and cut the political ground from beneath it by introducing from above a set of reforms that would meet the requirements of the liberal opposition parties and confront the economic crisis that had done so much to lead the masses to accept the leadership of the radical left. In this sense there was a unity of purpose between the military and the *Foro Popular*; they both sought to divert mobilisation. However, the civilians baulked at the degree of the repression this required. When they perceived that the armed forces were only prepared to undertake limited reforms under conditions of absolute and exceedingly violent control – precisely because they would otherwise be forced beyond acceptable limits by mass mobilisation – they resigned.

The second phase, from January to February 1980, saw the unification of the left in the *Coordinadora Revolucionaria de Masas* (CRM). This, combined with the collapse of the junta, compelled the US to take a much higher profile and step in to bolster the new junta by vetoing a challenge from the extreme right and throwing its weight behind the Christian Democrats as the civilian partner and the acceptable face of the regime. The essential content of the first junta's reforms was maintained but their form was changed; they would now be implemented within a framework of an extensive counter-insurgency campaign and a drive to annihilate the left. This did not reduce the vocal objections of the far right but it brought the junta much closer to the 'total solution' the ultras were demanding. While the remnants of the *Foro* remained in a vacuum as a consequence of the failure of their strategy, the CRM began to confront the evident exhaustion of its tactics of partial strikes, demonstrations and occupations.

The third phase runs from the beginning of March and the implementation of the agrarian reform. The level of violence that this provoked proved decisive in consolidating the opposition. Under Archbishop Romero the majority of the Church effectively disowned the PDC and threw in its lot against the regime. Romero's assassination in late March sealed this decision and finally split the PDC itself. In recognition of the fact that it had a choice – to disappear from history or to ally with the left – the rump of the *Foro* constituted itself into the *Frente Democrático Salvadoreño* (FDS) and then joined the CRM to form the *Frente Democrático Revolucionario* (FDR) on the basis of the CRM's programmatic platform. By April the principal blocs were consolidated and with the unification of the guerrilla groups military encounters increased in both frequency and scale. Henceforth the military question was to predominate. The civil war had begun.

The First Junta: October to December 1979

Much of the confusion over the nature of the new regime that replaced Romero derived from the fact that it was not entirely clear which faction of the military had led the coup. It was even less clear which faction had subsequently taken its leadership. Three broad groups inside the army had planned to stage a coup sometime over the summer or early autumn. The first was that led by the 'fascists' Alvarenga and Iraheta, but the rebel proclamation was manifestly not theirs. The second group was headed by Colonel Adolfo Majano, commander of the arsenal, and comprised younger field officers of a reformist cast of mind. This group had links with the rebels of 1972, was attached to the military institution rather than the PCN, and clearly aimed to establish a regime somewhat akin to that of General Velasco in Peru between 1968 and 1975: they accepted the need for basic reforms and some form of populist political project, but as much as they saw that this would mean a fight with the oligarchy they also sought to restrict its limits, eradicating the left by beating it at its own game. The Majano group was, therefore, politically close to UNO, the major difference being that it quite naturally placed greater emphasis on the role of the military and the importance of centralised authority. It was this faction, centred on the San Carlos and Zapote barracks in San Salvador, that staged the coup. Shortly after the removal of Romero it came together to form the *Consejo Permanente de las Fuerzas Armadas* (COPEFA).

The third principal faction was closely tied to the interests of the US. This group was headed by Colonel Jaime Abdul Gutiérrez, commander of the cadet school, and Colonel José Guillermo García. Both had links with Medrano and a more directly remunerative association with the state telecommunications agency, ANTEL, of which García was the president and Gutiérrez the manager. A third member of the group, Colonel Nicolás Carranza, had been ANTEL's technical manager. Through ANTEL these men had established close links with the US multinational ITT, with which they were accused of corrupt dealings, and the American Embassy. This connection was to bear fruit immediately: when COPEFA nominated Colonels Majano and Guerra y Guerra as their representatives on the junta, the US stepped in to rectify the balance. According to an officer belonging to

COPEFA,

> The United States opposed the naming of Guerra y Guerra and instead
> proposed to us two names: Colonel José Garcia and Colonel Jaime Abdul
> Gutiérrez. We needed American support, and we agreed to this. Gutiérrez
> became the second military man on the junta. Garcia became Minister of
> Defence. Guerra y Guerra accepted a lesser post as Under Secretary of the
> Interior.[2]

Carranza became deputy Defence Minister.

The initial institutional trade-off began a progressive
marginalisation of the 'young turks'. Although this was not fully
completed until the end of 1980 and the exiling of Majano, it
proceeded much faster and more emphatically than was generally
recognised by civilians. As a result of their political naivety, lack of
strong civilian support, loyalty to the institution and its informal
kinship groups of *tandas* or graduating fraternities, as well as the alleged
payment of bribes to the sum of $10 million, the Majano faction lost
control of COPEFA, which was effectively the supreme military body in
the first months after the coup. When asked why there had been no
move by COPEFA to end the repression, one of Majano's lieutenants
replied,

> Colonel Marenco is head of that now. He is 'Chele' Medrano's nephew and
> protege. He reorganised COPEFA in a few months. Eighty per cent of its
> membership changed, all of them loyal to Garcia. Garcia is not one of us.
> What you hear about the repression is true, and it comes from Garcia's
> group.[3]

The ascendant Garcia faction took care to minimise its previous
associations and acquiesced in the score of resignations by *romerista*
officers demanded by Majano and his backers, but it was quick to
realign itself with one of the key military groupings that had supported
Romero, ANSESAL *(Agencia Nacional de Seguridad Salvadoreña)*. Thus,
even before the fall of the first junta, the hardliners had recuperated
and formed a strong bloc inside the armed forces. Majano's group still
held important troop commands and had a voice in the regime, but
they did not control it. It could be said that there had been a coup within
a coup, but it would be incorrect to explain the continuation and
increase of repression on this basis alone; all the military factions were
agreed on the necessity for tight control and meeting the left with force.
It was Majano's faction that declared the month-long state of siege, the

tight curfew and the military occupation of all urban centres in the days after the coup. Social forces and political ideas inevitably resonate within an officer corps but only within determinate limits.

These developments can only have gratified the State Department, which, in view of all the frenetic activity before the coup, was not surprisingly held responsible for staging it. Little was done to upset this interpretation when, on the day following the coup, Hodding Carter enthusiastically declared the new regime to be 'moderate and centrist' and agreed that the coup was a relief for the State Department because it facilitated 'the search for peaceful solutions'.[4] According to the US Embassy in San Salvador, 'we listened, but we didn't take any action, either positive or negative. For the first time in history we didn't have anything to do with it.'[5] However, ten days before the coup a government official in Washington told a human rights activist, 'you're going to see positive changes in El Salvador in the next two weeks'.[6] The *New York Times* reported that the rebels had informed Washington of their intentions two weeks before the rebellion, giving rise to warnings to Romero to be ready to pack his bags on the 15th. Moreover, the *Times* commented, the plans of the *golpistas* to bring members of the Universidad Centroamericana (UCA) into their government had not diminished enthusiasm in the State Department.[7]

It seems probable that, once it had learnt of developments, the State Department saw things going so emphatically in its favour that it was not obliged to do anything other than sit back and positively not interfere. If so, it was most certainly the first and last time. Nevertheless, the State Department took a relatively low profile until late December, by which time it became clear that the civilian members of the junta could no longer be relied upon.

Some of Majano's advisers from UCA lacked political affiliation but others were close to the parties in the *Foro Popular*, which now came to the centre of the stage. The *Foro's* platform converged with the main points of the colonels' declaration but it still made acceptance of cabinet posts conditional upon a number of guarantees: an end to repression; the dissolution of ORDEN, UGB and other terrorist groups; investigation of the cases of those who had 'disappeared'; a general amnesty and freedom for all political prisoners; full rights of political organisation, association and to strike; an end to the state of siege; and initiation of major economic reforms, beginning with price controls and wage increases and leading to an agrarian reform.[8] These were fundamental democratic demands, at the base of the campaign of the popular organisations and the core of the old UNO programme; rejection would have meant denial of the proclaimed political logic of the coup. On 19 October, the colonels, including Garcia, formally approved them. The PDC proposed Morales Erlich as *Foro* candidate but he was defeated by the MNR leader Guillermo Ungo, who joined UCA Rector Román Mayorga on the junta. The third civilian member was a clear ally of the García faction. He was Mario Antonio Andino, manager of the local Phelps Dodge subsidiary, Conelca, which had a lucrative contract supplying cable to ANTEL. Andino's links with the De Sola's Miraflor group justified his place as representative of private enterprise.

This coalition of officers, liberal technocrats and reformist politicians was reflected in the nomination of ministers in the cabinet formed in the last week in October. The new government led by the junta (Majano, Gutiérrez, Mayorga, Ungo and Andino) contained five soldiers, four members of the *aperturista* sector of the landed bourgeoisie, six figures close to UCA, and ten members proposed by the *Foro Popular* with a further five suggested by it and accepted by the other groups. The PDC was compensated for the lack of a full junta member with the post of Foreign Minister going to Hector Dada and that of Minister of the Presidency to Rubén Zamora. Of the *Foro*, the PDC had five ministerial posts, the UDN five and the MNR four.

The entry of the UDN into the cabinet was effectively the entry of the PCS into government, where it dominated the Ministry of Labour. The presence of 'communists' in the regime certainly went down badly in the circles of the oligarchy, and it fared equally poorly with the left. As a result, the PCS went to some lengths to defend its decision, which was nothing if not consistent. According to its spokeswoman, Liliana Jimenez, the coup had not gone entirely according to Washington's plans. The oligarchy was divided, and it was now necessary to halt the threats of its right-wing faction. By joining the government the party was fulfilling Lenin's requirement that a part of the military should be neutralised. The PCS would support the progressive elements against the fascist threat but it was 'in no sense engaging in alliances with the bourgeoisie'.[9] A week after the coup Shafik Handal denounced claims that it was US-backed as 'simplistic and unilateral'. It was 'nothing new', however, that Washington should have a hand in it. The coup was 'not the expression of a homogeneous current', and there was room to build an alliance with the progressive sectors of the military as in 1944, 1960 and 1972. The critical issue was the formation of a democratic alliance against the fascists, and it was the responsibility of all on the left to support such an alliance.[10]

The left rejected this position unanimously not solely on the basis of its established critique of the 'stagism' and 'reformism' of the PCS but also because from the very start it perceived no effort on the part of the army to meet the conditions made by the *Foro*. The state of siege remained, and while Majano had personally released a few political prisoners, nine days after the coup Garcia had declared that there were none left, thereby tacitly admitting to the death of some 300 *desaparecidos*.[11] There was, moreover, to be no further action over those that had disappeared. As in Argentina, it was impossible for the military to admit that it had executed its prisoners. This refusal to entertain further discussion of the prisoners had a considerable impact, not least amongst those parties that had just entered the government. But the left had lost what few expectations it had of the regime as a result of the rapid action taken against it by the armed forces.

From the start the junta's rule was marked by an upturn in violence. On 16 October, following the high command's order to 'resolve any unforeseen situation', local commanders ordered their troops to take over all factories occupied by workers. This move was aimed at the *Bloque's* urban union organisation, the *Comité Coordinador de Sindicatos José Guillermo Rivas* (CCS), which had led a series of occupations not in support of or opposition to the coup but in order to exploit it in order to gain better conditions. Troops attacked the workers of the Arco, Apex, Lido, Sherwin, Williams and Duramás factories, killing ten and making many arrests. Three of the factories were badly burnt.[12] Six days later a FAPU funeral march for two of its militants killed by police was attacked. Six more members of the organisation were killed and 'consolidating operations' lasted for several hours. The new commander of the National Guard, Colonel Vides Casanova, denied eye-witnesses' claims that his force was responsible, asserting that the incident was no more than 'clashes between rival groups, some in favour of and others against the junta'. The Guard could not have been involved because 'everything it does and represents conforms to its philosophy of discipline, loyalty and respect'.[13] However, when, a week later, the *Ligas* held a march in support of the demands of the *Bloque*, FAPU and the mothers of the disappeared for the release of political prisoners and investigation of the cases of the disappeared, the scale of the slaughter was too great to permit such ingenuous disclaimers. Cameras caught the movement of troop-carriers and armoured cars towards the demonstration as well as the subsequent shooting and body-count; 86 died and more than 200 were wounded. An American journalist went to the junta for an explanation and was told by Majano that what had occurred was 'violent aggression against public authority' on the part of the demonstrators. When the journalist responded that he had been there and that the marchers had not used firearms, there was a long silence, finally broken by Ungo, who stated firmly that, 'the state also has the right to legitimate defence'.[14] As if to prove this, troops attacked the traditional student *bufonada* organised together with the BPR; 29 people died.[15]

These four massacres in the last twelve days of October were the most outstanding incidents of military repression of peaceful protests. Others occurred on a lesser scale; they would continue to occur with increasing frequency. However, Ungo's remarkable statement, which appeared to be nothing less than an abdication of all the *Foro's* demands and capitulation to the hardline officers, may be explained at least in part by the fact that it had been the *Ligas* which had been the victims of 29 October. On 24 October, the *Ligas*, the only mass organisation to join the *Foro*, withdrew from it, accusing it of compliance in massacres, petty bourgeois opportunism and betraying the interests of the masses. The *Ligas* called upon the workers not to participate in any activity that these opportunists organise and not to pay any attention to what these demagogues say, however prettily they speak'.[16] This about-turn was not inconsistent with the political erraticism of the LP–28, but it was all the more repugnant to the MNR leader because the organisation had backed the call for a popular insurrection made by its guerrilla affiliate ERP while the *Ligas* were still part of the *Foro*.

Faithful to its insurrectionary strategy, the ERP had been the only group to respond to the coup with a call to arms. On the day after the removal of Romero, militants of the ERP had occupied sectors of the shanty towns of Soyapango, Mejicanos, San Marcos and Cuscatancingo, engaging the army in a series of long battles. The insurrection failed to spread, and led instead to extensive destruction, the loss of 50 lives and a rapid retreat by the *erpistas*.[17] The political lessons of this failure were considerable, and although the *Ligas* did not execute another complete volte-face, their positions began to draw closer to those of the rest of the left. The *Ligas* still spoke of the junta as *'romerismo sin Romero'* and as the product of a US-backed right-wing coup. They argued that because of the distinct class structure of El Salvador the revolution would proceed much more rapidly than in Nicaragua. Yet, they admitted to the suspension of military activity and began to back the campaigns of the BPR and FAPU to force the regime to act on the *Foro's* demands.[18]

Although FAPU had not itself entered the *Foro*, it had been well represented by FENASTRAS, its largest affiliate. It argued that this was to preserve its political independence, but this position was scarcely tenable and on 24 October FENASTRAS joined the *Ligas* in retiring from the *Foro*.[19] This brought FAPU more into line with the *Bloque*, which had rejected participation from the start and hardened its position after the coup, arguing that it was impermissible to form alliances with the bourgeoisie and join a government that was 'massacring the people'. The leading theoretician of the BPR, Rafael Menjívar, identified the coup as the product of only the second major crisis of hegemony in the dominant bloc, the first being that of 1927 to 1932. The project of the US was, on the one hand, to effect a categorical repression of the popular movement and prepare the way for the electoral victory of the PDC, and, on the other, to compel a shift of capital and power towards the industrial sector.[20] This very prescient analysis was shared to some extent by FAPU, which saw the regime as incorporating a number of distinct currents: an openly pro-imperialist group headed by Gutiérrez; the young officers, who were neutralised, outmanoeuvred and 'haven't understood that popular aspirations cannot be drowned in blood'; the *aperturista* sector of the landed bourgeoisie headed by the De Solas; 'petty bourgeois reformists' led by Mayorga and the UCA group; and the *Foro*, which 'could have been the expression of the popular political forces had it not involved itself in the treason and opportunism of Christian Democracy . . .'[21]

FAPU's interpretation of the degeneration of the *Foro* as the result of the dealings of the PDC and the 'recognised affinity with imperialism' of many of its leaders, and its remarkably soft line on the *majanistas*, betokened continuing differences with the *Bloque*. None the less, both groups now shared the immediate tactical task of forcing the regime to comply with its avowed democratic intentions and economic reforms. For the *Bloque* at least, the corollary to this was that while the junta might make a number of minimal concessions, it would soon be shown to be incapable of any major opening, thereby losing its democratic facade and the still appreciable popular support it enjoyed by virtue of the backing of the unions in the *foro*.

This campaign took the form of a succession of marches and occupations, the most celebrated and important of which was that of the BPR of the ministries of labour and economy between 24 October and 6 November. In these actions a number of ministers, including two from the PCS, and public employees were held hostage by *Bloque* militants to force concessions from the regime. Many of the demands were no different from those of the *Foro*, some were designed to protect the popular economy, and others were manifestly political with no chance of being negotiated but valuable in their propaganda impact. Amongst the conditions for the release of the hostages were a general 100 per cent wage increase; reductions in the prices of meat by 40 per cent, of vegetables by 30 per cent and of fruit by 40 per cent; reductions in petrol prices by an average of 45 per cent and in the price of clothes by 50 per cent; a freeze on transport prices; an end to repression; freedom for all political prisoners; dissolution of ORDEN, the National Guard, the National Police and the Treasury Police; and the removal of all foreign military advisers.[22] Although it organised a counter-demonstration outside the ministries, the *Foro* was unable to launch a major political offensive precisely because the *Bloque's* demands were substantially its own. After two weeks the civilians in the junta prevailed upon their military colleagues to concede the bulk of the economic demands and reiterate their good intentions as to repression by accepting the *Bloque's* offer of a 30-day truce to enable it to fulfil these requirements.[23] The occupation was lifted, as were the others undertaken in solidarity with it. For the first time in three weeks there was a lull in the conflict, but it was not to last for long.

The occupation of the ministries highlighted the ability of direct mass action to obtain that which discrete pressure from within the government had failed to deliver. It gave the coup de grace to the *Foro* as a popular movement, boosted the mass organisations, and demonstrated to the reformist *politicos* in the regime that they were being outmanoeuvred to the left as well as to the right. It had, moreover, drawn international attention to El Salvador at the time of the massacres, just as the junta's representatives at the OAS meeting in La Paz were claiming that human rights were now fully respected.[24]

The parties in government were obliged to take stock and defend their positions. Through Ungo the MNR apparently maintained its intransigence against the left. The social democratic leader responded with formidable political logic to a question as to whether he would leave the junta because of the repression:

> I would not speak of repressions because this is not a selective repression with political persecutions, ideological persecutions. I would speak of

confrontations which are occurring as a result of objective and subjective causes which so far it has not been possible to overcome.[25]

If the MNR was seeking to disguise its defeat, the PDC was endeavouring to take the initiative. At the end of October it celebrated the return of its exiled leader José Napoleón Duarte, who told the crowd waiting at the airport that he believed in the junta's promises and then led his supporters in a march to the city centre, where they clashed with a demonstration led by the mothers of the disappeared. This led to prolonged street fights and conveniently enabled the US press to multiply by the power of three the numbers that had 'greeted' the man who was increasingly depicted as the potential saviour of the Salvadorean political crisis.[26] At the first major press conference given by the party after Duarte's return, the PDC emphasised that its support for the junta was conditional upon the fixing of a date for presidential elections; the junta itself should take only emergency measures and prepare the ground for the return to democracy.[27] With or without its allies in the *Foro*, the PDC was plainly set on obtaining office.

Of all the parties in government, the PCS suffered most political damage. This was evident in a TV broadcast given by Handal on 5 November, when he accepted that the junta had committed brutal massacres but claimed that those responsible were 'the fascists infiltrated into the government' and not government functionaries. He then proceeded to identify officers who were preparing a coup against the junta.[28] Whatever the truth in the coup claim, it barely sufficed to extricate the party from the absurd position of serving in a government alongside fascists, even those who had been infiltrated into it only to overthrow it.

The centre was powerless. Its sole achievement had been the removal of 60 members of the National Guard, only twelve of whom were sent for trial. Of the rest of its demands, only those for increased wages and a price freeze had been conceded, and those by virtue of the BPR's mobilisation. ORDEN had nominally been dissolved but it was an open secret that Medrano had kept it in action by the simple expedient of changing its name, to the *Frente Democrático Nacional* (FDN). Not only had the repression increased but further death squads, such as the *Escuadrón de la Muerte*, had appeared. In the first two weeks of the junta alone the death toll had exceeded the number of deaths for the rest of 1979. Attempts at introducing structural reforms in the midst of this carnage had been blocked either on constitutional grounds by

Justice Minister Luis Nelson Segovia or by refusal to implement them by Economy Minister Manuel Enrique Hinds, both of whom had close links with ANEP.[29] A US military mission visited to discuss substantial increases in aid to the armed forces but neither Ungo nor Mayorga was informed of this until after agreement had been reached.[30]

In December the position worsened considerably. The *Bloque's* truce elapsed and the cycle of conflict returned with the occupation of a score of sugar haciendas and a number of cotton mills by BPR and LP–28 militants demanding the implementation of the November agreements; 40 people died in the ensuing clashes with the National Guard. The guerrillas returned to the fore with raids on government buildings and radio stations, brief occupations of villages and city suburbs, and the execution of two members of the 'fourteen families', Federico Aguilar Meardi and Francisco Vives Ceballos. The junta was unable to make any headway in negotiating the release of Archibald Dunn, the South African Ambassador, and Jaime Alberto Hill, son of the most powerful oligarchic family, kidnapped by the FPL and ERP respectively. The right responded with a partial business strike and a march by the 'Committee for Peace', composed of right-wing women's groups, which met with Colonel Carranza and demanded that 'the bandits be exterminated'.[31]

In their first concerted initiative since October, 27 ministers and senior government officials sent an ultimatum to COPEFA on 30 December. They accused Garcia of being responsible for the repression and demanded his removal. They also proposed to remove Andino from the junta, which would now take command of the armed forces through COPEFA.[32] If these terms were not met in full the signatories would resign. On 1 January 1980 the ultimatum was rejected. The civilians' bluff had been called. Over the next few days Ungo and Mayorga resigned from the junta and 37 ministers left the government. One of them, Salvador Samayoa, the young UCA professor and Minister of Education, simultaneously announced his resignation and enlisted with the FPL in front of the TV cameras.

All that remained from October was a junta composed of Gutiérrez and Andino, with Garcia as Minister of Defence. Within two weeks Andino himself was forced to flee the country by threats from the left. With the end of the the 'first junta', the supposedly independent strategy of the *majanistas* disappeared; so also did that of the majority of the parties that had formed UNO and the *Foro Popular*. Of these only the PDC remained in the same camp as the military. In the space of ten weeks the attempt to form a 'bloc of the centre' against the left had collapsed under the weight of its own contradictions.

Polarisation and Unification

It was the left that responded most quickly and decisively to the new situation. On 10 January, the FPL and RN issued their first joint statement with the PCS, calling for an armed popular revolution based on the collaboration of democratic and revolutionary forces, exhorting 'honourable' officers to join the fight, and stressing the paramount importance of unity. Although this document bore the separate slogans of all the groups, it was clear that the process of convergence was underway.[33] The experience of its short spell in government and the resulting political crisis it had suffered had driven the PCS to engage once more in armed struggle. Henceforth it would rank as a 'politico-military organisation' alongside the guerrilla groups, although with nearly 90 per cent of its cadre formed during the UNO period, it lagged far behind them in military capacity.[34] The document was not signed by the ERP because of continuing difficulties between it and RN, but it could not afford to marginalise itself for long and, after much pressure, finally joined the front in March.

This agreement between the guerrilla forces was followed the next day by the far more public declaration of alliance between the mass organisations, including the *Ligas*, in the *Coordinadora Revolucionaria de Masas* (CRM), founded at an open meeting in the National University. The establishment of the CRM was, for many, five years overdue and had an enormous impact upon the mass movement. This was shown in the demonstration it called for 22 January to mark the 48th anniversary of the 1932 uprising; the march drew some 250,000 people and was the last truly open popular event to take place in El Salvador. Its size was all the more remarkable because it took place during a strike by transport workers and after several days of a concerted media campaign, in which the newly-created *Frente Amplio Nacional* (FAN), headed by Roberto 'Major Bob' 'D'Aubuissón, warned of a 'communist plot' and urged 'patriots' to stop the demonstration. The UGB, with which D'Aubuissón was also linked, declared that if the military 'didn't do the job' they would.

Early on the morning of the march the offices of the *Bloque* were bombed, those of FENASTRAS machine-gunned, and the university subjected to a number of attacks by civilians. At 10 a.m., when people had already been congregating for a number of hours, the *campesinos* who had arrived over the previous days started to move into the centre from the university. Crop-dusting planes and helicopters passed overhead and released cargoes of insecticide on the marchers, but this failed to break either the ranks of the demonstration or the spirit of its participants. Some declared simply that, 'we have to be one single body in the battle against the rich', others that they had come 'so that people can see that we are not few' or that 'we're not going to run, they are not going to terrorize us'.[35] This sense of determination met a predictable response when, at about 1 p.m., the 40,000 supporters of FAPU passed the presidential palace and turned into the cathedral square. Shooting broke out from a number of surrounding buildings, most of them government offices. The march was not undefended and members of FARN returned fire but in a highly undisciplined and dangerous manner, undoubtedly resulting in the death of some of their comrades. Although the death toll of 21 was not as high as on other occasions, the political impact was substantial. According to the government there had been no troops in the vicinity and the shooting was a result of the 'anger of private citizens' provoked by the march. These citizens had possessed heavy arms of the same calibre used by the armed forces, and no effort was made to trace them.[36] It was clear to all that the unity of the left had not prompted any shift in the regime's position; popular demonstrations would be met with repression either from the military or the paramilitary right with which it liaised. Occupations of embassies and public buildings continued for a number of weeks but their domestic political value was not great. There were no further mass marches. The challenge facing the left was to find alternative means of sustaining and deepening popular support and mobilisation.

The political basis for the unity of the left was laid down in the 'Programmatic Platform of the Revolutionary Democratic Government', signed by the parties of the CRM on 23 February. The looseness of the terminology employed in the document was designed to achieve a working compromise between the positions of the parties of the left; in this it succeeded to such a degree that it was later to serve as the programme for the entire opposition. In this the *Bloque* made the greatest concessions: capitalism and socialism were not even mentioned. The 'Platform' was built around democratic, anti-dictatorial, anti-imperialist and reformist motifs. It spoke of a 'new

society' and 'social progress', containing the October demands of the
Foro but also calling for the 'dissolution of the existing state powers'.
While it laid down the dismantling of repressive bodies such as
ANSESAL and ORDEN, the National Guard and the other police
forces, it did not stipulate the destruction of the army. A new army
would be built from the guerrilla forces and the 'healthy, patriotic and
worthy elements that belong to the current army'. The government
itself would 'rest on a broad political and social base, formed above all
by the working class, the peasantry and the advanced middle layers'
united with those who supported the programme amongst the
'medium-sized industrialists, merchants, artisans, and farmers (small-
and medium-sized coffee planters and those involved in other areas of
agriculture or cattle raising)'. To these forces would be added 'honest
professionals, the progressive clergy, democratic parties such as the
MNR . . . advanced sectors of Christian Democracy' and honest
military officers. The government would 'put an end to the political,
economic and social power of the great lords of land and capital' but
small- and medium-size owners would not be affected by
nationalisations, which would be limited to land, the banks, foreign
trade, electricity and petrol refining. Only 'monopolistic enterprises'
and the 'big landlords' would have their property expropriated. On
this basis effective planning would be realised, an extensive agrarian
reform undertaken, proper mechanisms for credit for small and
medium enterprises established, jobs created, a 'just wages policy'
introduced and social services expanded massively to include health,
housing and literacy campaigns. The aim was to 'liquidate once and
for all the . . . dependence of our country on Yanqui imperialism'; the
new regime would adopt a non-aligned position, withdraw from
CONDECA and other military treaties and organisations and
maintain close fraternal relations with Nicaragua.[37]

The programme manifested the influence of the FSLN, whose
alliance with the anti-Somoza bourgeoisie was undertaken as a
blueprint for the 'popular government' which, whatever precise term
was used, all the left agreed was not but would precede a socialist
government. Given the omnipotence of the oligarchy, expropriation
of its property would constitute a much greater step towards
nationalised property relations than had occurred in Nicaragua after
July 1979. Although mention was made of representatives rather than
delegates, only municipal authorities were identified as 'organ(s) of the
new people's power'; no precise format was laid down for the structure

of government, which could be interpreted equally well as based either on soviets and workers' councils or parliamentary democracy. The 'Platform' was neither socialist nor a classic manifesto of bourgeois democracy but, above all else, populist and radical. In this respect it was true to the traditions of post-war national liberation movements in the neo-colonial states. Its prime targets were imperialism not capitalism, dictatorship not bourgeois government, the oligarchy not entrepreneurs as a whole. In its elisions and omissions, its concentration on form rather than substance, it reflects precisely the backwardness of Salvadorean capitalism. In endeavouring to provide a programme for the eradication of this backwardness and its political and social consequences, the 'Platform' was a manifesto shared by all those who sought modernisation and democracy, whether they held that this could be achieved through capitalism or not. On this issue it had nothing to say and was, therefore, an optimum basis for alliance against the prevailing system. The leadership of the alliance remained an open question, to be contested in the process of realising the points of the programme.

Yet, neither in mid-January, when the CRM was established, nor in late February, when it issued the 'Platform', were the conditions for such an alliance fully given. Of the parties in government until the end of the year, only the PCS had joined the left, most of the *foro* was in a vacuum, while the PDC now took the opportunity to be the sole political party ruling with the military. This decision was the source of some conflict inside the party, which had gained little popularity over the previous months. But it is an indication of the fundamentally reactionary nature of Christian Democracy that the principal issue was not whether to enter the government, but what the terms of that entry should be. The 'progressive' elements won the day by making their support for the regime conditional upon the removal of any representatives of private enterprise from the junta and agreement to nationalise the banking system (demands opposed by Duarte and the right of the party), as well as dialogue with the popular organisations, a pluralist government, agrarian reform, effective control of the military by the junta, nationalisation of the export of sugar, cotton and fish, and unionisation of the peasantry.[38] As can be seen, these requirements were, on paper, not very distinct from those of October; the major difference was the experience of the intervening months. The PDC – or at least those sections of it that genuinely held by these conditions – still believed it was possible to democratise the armed forces while the

CRM proposed to confront them in combat. The officers themselves accepted the terms just as three months before. Joining Gutiérrez and Majano on the junta were Antonio Morales Erlich, Hector Dada (who had just resigned as Foreign Minister) and an independent, Dr Ramón Avalos, a physician who, as somebody unkindly put it, was not even known by his mother.[39]

The entry of the PDC into government galvanised the opposition of the extreme right. This was partly due to the fact that however anti-communist Christian Democracy might be, it was seen as intent upon an agrarian reform in which it would have the support of both the US and sectors of the military. It was, in short, the most dangerous competitor. However, the renaissance of the ultras was also due to the extreme weakness of the regime after the departure of the *Foro* and the rise of the CRM. Thus, ANEP condemned the 'manoeuvres' and 'ambitions' of the PDC, on which it laid total responsibility for the regime's actions because the Christian Democrats had specifically vetoed any representative of private enterprise.[40] ANEP then withdrew from all state corporations and agencies, began to boycott the new state coffee-exporting agency INCAFE, and fought a vociferous campaign against the nationalisation of the financial sector which, despite a firm stand by Majano, won a delay in the measure.[41] In view of Washington's open support for these reforms it was not surprising that ANEP, indignant at its old ally's switch of allegiance, also proclaimed the 'right to self-determination' and adopted a strong nationalist position.

The political challenge of neo-fascist hardliners was led by D'Aubuissón and Medrano. Although the former was now retired, he still had many links with officers through ANSESAL, of which he was a former chief. Medrano, of course, exercised considerable influence through ORDEN/FDN; but both felt sufficiently threatened to launch an open campaign in the first months of 1980. D'Aubuissón and FAN demanded the removal of Morales Erlich and Dada from the government, which they treated as co-substantial with the left. Medrano took a somewhat different line in demanding a 'decisive repression of subversion' followed by elections for a constituent assembly. The 'delinquent guerrilla subversives' had abdicated their rights to constitutional guarantees: human rights were irrelevant for people 'who seek to destroy the country'. The regime should remove 'all corrupt and partisan men . . . the most important thing is that its senior members are people who are friends of the armed forces and in touch with its thinking'.[42] A week later Medrano called on the military to take the law into its own hands and smash the left. Washington's speedy intervention to prevent a coup was made no easier by the fact that several days before it was believed to be taking place the debonair D'Aubuissón proclaimed on television that the US was 'the bastion of freedom which will, when the time is right, elevate us and the great Central American fatherland out of this Communist misery'.[43]

The coup was narrowly averted but the problem would not go away. In April, D'Aubuissón appeared in Washington accompanied by Alfredo Mena Burgos, a leading Salvadorean businessman. With the aid of right-wing organisations, such as the American Security Council and the American Legion, D'Aubuissón and Mena Burgos set about lobbying senators and congressmen against the junta. This caused discernable discomfort inside the State Department, but the administration was saved from the embarrassment of taking any action when D'Aubuissón, finding this type of activity unsuited to his buccaneering style, returned home. When he returned to San Salvador he accused Morales Erlich of having links with the armed left (true, in so far as his son was a member of the FPL) and Majano of being a member of the Mexican Communist Party. Availing himself of all the advantages of modern technology, D'Aubuissón circulated a video of himself making these changes around the country's barracks. With the assistance of 'Chivo' Iraheta and a group of hardliners based in Usulután, Gotera and Sonsonate, he tried to stage another coup at the end of April. This was prevented by a rapid tour of the main units by Majano and Duarte; a few days later D'Aubuissón was arrested red-handed with the plans for the uprising in his briefcase. The *majanistas* wanted him either shot or jailed for life, and the PDC threatened to leave the government if he was not punished. But by this stage the right was fully consolidated inside the regime and eight of the country's fourteen garrisons demanded that he be set free. While upper-class families gathered outside the residence of the US Ambassador calling for their hero's release and chanting 'White is Red', 'Viva Reagan' and 'Viva Jesse Helms', Garcia implemented for the first time in six months the constitutional clause that stated nobody could be held without being charged for more than 72 hours. D'Aubuissón was released, held a press conference where he repeated all his charges against Majano, and slid off to a boisterous and temporary exile in Guatemala.

By the time of D'Aubuissón's exile in May 1980, the military challenge of the ultra-right had largely been neutralised. But in January and February it posed a serious threat to the military–PDC alliance, which would almost certainly have fallen had Washington not taken precipitate action and forcefully intervened. Along with Afghanistan and Iran, El Salvador had become a priority for the State Department. William Bowdler, who had now replaced Vaky as Assistant Secretary of State, flew once more to San Salvador and announced that there was no crisis, only a 'transition'.[44] Bowdler's visit was intended to beef-up the new junta and consolidate the 'centre' so critical to US strategy. Frank Devine, who had replaced Lozano as ambassador, proved unequal to this task, being true to the tradition of staid and somnambulant Cold War warriors who had long occupied diplomatic posts in Central America. Bowdler's tactic was to talk of reforms to the PDC and figures such as Archbishop Romero, and stress public order in his meetings with ANEP and the military. On 23 January Bowdler and Devine met Romero to seek his support, which they correctly judged to be critical to their cause. Given that the Archbishop had stated after the fall of the first junta that 'the hour of legitimate violence is approaching', there were no surprises when little common ground was discovered.[45]

> Bowdler: We want to continue talking in favour of urgent changes, but for the future.
> Romero: It is the people that want change.
> Devine: The popular groups want power, not change.
> Romero: People want rapid change, and the faster it comes the less violence there will be.
> Devine: The problems in El Salvador are being manipulated by international communism.[46]

Moving on to address a meeting of ANEP, Bowdler reportedly stated that he knew about communist infiltration and that it was very active. Nevertheless, the existing regime was still the best way to deal with it, although 'we have to move the Christian Democrats to the centre and ensure that they act less demagogically than they are at the moment'.[47]

This approach was insufficient. Late in February D'Aubuissón went on television and 'fingered' Attorney General Mario Zamora of the PDC as belonging to the FPL. When, a week later, Zamora was shot dead by 'unidentified gunmen' and rumours of a coup spread rapidly, the US had to stiffen its approach. Devine's temporary replacement, James Cheek, warned that any coup would lead to an embargo on military aid. State Department spokesman Tom Reston reiterated that 'there should be no misunderstanding that our willingness to cooperate is predicated on a government committed to reforms'.[48] The next day Washington issued another firm warning against a coup and confirmed that all aid was conditional upon the implementation of an agrarian reform. Colonel Gutiérrez, who had gone to Houston for surgery on a severe stomach complaint, was raised from his hospital bed and flown home to impose discipline on his confrères.[49] The immediate crisis was overcome but it was clear that the right would have to be held constantly in check. To do this Washington appointed as its new ambassador Robert White, a career diplomat with some experience of handling recalcitrant Latin American rightists after dealing with Paraguay's 25-year long dictator Alfredo Stroessner as ambassador to Asunción. White was hailed as a liberal and a forceful advocate of Carter's human rights policy. The urgency of his designation was underlined by the fact that between January and mid-March 685 people had been killed, 193 of them in the fortnight before White's appointment. If the US was to act as a 'stabilising factor' amidst this mayhem it needed an accomplished propagandist and skilled manager on hand.

White lived up to these requirements, energetically complying with the State Department policy of enumerating with precision the violations of human rights under Romero whilst ignoring those under the junta and stressing its good intentions, the threat from the left and, particularly at this stage, that from the right. In a speech to the El Salvador–American Chamber of Commerce on 28 March the new ambassador asserted that businessmen funded death squads, causing an uproar. One landowner remarked, 'Next the USA will just send in the marines to kill anyone in a three-piece suit.' Another protested, 'now we are made to fear the Yankees as much as the communists. We thought the USA would defend free enterprise.'[50] This disillusionment was not entirely unfounded, but in practice Washington's campaign against the excesses of the oligarchy was a very small affair indeed when compared to its support and direction of the regime's agrarian reform, designed with the clear intention of complementing a counter-insurgency campaign that would result in greater death and destruction than the terror squads of the right could conceivably inflict.

'Reform' in Action

On 6 March 1980 the Basic Agrarian Reform Law, Decree 153, was announced. To ensure that the reform was undertaken in 'a climate of order', a state of siege was declared on the following day; it was not to be lifted. With the implementation of the reform the crisis of the Salvadorean state took on a new character and the country entered civil war. There is, then, a certain irony in the fact that Washington pushed the reform as the last chance to avert such a war. However, as Bowdler made clear, the greater worry was that the left might win it:

> We are convinced that if the Government doesn't move drastically to undercut the popular attractiveness of the Radical Marxist solutions to the grave economic and social problems in El Salvador through means of a significant program of reforms, the result will almost certainly be a bloody civil war with a subsequent victory of the radical left.[51]

John Bushnell of the State Department told Congress that the measure to expropriate all properties over 500 hectares was inoperable without a military presence, and that the US was therefore treating requests for military assistance as an integral part of the reform.

> The principal obstacle to the reform . . . is that the extremists from both the left and the right are intent on dividing the Government and preventing the consolidation of a powerful moderate coalition which it will attract to its program if it is allowed to prosper . . . I want to emphasize that contrary to a common misconception, our proposals for security assistance are not disconnected nor contrary to our support for reform in El Salvador. The redistribution of land would not be possible if it wasn't for the protection and security provided by the Salvadorean army to the new property holders . . .[52]

Since October US support for such 'protection and security' given by the armed forces had amounted to $500,000 worth of military supplies and training facilities together with the posting of a six-man Mobile Training Team (MTT). The employment of a further 36 advisers was under urgent consideration, but the most important move was the US administration's decision to issue $5.7 million in military credits to the Salvadorean government. This was passed on 1 April. In six months US military aid to El Salvador had surpassed the sums disbursed under the Military Assistance Program between 1950 and 1969.[53] Washington had set itself on a course that meant either complete withdrawal or massive escalation; there were no half-measures.

The majority of the PDC was no less enthusiastic about the reform than its US patrons. According to Duarte,

For twenty years we have been fighting for that day when an agrarian reform would be carried out that would take power from the oligarchy and give it to the people. Now we have accomplished the beginning of this democratic and anti-oligarchic revolution.[54]

In the event, one of the few concrete aspects of the measure in which the PDC was to have any say was its presentation in the media which, as outlined in confidential instructions to the radio stations, was very much tailored to the party's self-image:

The Reform should be presented in a simple, serious, tranquil and professional tone in order to diminish completely any note of fear. The format should avoid at all cost any martial music and should instead employ traditional Mexican songs, tropical boleros and classical music . . . Most importantly, announcers should avoid any form of paternalism, such as the terms 'Papa government' or 'Papa ministry of agriculture'.[55]

The slogan was 'The Reform is for Everyone', but the press was prohibited from any 'prior investigation', detailed testing of public opinion, 'creative investigation' or 'detailed plan of action or argument for it'.[56] The reason for this was not simply due to the high profile of the military but also to the fact that the programme had been rushed through at extraordinary speed. On 3 March there was no public word on it; on 4 March the dormant Institute for Agrarian Transformation (ISTA) was suddenly revived, and two days later the law was passed.

The immediate impact of dispossessing the owners of estates larger than 500 hectares and turning them into collectives to be run by the workers did not, as might have been expected, take the form of a substantial redistribution of land, jubilation on the part of the *campesinos*, and a backlash from the owners. The immediate result was a transfer of property rights on paper, a massive movement of troops across the countryside, and considerable apprehension on the part of the peasants, who in the majority of cases refrained from taking possession of their new property out of fear. In this they were justified. One ISTA technician assigned to oversee the reform related that,

the troops came and told the workers the land was theirs now. They could elect their own leaders and run the co-ops. The peasants couldn't believe their ears, but held elections that very night. The next morning the troops came back and I watched as they shot every one of the elected leaders.[57]

This was not an isolated case. Jorge Alberto Villacorta, who resigned as deputy Minister of Agriculture on 26 March in protest at the violence, provided further evidence in his departing note to the junta:

> During the first days of the reform — to cite one case — five directors and two presidents of the new *campesino* organisations were assassinated and I am informed that this repressive practice continues to increase. Recently, on one of the haciendas of the agrarian reform, uniformed members of the security forces accompanied by someone with a mask over his face, brought the workers together; the masked man was giving orders to the person in charge of the troops and these *campesinos* were gunned down in front of their co-workers . . . [58]

This use of the reform to liquidate peasant militants registered immediately in the death tolls kept by the Church: 234 people died in February, 487 in March. The figure was to go on rising, to 1,000 in June. Many more fled their homes, to become part of the rapidly accumulating refugee population for which the regime made no provisions. On the other hand, the unambiguously violent nature of the reform led 700 ISTA agronomists to declare a strike, but their absence appeared to make little difference, demonstrating the minimal degree to which the measure depended upon specialised advice and direction.

The impact of the reform in the towns and national political life was no less acute. It had been preceded by Hector Dada's resignation from the junta on the grounds that no attempt had been made either to halt repression or to enter into negotiations with the mass organisations. Dada was replaced with Duarte, taking his first official position since returning to the country and consolidating the position of the right of the PDC inside the regime. There were to be a number of further resignations by more minor officials over the next weeks, by which time the civilian membership of the government remained stable. On 10 March the PDC confronted within its own ranks the political crisis faced by the rest of the bourgeois opposition. One sector, headed by Dada and Rubén Zamora, charged the leadership with complicity in dictatorship, acquiescence in repression, and destroying the party's principles and popular base. The PDC could no longer organise a meeting of over 1,000 compared with the 100,000 it had massed in days gone by.[59] The dissidents resigned and took a quarter of the party's remaining activists with them.

The CRM's response to the junta's offensive was to call a 24-hour general strike on 17 March as a 'rehearsal for the people'. This, the first test of its ability to provide a united leadership for the working class, closed down the capital and achieved 80 per cent support across the country. The *Coordinadora* proved that it possessed the allegiance of the workers, but it was still unable to protect them adequately; 54 people were killed in San Salvador on the day of the stoppage. The scale of military operations in the city was as great as if there had been an insurrection. Dr Avalos, the junta's medical 'independent', warned that 'activists must be willing to vanquish or die, just as in any other type of war'.[60]

The only institution that remained between the two major camps was the Church. Yet, by mid-March this position was no longer tenable, and Romero, who had at times been strongly critical of the activities of the groups of the left, took a firm stand against the regime. On 17 February the Archbishop had written a much-publicised and forceful letter to Carter in which he denounced the new military package and urged authentic non-intervention. There was abundant evidence that the equipment already sent was being used to repress the people and violate human rights by a government that had not 'demonstrated any ability to solve structurally or in political practice our serious national problems'.[61] Vance's pious reply indicated no disposition to alter the position. Five days later Romero gave a sermon in which he asserted that the regime 'lacks any popular backing, and can count only on the support of a few foreign powers'; the PDC presence in the government was only to cover up its repressive character.[62] On 24 March Romero used his sermon at Sunday mass, which was always packed as well as being broadcast nationally by the diocesian radio station, to break from general comments about the state of the nation and the character of the government. In stating that, 'no soldier is obliged to obey an order to kill if it runs contrary to his conscience', he issued what was both an unremarkable restatement of basic doctrine and an explosive political challenge. The Archbishop had sanctioned mutiny. A day later he was assassinated by a single shot in the heart when celebrating mass.

More than any other single act this killing brought El Salvador to the attention of the world. Although the regime itself faced little alternative other than removing its most visible and popularly respected opponent, it was scarcely inept enough to rid itself of the accursed priest in such a manner. It was generally accepted that a death squad had done the deed, either under the direction or with the complicity of a sector of the military. The Church itself claimed that it was an ultra-right manoeuvre to provoke a precipitate popular uprising and enable the destruction of the left. Duarte opined that the crime 'could have been committed by any one of the two extremes . . . it's in the interest of both to have a state of violence'.[63] To tar the left in this manner was an idiocy only too plainly required by the fact that if it was otherwise, the party of Christian Democracy was linked through its allies in the junta to the authors of the assassination of the leader of its national Church. A year later Robert White, now in disgrace, revealed that the contents of D'Aubuissón's plans for a coup in April contained evidence that linked him with the killing, which was probably undertaken by a hired Cuban 'hit-man' capable of killing a man with a single shot of a .22 calibre weapon; Salvadorean terrorists preferred to rake their victims with machine-gun fire if they were not already tied up.[64] The judge appointed by the junta to investigate the case left the country in a few days when he began to receive death threats, and little more was done to identify the killers. Washington's reaction was to offer the assistance of the FBI, but it saw no reason to let the event interfere with its support for the regime: the day after the killing William Bowdler, nominally a diplomat, announced that the US was giving $55 million in economic and military aid to the junta.

The international image of the regime lost what few remaining vestiges of credibility it had when, four days after the assassination, troops attacked Romero's funeral procession and killed 40 of the 80,000 mourners gathered in front of the visiting dignatories, who were themselves forced off the plaza into the cathedral, where the body was hurriedly interred. This further massacre seemed positively designed to attract international opprobium, but its real cause was the eight-day general strike declared by the CRM two days before in homage to Romero. As with the strike a fortnight before, this stoppage received widespread backing, especially in the capital which was paralysed for a week. Guerrilla activity was more pronounced, but the *Coordinadora* declared that it would not embark on a hasty insurrection; the moment had not yet come.

Although it proved extremely difficult to mask the dictatorial nature of the regime, the US continued to argue that this was the result of threats from extremists and lack of professionalism within the military; however violently it might be implemented, the agrarian reform testified to the government's commitment to crippling the oligarchy. The reality was somewhat different.

As we have seen, the military character of the measure indicated that the left was a principal target, and this fact was identified as central by one of the reform's leading advisers, Roy Prosterman, a Washington university professor who had previously been involved in the 'Land to the Tiller' programme in Vietnam in the 1960s and now headed the AIFLD team ensconced on the top floor of the San Salvador Sheraton. Prosterman considered that 'if the reforms are successfully carried out here [El Salvador], the armed leftist onslaught will be effectively eliminated by the end of 1980'.[65] Such 'elimination' cannot be taken as meaning only physical destruction by the military: it was also to be brought about by removing the left's support amongst the *campesinado*, the radicalism of which would fall off as it received land. As one US official put it, 'there is no one more conservative than a small farmer. We're going to be breeding capitalists like rabbits.'[66] For the US this was the aspect that deserved most attention. The AFL–CIO union confederation hailed the programme as 'the most complete agrarian reform in the history of Latin America', while the *New York Times* asserted that it would expropriate '60 per cent of the country's best farm land'.[67] These expectations were far too grand.

The reform devised by the AIFLD fell into three phrases. The first, Decree 153, was the expropriation of all holdings over 500 hectares; this was implemented on 6 March. The second would affect all units between 150 and 500 hectares. Since 60 per cent of all coffee production took place on farms of this size, it was Phase Two that was at the heart of the reform and posed the real threat to the power of the oligarchy. Compensation for lost land would take the form of 25 per cent in cash and 75 per cent in government bonds, which could only be reinvested in industry. This strategy of diverting capital into the manufacturing sector was a key aspect of the scheme and gave it its 'modernising' credentials; but it was not overly attractive to many landlords because compensation was based on tax evaluations, which were inevitably much lower than the market price of the expropriated land. The third phase, announced on 28 April, was Decree 207 or the 'Land to the Tiller' programme. This gave the right of all tenants to ownership of their plots once they had met the market price through aggregate payments of rent. Whereas the first two phases would expropriate the property of the landed bourgeoisie and be run by co-operatives, this one was designed to stall the mobilisation of tenants on subsistence plots with the guarantee of freehold.[68] The 65 per cent of the rural population who were landless labourers, rather than *colonos*, sharecroppers or permanent employees, received nothing from the reform.

On the first day Phase One was put into effect with the seizure of 30 estates. This phase officially covered 238 estates. Of these, 60 per cent of the land is in fallow or pasture for cattle; land affected by Phase One accounted for only 9 per cent of coffee production.[69] Moreover, under what was known as the 'right of reserve', owners had the right to claim back up to 150 hectares plus 20 per cent more if they made improvements on the land. If this right was taken up in full, Phase One encompassed only 10 per cent of the country's cultivable land. In practice it came nowhere near this figure since after two months the reform was brought to an abrupt halt. On 14 May Gutiérrez ordered an immediate end to all expropriations under Phase One and postponed Phase Two indefinitely. Over 50 per cent of the land potentially covered by the measure was now cut out and – most importantly – this land covered the vast majority of El Salvador's coffee plantations, the power-base of the oligarchy. Resistance had been very strong, taking the form of a substantial flight of capital, which was clearly well under way in the industrial sector and by April had led to the loss of 11,000 jobs, export of up to 40 per cent of the country's farm machinery to Guatemala, and the slaughter of 30 per cent of its cattle.[70] Furthermore, pressure from the landlords had led the military to set up a 'Committee for Devolution', which, although it was outside the law, oversaw the return of certain estates to their original owners. It is estimated that 200 estates were expropriated and 45 returned through 'sweetheart deals' between senior army officers and owners.[71] According to Leonel Gómez, assistant director of ISTA until his exile early in 1981, this process was the site of extensive corruption with some officers amassing substantial sums.[72] On the new co-operatives it was the permanent employees – the foremen and mechanics – not the *colonos* who took control. USAID officials visiting the new co-operatives found the majority run by these employees and ISTA technicians. The army or National Guard was never far away, either physically or in the decision-making process.

The blocking of Phase One and indefinite postponement of Phase Two left Decree 207, the ideological centre-piece of the reform. However, the tenets of possessive individualism were very badly applied indeed. In the first place, the 'Land to the Tiller' programme was launched out of the blue, taking even ISTA by surprise and preventing essential preparation. Its introduction in late April was, in all probability, to compensate for the ditching of the rest of the reform, but Prosterman's effort to emulate his Vietnamese schema foundered on a profound ignorance of Salvadorean agricultural methods. In seeking to give freehold to tenants, Phase Three was directed almost exclusively at plots under two hectares in size since these comprise 80 per cent of rented lands. These tiny plots provide 50 per cent of all the country's subsistence foodstuffs and are concentrated in the northern departments of Chalatenango, Morazán, Cabañas and Cuscatlán, the main centres of guerrilla activity. However, individually the plots cannot provide subsistence for a family; because of poor soil quality they must be rotated and allowed to lie fallow to avoid erosion. Few are cultivated for more than two years in succession and families work several simultaneously. Thus, the programme would have the effect of freezing a necessarily mobile market in rented land and lock peasants onto single units for 30 years when the fertility of the land itself would be exhausted in a fraction of this time. It further failed to take into account the fact that many owners are themselves *minifundistas* and tenants, small peasants who rent land amongst family and friends in a process that approximates more to reciprocity than exploitation.[73] Not surprisingly, a year after the opening of Phase Three only 1,000 provisional titles had been handed out when 150,000 had been envisaged. The agrarian reform had achieved the peculiar distinction of drawing resistance from *campesinos* as well as landlords without making significant alterations in the structure of power in the Salvadoran *campo*; claims that it constituted the junta's reformist *bona fide* were politically necessary but utterly fraudulent.

The counter-insurgency campaign launched in the countryside and the full backing for the strikes called by the CRM in March had the effect of impressing upon the centrist parties displaced from the first junta that there was no longer room for equivocation or space for *rapprochement*. On 4 April, the MNR combined with the Popular Social Christian Movement (MPSC) formed by Dada and Zamora after their split with the PDC, and ten unaffiliated union federations and professional associations to form the *Frente Democrático Salvadoreño* (FDS) to pursue the policies of the *Foro* outside the government. The FDS lacked any military capacity, and under conditions which were rapidly approaching those of a full civil war its existence as a viable independent force could only be transitory if it was not to fuse with the CRM, the programme of which was as accessible to a 'democratic' reading as it was to a 'revolutionary' interpretation. In fact, the establishment of the FDS was preparatory to precisely such a move; on

18 April a rally that attracted 100,000 people to San Salvador marked the alliance of the CRM and the FDS to form *Frente Democrático Revolucionario* (FDR).

The FDR was founded upon agreement on the CRM's programme, which had envisaged just such a bloc of 'progressive forces'. The extent to which the regime had destroyed the political centre and driven it to ally with the 'subversive left' was evident in the fact that *Frente* was headed by Enrique Alvarez Córdoba, a member of the 'fourteen families' and an ex-Minister of Agriculture for Molina and the October junta. The effect on the left had, however, been no less great; it was now fighting alongside men such as Dada and Zamora whom two months earlier Salvador Cayetano had described as being 'in close alliance with the US State Department'.[74] In January FAPU had denounced Mayorga and Ungo as 'petty bourgeois reformists fully entwined in the web of the oligarchy'.[75] These figures were now to play a central role in the FDR and lead its international campaign; outside Central America they were its 'public face'. As Zamora was to tell *Newsweek*, they wanted a 'democratic society' and a mixed economy, in which foreign investment would play a part. Indeed, somewhat later Zamora went so far as to opine that, 'a military victory [of the rebels] will find the US completely hostile . . . under these conditions, what are the chances of pluralism?'[76] There was considerable political space between this position and that of the BPR. It was even open to doubt whether they shared the aim of defeating the junta; the parties of the FDS seemed more intent upon forcing it to make major concessions after a negotiated solution, but this could be neither declared nor achieved without allying with the mass organisations and relying upon their armed might, which was led by the left. Political differences were subordinated to military considerations, which henceforth were to dominate the course of the Salvadorean Revolution.

10
CIVIL WAR

The United States could never permit another Nicaragua, even if preventing it meant employing the most reprehensible measures.

Zbigniew Brzezinski, June 1980

We call on the entire people to rise up as one single person, using all possible means of combat, on all fronts of the war and throughout the length and breadth of the national territory. We call upon the entire people to fight valiantly under the orders of their immediate commanders until the definitive overthrow of the oppressive, genocidal regime of the privileged oligarchy and imperialism.

FMLN, General Order No. 1, 10 January 1981

It isn't just El Salvador. What we are doing is going to the aid of a Government that asked for help against the guerrillas and terrorists . . . who aren't just aiming at El Salvador but who are aiming at the whole of Central and South America. I'm sure, eventually, North America.

Ronald Reagan, 6 March 1981

If El Salvador may legitimately be said to have entered a state of civil war in April 1980, there is no precise point at which we can say this war 'broke out'. It was not a war of large formations but a guerrilla war and therefore ill defined in terms of lines of control, with a highly variable intensity of conflict. Over two years (1980–January 1982) over 30,000 lives were lost in an extended war of attrition that only occasionally came to determinate critical encounters such as the guerrilla 'general offensive' of January 1981, which may be seen as El Salvador's Tet. The war, as a result, differed from that in Nicaragua, where the FSLN concentrated primarily on attacking and holding key centres, from which they would withdraw if necessary but always with the aim of returning to establish liberated territory. This difference was largely because the Nicaraguan civil war was relatively short; by the late spring of 1979 the FSLN was in a position to embark upon an insurrectionary strategy, employing its troops in formal encounters after only a year of mobile operations at a national level. Moreover, in Nicaragua the key instances of conflict had taken the form of mass urban insurrections, first in the provincial centres and then in Managua; in El Salvador this did not occur.

The principal reason for the extended nature of the war was the capacity of the junta to hold its piecemeal military apparatus together to the extent that it was able to ward off guerrilla offensives and impose a repression that held the population in a state of terror, preventing the *levée en masse* that characterised the later stages of the Nicaraguan revolution. It could only have achieved this or, indeed, survived for more than a few weeks with the resolute support of the US, which Somoza was, in the last instance, denied. First Carter and then Reagan, who followed the same line but with a much more concerted bellicosity, poured in money, equipment and men to hold the line. At no stage has this been a discrete operation; it is a function of the return to the Cold War and increasingly acute confrontation with the Soviet Union. El Salvador has joined Poland and Afghanistan as a region of absolute importance in the 'struggle against Soviet expansionism'. This internationalisation of the domestic conflict has given it a new character and made its implications for the rest of Central and Latin America all the more acute. The defence of Cuba, the protection and deepening of the gains made in Nicaragua, and the expansion of the newly unified guerrilla movement in Guatemala have all become part of a single movement that depends vitally upon a popular victory in El Salvador. By early 1981 the Salvadorean conflict had become so critical to political control of the region that Washington resolved to take a position which was not simply 'interventionist' but raised the possibility of either categorical defeat or sending in troops, neither of which was an acceptable option with respect to domestic public opinion or the balance of forces on a world scale.

Preparing for Insurrection

The regional implications of the struggle were not lost on the Salvadorean military which, like its colleagues in CONDECA, had identified one of Somoza's major weaknesses in the half-hearted neutrality of Honduras and frank animosity of Costa Rica, states that bordered on Nicaragua. This isolation limited 'hot pursuit' operations by the National Guard and denied support from the armies of neighbouring countries as well as giving the FSLN an extremely important rearguard. While the Salvadorean high command could be certain of the support of the Guatemalan military, it faced greater problems with Honduras which, after the 1969 war, had no formal relations with El Salvador. Moreover, it did not possess total control over their common border, which was patrolled in part by OAS peace-keeping troops under the terms of the truce. The neutrality of this force overseeing the *bolsones* of disputed territory on the frontier threatened to enhance the mobility of the guerrillas, especially the FPL, which was particularly strong in Chalatenango, and the ERP, concentrated in Morazán, both bordering on Honduras.

This problem was confronted very quickly. On 9 May 1980, high-ranking Salvadorean officers met their Honduran and Guatemalan counterparts at Nueva Ocotepeque in Honduras, and agreed to a plan known as 'Iron Pincers' which provided for a joint flanking operation against the guerrillas.[1] It was made plain that this was no mere paper agreement when, within a matter of days, senior members of the Salvadorean airforce staff were killed in the crash of a Guatemalan plane on a domestic flight, and the guerrillas announced that the bodies of some of the troops they had killed were clothed in Salvadorean uniforms but lacked any form of identification and had foreign coins in their pockets.[2] These troops were believed to be ex-members of Somoza's National Guard being trained in Honduras by Israeli advisers.

These were telling occurrences, but they paled into insignificance when compared with the joint operation between Salvadorean and Honduran troops on the Sumpul river in northern Chalatenango on 14 and 15 May. A 'mixed corps' of National Guardsmen, regular army troops and members of ORDEN advanced on the villages of San Jacinto and Las Aradas in a 'mopping-up operation' which consisted of nothing less than the razing of all buildings, firing of crops and execution of inhabitants in the zone. Some 1,500 villagers were forced to flee across the Sumpul, which was in full flow, into Honduran territory, but once there they were forced back by Honduran troops into the arms of the waiting Salvadorean military. Many were drowned in the two crossings, scores more were lined up and shot down on the Salvadorean bank. For several days afterwards Honduran fishermen found their nets clogged with the corpses of children. The estimates of Honduran missionaries and the Salvadorean Human Rights Commission were that at least 600 people had died, most of them women, children and old men since the young men had already left the area upon hearing of the operation. Within El Salvador it quickly became clear that *operaciones de limpieza* should be considered as tantamount to creating free-fire zones in which everybody was considered a potential *subversivo* and likely to be killed. Outside the country the 'Sumpul massacre' was reported by the left but the 'respectable' press, ever willing to treat such reports as 'allegations' or the inherent hyperbole of radicals, was over eight months in picking up the 'story'. When it finally did, the accounts of the survivors made it impossible to deny that the counter-insurgency campaign in the Salvadorean countryside was nothing less than a regime of terror and barbarism.[3] Henceforth almost every newspaper report from the country would contain reference to new slaughters on the part of the military – usually the National Guard or the Treasury Police – and Washington was obliged less to challenge the veracity of reports than to express its desire that 'methods' were improved.

The adoption of the strategy of rural 'sweeps', which led to the forced removal of thousands of peasants and the flight of many more over the ensuing months, coincided with the removal of Majano from the post of joint-commander of the armed forces and his replacement by Gutiérrez alone, an act of purely political motive because, as an engineer, Gutiérrez had little military standing amongst his peers. The demotion occurred as a result of the 'D'Aubuissón affair', in which the *majanistas* had been thoroughly outmanoeuvred; Majano still remained in the junta but had lost much authority within the military. The hardliners now held the upper hand and the military as a whole was showing a greater disposition for the 'total solution' urged upon it by the likes of Medrano. The need for such an offensive was underscored by the fact that in May the guerrillas had agreed to unite in a single command, the *Dirección Revolucionaria Unificada* (DRU). This did not bring about an immediate agreement in tactics; in June RN was to call for an insurrectionary line while the FPL still declared that there would be no full-scale mobilisation until victory was assured.[4] None the less, the forces of the left were demonstrating an ability seriously to damage the military: in May they claimed to have inflicted 122 casualties on the army, and 41 attacks on convoys were admitted by the high command.[5] Operations continued at this level throughout the summer months with the armed forces experiencing difficulty in maintaining control over outlying regions, especially in the east. The opposition also made its first substantial diplomatic advance when, in June, the FDR received the support of the Second International, which declared at a meeting in Oslo that the US was mistaken in its policy towards El Salvador since 'support for the junta is not a viable option'.[6] This move resulted directly from the establishment of the FDR as a broad front in which social democracy could identify the interests of its local co-religionists in the MNR.

The FDR concentrated upon urban organisation over the summer of 1980. On 24 June a 48-hour general strike was called to demand the ending of the state of siege, repression and US intervention as well as the right to strike and access for the Red Cross to verify violations of human rights. In terms of its industrial effect the strike was successful: 85 per cent of the capital's economic activity was brought to a halt with 150,000 workers, 80,000 of them state employees, coming out.[7] The response was so emphatic that Ambassador White had cause to tell the press that 'right now there is a real question of who rules this country'.[8] The strike was directed by the CRM rather than by the DRU; it was not intended as an insurrectionary move and the guerrillas desisted from any overt action. According to Alberto Ramos, a leading member of FAPU, this was because the left wanted to show that it was not responsible for the violence.[9] Probably more important than this, however, was the intention of avoiding conflict under adverse conditions, the CRM concentrating upon building discipline amongst the local militias and food distribution committees it was setting up in the towns. The fact that it still lacked the capacity to resist the military in the cities and particularly San Salvador was made clear when on the day after the strike the airforce launched an attack on the university and the working-class neighbourhood of La Fosa which bordered onto it. The number of deaths was high.

On 13 August the FDR moved again, calling another general strike, this time for three days and in a manner that undoubtedly had insurrectionary overtones. This action yielded less positive results than that of June. In the capital absenteeism was high but many shops and factories were kept open, and the police commandeered many buses, forcing them to cover their normal routes at gunpoint. The armed forces were well prepared and deployed in force: although they did not attempt to enter *barrios* such as Soyapango and Mejicanos, where the militias had erected barricades and set up 'no go' areas, their control of the city centre was unchallenged. Guerrilla actions in the city were disparate and badly co-ordinated: more than 50 people died in clashes with troops, but no major gains were made. There were interruptions in the supply of water and electricity, and the strike received full support in the provincial towns, but within a day it was obvious that the strike was not going to precipitate an insurrectionary situation. By the second day the FDR was making a very cautious appraisal of events while Associated Press sent out despatches that described the strike as a complete failure, an opinion not surprisingly shared by the junta.[10] The failure of the strike lay not in the lack of popular support, although this was visibly less than in June, but in the tactics of the left, and the conclusions drawn by the government were therefore misconceived. Although the August strike was organised around the same demands as that of June, the issue at stake was state power, and the FDR clearly hoped for an insurrectionary outcome or, at least, one that resulted in a grave crisis for the regime and posed the question of a major political and military offensive. But in limiting such a mobilisation to a three-day period it simultaneously negated this aim and dampened radicalism. In addition, the FDR had overestimated the capacity of the workers to respond to two general strikes within six weeks as well as gravely underestimating the preparedness of the armed forces. This was not purely the result of misreading the conjuncture; the FDR had wanted to call a second strike in mid-July but had been stopped by the objections of FAPU, which despite adhering keenly to an insurrectionary line had a more sanguine assessment of the conditions under which it could be realised. Indeed, FAPU had so strongly opposed the timing of the strike that it only supported it on the last day, but this alone cannot be held responsible for the failure of the mobilisation to develop into a full popular offensive.[11] One interpretation of the FDR strategy over the summer is that the reformists in the leadership were keen to avoid extended conflict and bring matters to a head rapidly as possible. This would avoid the complete destruction of the military and facilitate negotiations in which they could determine the terms before the guerrillas had amassed the strength to impose a radical solution. However, it was apparent that no general strike could succeed without a military offensive, which the DRU did not yet have the capacity to launch.

It was not the strategy of mobilising the urban working class but the working class itself which was exhausted. It had seen little return for five days of general strikes; its self-defence organisation had improved but at a high cost, and it had cause to doubt the tactics of its leaders. The outcome of the strike movement had not been a major defeat but an important setback with the urban masses pushed into partial retreat by the strength of the regime's repression. The response of the FDR was to pass the initiative to the DRU and the predominantly rural guerrilla campaign implicit in the *guerra prolongada* strategy; the focus of the struggle swung decisively towards the countryside.[12] This move was taken in an exaggerated manner and on the basis of an empirical reading of events that was consonant with the mistakes in organising urban mobilisation. Although they were not immediately apparent, the counter-productive consequences of this were later recognised and admitted by the left.

The response of the junta was predictable. In the face of the August strike it had for the first time received the full backing of ANEP, and this bolstered the success of holding the left at bay. Morales Erlich offered talks to the MNR and the PDC dissidents if they broke from their alliance with the 'semi-delinquent extreme left'. The army, while it admitted to problems in the north and east, reiterated that the threat had been contained without major difficulty and would soon be rolled back.[13] This was soon shown to be unduly optimistic, but throughout August and September 1980 the junta displayed a certain revival of fortune as a result of the dislocation of the left; this was its most secure period.

This shift in the balance of forces seemed to be confirmed in late August when the FAPU-affiliated power workers' union, STECEL, launched a strike on its own. Electricity was cut for 20 hours and the union withdrew from the stoppage intact, but it was manifestly an isolated act bred of appreciable disunity in the labour movement; STECEL had not been brought out permanently during the general strikes. The fact that the guerrillas of RN had not been deployed to protect their comrades suggested further fissures. These became public on 12 September with the announcement that RN had left the DRU a fortnight earlier and that FAPU had lost its executive position inside the CRM although it still remained a member. The question of the timing of the strikes had played a major part in this dissension but even more important was the divide between the prolonged war and insurrectionary strategies which the formation of the DRU had only papered over. Having failed to implement its line on the handling of the strikes, RN now faced the prospect of the *guerra prolongada* strategy achieving dominance as a result. There was also deep disagreement over RN's insistence upon the importance of allying with the *majanistas* and throwing the popular forces behind any coup that they might stage. The rest of the DRU held that Majano and his group should join them, and that the popular movement should not subordinate itself to sectors of the military simply in order to achieve a quick result.[14] The whole affair was further blackened by the death of the leader of RN, Ernesto Jovel, in circumstances that at first led observers to evoke the killing of Roque Dalton, but RN later announced that Jovel had died in an aircrash off Panama and suspicions of foul play were dismissed.

In one respect this issue was resolved quite speedily, for in September Majano's position in the government came under challenge once again. At the beginning of the month Gutiérrez and Garcia exploited the former's command of the armed forces to issue 'Battle Orders' – the yearly postings and promotions – which deprived the *majanistas* of control of important garrisons with many of them being posted abroad. If these appointments were accepted, complete control of the military apparatus would fall into the hands of the hardliners. The dissidents replied by demanding the removal of Garcia and Carranza and negotiations with the FDR. Majano set up his own general staff in the Zapote barracks and a coup looked highly likely. Within the junta Morales Erlich and Avalos backed Majano but Duarte sided with the Garcia camp and toured the barracks with Gutiérrez urging 'unity'. The US Embassy, now skilled at arbitrating between these factions, found against Majano, whom it considered incompetent and potentially dangerous. By 9 September it was clear that the orders would go through and that Majano had lost all his authority although Garcia still held back from removing him from the junta in an astute move that dissuaded the dissidents from rebelling.[15]

With the possibility of a split in the military greatly diminished and no sign of insubordination, RN was forced to reconsider its position. On 21 October its request to re-enter the united guerrilla command was accepted in generous terms, and it took its place in the new organisation that now replaced the DRU, the *Frente Farabundo Marti para la Liberacion Nacional* (FMLN). The formation of the FMLN consolidated the guerrilla movement in a manner that the DRU had failed to achieve. The lessons of June and August were not wholly learnt and RN was to continue to pressure for an insurrectionist line, but this was held firmly in check and co-ordination of operations substantially improved over the following months under the general command of Salvador Cayetano (FPL), Shafik Handal (PCS), Joaquin Villalobos (ERP),

Fermán Cienfuegos (RN) and Roberto Roca (PRTC). The FDR was now manifestly beholden to the guerrillas for its political authority.

This revived unity and efficiency of the opposition's organisation had hardly begun to manifest itself before it was dealt a severe blow. At the end of November, an evening meeting of the national leadership of the FDR in a San Salvador school was surrounded by a large number of armed men in civilian clothes. The meeting was not properly protected and there was no fight. The next day, 28 November, six mutilated bodies were found at Ilopango, just outside the city. They belonged to Enrique Alvarez, dissident landowner and president of the FDR; Juan Chacón, the young secretary general of the BPR; Manuel Franco of the UDN; Humberto Mendoza (MLP); Enrique Barrera (MNR); and Doroteo Hernández (FAPU). Leoncio Pichinte of the *Ligas* saved his life by arriving late for the meeting and, seeing the attack, fleeing. The murders were claimed by the *Comando Maximiliano Hernández Martínez*, which two weeks earlier had announced its intention to eliminate 'communist thieves and prostitutes'.[16] The FDR had lost some of its most experienced and popular leaders; they were replaceable, but the loss of men like Chacón was very grave since they had gained enormous personal respect for their leadership of the struggles of the previous years. The assassinated leaders were quickly replaced, with Ungo later taking Alvarez' place as president, but a mass funeral march had to be cancelled for fears of another massacre; looseness over matters of security was recognised to have reflected badly on the FDR and tightened up.

The US had little to say about this, but it was scarcely going to mourn the FDR leaders when White had some months previously falsely announced Chacón's death upon hearing that he had been captured. However, within a week the same violence that had been inflicted on the FDR struck much more mindlessly when, on 4 December, three US nuns of the Maryknoll order and a woman lay worker were found shot and raped on the road from Ilopango to the capital. The immediate evidence indicated that the women had been killed at a roadblock by National Guardsmen; several months later it transpired that their murder had been planned by the security forces in the region, and early in 1982 several members of the Guard were finally sacrificed to the requirement of the US that culprits be presented.[17] The news of the murders drew an immediate outcry that was far too strong to be brushed off; the women were known to have been progressive in outlook, and it was impossible to attribute their deaths to the left.

Moreover, the line that actions of this type were undertaken by a few isolated criminals was clearly an insufficient response when the victims were US citizens and the personnel of death squads generally accepted to be members of the official state paramilitary forces. A day later all US aid was suspended and the junta's position once more became highly precarious.[18]

By this time, of course, Ronald Reagan had won the US presidency, cause for much celebration on the part of the Salvadorean ultras. Nevertheless, the Reagan campaign had the effect of consolidating lingering doubts within parts of the Washington establishment as to the efficacy of the policy towards El Salvador. While the strike movement had failed to bring down the regime, it had demonstrated the enormous popular support enjoyed by the FDR, and the guerrillas were continuing their attacks with little difficulty. Internationally the junta had an extremely poor reputation, and the notion that it was 'centrist' could not be sold to any foreign ministry that was not already disposed to give it support. It was not only the European social democrats who refused to accept the Carter line. Mexico and the majority of the Andean Pact countries were also unsympathetic towards it, while Costa Rica and Panama were less than enthusiastic in their neutrality. The regime could only rely on Guatemala, Colombia and the Christian Democrat government of Herrera Campins in Venezuela. These factors could not have failed to have worried any half-serious Washington bureaucrat; the US was neither winning the war nor supplying a presentable rationale for its activity in El Salvador. The only viable option appeared to be a measured withdrawal or a massive escalation.

One response to these problems was contained in a document that appeared in Washington early in November, before Reagan's election, which brought him to office in January 1980. This paper was supposedly written in consultation with members of all the US government departments concerned with operations in El Salvador and went under the title 'Dissent Paper on El Salvador and Central America'.[19] Some months later, when Reagan was in power, doubt was thrown on the authenticity of this document,[20] but its contents were not so remarkable that they could not be made to square with the viewpoint of disenchanted State Department managers of the human rights school.[21] The 'Dissent Paper' argued simply that in order to find a 'middle way' it was now necessary to appreciate the power of the right in the regime and the mass support for the FDR. The US should recognise and negotiate with the FDR, halt military aid to the junta, condemn Guatemalan and Honduran interference, reduce the creeping involvement of the Southern Cone countries, and maintain a much lower profile if it was to avoid being locked into an irretrievable position of support for dictatorship and suffer the extreme consequences if this collapsed, which did not seem too improbable. This Zimbabwe-style solution was virtually indistinguishable from the alternative strategy urged by social democracy but the chances of its implementation by a US administration were dramatically reduced by Reagan's election.

There had been little or no ambivalence as to the Republican party's policy on El Salvador for some time. Over the summer of 1980 the Cold War warriors of the 'new right' and the 'moral majority' as well as more pragmatic but no less ambitious displaced 'experts' in international relations of the Nixon era emerged from their obscure covens to give vent to their views. One of these aspirants to high office, Roger Fontaine, told the *Miami Herald* in August that a Reagan administration would 'act a good deal more aggressively in preserving what's left of, and preserving what opportunities are left for, democracy . . .' When asked if the US might stage a military intervention in Latin America, he replied, 'the use of military force is an option any nation, in terms of its vital national interests, has to maintain as a possibility'.[22] For the next two years the Reagan administration was not to waiver from this position. Fontaine later produced a document in collaboration with Cleto Di Giovanni, a former CIA agent close to the Reagan transition team, which showed marked differences with the Carter government's assessment of the junta and approximated more to Senator Jesse Helms' view that it was 'socialist'. Fontaine and Di Giovanni argued that,

> A pro-US military government in El Salvador, which had been economically viable, has been replaced with a Center–Left Government which has brought the country to economic ruin by desperate and sweeping reforms.[23]

In December Di Giovanni visited San Salvador and stated that the public denials of support by the Reagan team for a right-wing coup should be disregarded as necessary politicking.[24] This apparent move to ditch the entire 'centrist' strategy and fall back on an unadventurous dictatorship of the Romero school was not, in fact, to be implemented in full, but it signalled the direction the new administration would take.

This, combined with the drawing up of a 'hit list' of reformers in government service who would be purged, drew a decidedly undiplomatic response from Carter's man in San Salvador, Robert White, who declared to the press, 'When civil war breaks out in this country I hope they get their chance to serve.'[25]

This squabbling formed the backdrop to the emergency operation to salvage both the junta and US policy from the effects of the murder of the nuns. On 7 December, three days after the killing, Bowdler flew to El Salvador with his Republican counterpart, William D. Rogers, who had been assistant Secretary of State under Nixon and Ford. Their 'investigation' of the killing revealed very little, but three days after their return to Washington it became clear that the mission had had a very different motive. The case of the nuns made it imperative to reshuffle the junta and give it a new image if US aid could be restored with any credibility. The solution proposed was one that had been pending for most of 1980 and prophesied by Rafael Menjivar as early as November 1979: the appointment of José Napoleón Duarte as president of the republic. This required the final removal of Majano, who had been out of the country for most of the autumn and the target of a bomb attack, almost certainly from the right, shortly after his return. On 12 December, the officer corps voted 300 to 4 in favour of Majano's removal from the junta. This certainly did not represent the feelings of the entire military establishment since several hundred officers did not vote and Majano's supporters numbered more than four, but the colonel was still out. After 15 months of prevarication, ineptitude and a string of defeats he made something of a stand, claiming that the regime 'has a popular appearance but is of clear rightist tendencies. Barbaric acts have been committed against the people with the complicity or tolerance of this group, or its negligence. I call upon the Salvadorean people to unite and fight . . . in the face of an imposter government.'[26] It was to no avail; Majano's refusal to accept a diplomatic post only led to the order for his arrest. He took with him into clandestinity only two supporters: Colonel Vladimir Cruz and Captain Ricardo Fiallos. Duarte, appointed on 14 December, became the country's first civilian president for 49 years, but it was a privilege granted him only because of US pressure and his loyalty to the institution. As he himself said, 'The only reason I am in this position is because I have the support of the army.'[27] Gutiérrez became vice-president, and García, now unquestionably the power behind the throne, was the only cabinet minister to retain his position.

The fanfare that surrounded these changes obscured the extraordinary weakness of the regime. It had certainly avoided a division of the armed forces (eight officers in all were to defect), but it lost the support of the UCS peasant union and ISTA, both of which were headed by Rodolfo Viera, a firm supporter of Majano. Moreover, it was not possible for Washington to use Duarte's appointment alone as a reason for re-establishing aid; until the case of the nuns was more conclusively tackled, or other mitigating circumstances arose, all that could be done was to prepare the ground and boost the regime's image by stressing Duarte's democratic credentials, which were now commonly described in the international press as 'impeccable'. This task of buoying up the regime was no secondary matter, not least because the economy was now in acute crisis and would soon collapse completely if it were not given substantial external aid. The budget deficit was estimated at ¢1 billion ($400 million). By the end of 1980 fixed private investment was 48 per cent below that at the end of 1978, with an estimated $1.5 billion of capital leaving the country in just over a year. GDP had fallen by up to 15 per cent, and foreign reserves had fallen from $777 million in 1978 to just $10 million. Industry was working at 50 per cent capacity, unemployment had risen by 15 per cent in a year and inflation by 40 per cent.[28] Poor prices on the world market for sugar, cotton and coffee had done nothing to help this situation, and the damage and disruption caused by the war seemed certain to make the following year's harvest one of the worst since 1932. For the first time in memory El Salvador had become a nett importer of corn and beans, further depleting its reserves of foreign exchange.[29]

This economic crisis was paralleled by one on the military front. The setbacks of the August strike and the killing of the FDR leadership had not, despite claims to the contrary, affected the capabilities of the FMLN. Throughout the autumn a process of consolidation had taken place with the groups harassing garrisons and inflicting increasing casualties on the military. The level of repression in the countryside had certainly instilled terror into the *campesinado* but it also had the effect of boosting recruitment to the FMLN, for one's chances with a gun were appreciably greater than without. The FMLN continued to grow consistently, one of the notable features of which, in a country traditionally beset by *machismo*, was the very high proportion of women in its ranks. Moreover, it was able to draw on the support of the peasants who fed it and gave it information in return for medical care and other assistance. This necessary reciprocity had led to several areas of the country becoming denominated 'liberated zones', which in effect meant that the armed forces could only enter them in force and for limited periods since they lacked the men to establish a secure presence for any length of time and received little or no help from the peasantry. In the east of the country the situation was so bad that refugee camps had to be established for members of ORDEN and their families. By November the army had lost permanent control of most of Morazán and La Unión, northern Chalatenango and some parts of Sonsonate, where RN had established a presence. In these regions it maintained a garrison in the major town and left the rest of the territory to the guerrillas until it could muster sufficient forces to launch an offensive, which would oblige the temporary withdrawal of the *subversivos*. In San Vicente and the RN stronghold around the Guazapa volcano, so close to the capital that its camps could be seen from hotel windows in the city, the FMLN withstood a score of offensives without major loss.

In November 1980 the army made a concerted effort to destroy the two main guerrilla centres: Chalatenango (FPL) and Morazán (ERP). On the northern front the FPL conducted a mobile defence but in the east the offensive was conclusively beaten back by the middle of the month. The army's control of San Francisco de Gotera and Perquín, the two largest towns in the department, was permitted more by the demands of guerrilla strategy than by the strength of the garrisons. At the end of December there were clear signs that the FMLN was moving to the offensive. Attacks in Santa Ana and Usulután required deployment of extra forces but the major threat was in Chalatenango, where a force of 1,500 guerrillas had advanced 18 miles from the Honduran border and was only halted with difficulty at the village of Dulce Nombre de María. Garcia announced that the force was encircled and would be wiped out before the new year but he lacked the resources to effect this manoeuvre and the FMLN column escaped.[30] 1981 opened with the army badly stretched and the undefeated FMLN poised for a major offensive.

Regionalisation and Cold War

By the end of the first week in January the imminence of this offensive was public knowledge. A spokeswoman for the FPL told Raymond Bonner of the *New York Times*, 'I cannot give you the exact date or hour, but we are very close to our final battles. This is the decisive moment.' Stressing that, unlike RN or the ERP, the FPL had never before declared a final offensive to be imminent, 'Ana Maria' was categorical: 'The FPL has always been very cautious, but I can tell you we are in the final phase.'[31] On 7 January, the army launched an attack against Guazapa, where the FMLN was reported to be amassing a large force; after two days the attack had yielded nothing but unacceptably high casualties. On the 9th the FMLN announced preparations for a 'final offensive' over *Radio Liberación*. According to RN, the aim was to present the Reagan administration, which was to take office on the 20th, with a fait accompli.[32] The changeover of US governments was judged – not without good reason – to be an opportune time to strike at the junta, exploit the lack of co-ordination in Washington and pre-empt the anticipated escalation of US intervention.

The offensive opened late on the 10th, which, being a Saturday, allowed a day of preparation before the general strike called by the FMLN came into effect. Fighting lasted for a week and covered the entire country, the guerrillas reporting 43 principal actions, some of which were battles lasting for a number of days.[33] Their forces reached Ilopango, 14 miles from the capital, and there was heavy fighting in the working-class *barrios* of San Salvador. The government lost control of Santa Ana early on when, after the first FMLN attack, Colonel Bruno Navarrete, a man not known for leftist sympathies, led a mutiny of the town's garrison, killed the local commander, burnt the barracks and led more than 100 troops over to the guerrillas. This did not occur elsewhere, the junta's forces holding out against very fierce strikes against the traditional targets of Gotera, Perquin, Chalatenango, Metapán and Arcatao as well as important provincial centres such as Zacatecoluca, Sonsonate and Cinquera. Within the first 48 hours of fighting an estimated 500 people died, a casualty rate that did not diminish over the following days as the outcome of the offensive remained open. But in the capital the general strike failed to gain the support of those of the previous summer, and by the 14th it was clear that the FMLN was undertaking a measured retreat. This lasted for three more days with major rearguard actions at Zacatecoluca and Gotera preventing the armed forces from launching a counter-offensive. A week after it had started the offensive was over; it had failed to precipitate a mass uprising but the FMLN had not been defeated – a fact that many army officers did not hesitate to point out.

It was, however, clear that the guerrillas did not yet possess the capacity to defeat the military in an open war for fixed positions. The FMLN accepted that the move to the insurrectionist line had been mistimed, and the offensive was henceforth described as 'general' rather than 'final'. It was admitted that too much had been attempted too soon, with the inference that decisions had been taken with excessive attention to external factors and insufficient consideration of internal conditions.[34] The FPL's overall strategy had been substantially vindicated and its concession to the other groups was reversed. Henceforth the guerrilla command would concentrate on escalating its campaign in a more measured manner. Nevertheless, the offensive had so severely shaken the regime that it is unlikely that it would have survived for long had Washington not taken fright and re-established military aid on the 14th, stipulating that this assistance would, for the first time, include 'lethal' equipment (as opposed to equipment, such as helicopters, which facilitates killing but does not itself kill; the distinction appears to be treated with enormous respect in Washington).[35]

According to the Pentagon one of the main reasons for the resumption of military aid was the receipt of evidence that the FMLN was obtaining Soviet-made arms from Cuba and other sources. This 'evidence', it soon transpired, consisted of a Salvadorean army report that a group of several hundred men had landed in the east of the country from boats that could only have come from Nicaragua because they were constructed with a type of wood that was not to be found in El Salvador. At the height of the offensive White made much of this claim, stating that the 'proof' of Nicaraguan intervention and Cuban involvement 'clearly changes the nature of the insurgency movement here, making it clear that it depends on outside sources'.[36] No sign of the invaders, either dead or alive, was ever found, despite the claim of the high command that they had been dispersed in a fierce fight with high casualties. White later admitted that the report had no basis in reality, but it proved to be a well-timed propaganda coup by García, who succeeded in regaining US aid and distracting attention from the fact that he was now readmitting and giving favour to leading *romerista* officers who had been purged in October 1979; of these, the most important figure was Colonel Flores Lima who was appointed armed forces Chief of Staff. More important than this, however, was the boost the claims of Nicaraguan intervention gave to the already advanced regionalisation of the conflict. This was the most secure way for the regime to guarantee continued US support and therefore survive; for the US it provided the central rationale for escalated support for the regime and the pretext to embark upon a concerted campaign against 'subversion' in the region as a whole.

Allegations of Nicaraguan and Cuban involvement were at the heart of the Reagan policy on Central America. Yet it is important to note that the Carter administration had been consistently making such allegations before this flurry of activity in its last days; from the time of the Caribbean manoeuvres in November, the destabilisation of Nicaragua and Cuba had been high on the agenda. None the less, following the January offensive the US presentation of the Salvadorean conflict underwent a discernible change; protestations of the moderation and democratic aspirations of the Duarte regime were continued but they became increasingly listless and were progressively subordinated in emphasis to the external threat. The tenor switched from positive to negative, from backing one side to opposing the other. The issue was no longer how to suppress communism with reforms in El Salvador but how to fight communism on a world scale with the front line in El Salvador.

Given the publicity the accusations of 'communist intervention' received, it was not surprising that little attention was paid to reports of 1,000 Guatemalan troops and 500 from the Honduran army being deployed on the Salvadorean border during the offensive. As far as intervention was concerned, White had secured the monopoly on pronouncements, and few column inches were spared to quote the Honduran army officer who declared that 'There are 3,000 of us Hondurans and 2,000 Guatemalans from the third division, seventh battalion; we'll go in and kill those communists.'[37] Equally sparse coverage was devoted to claims that 500 ex-members of Somoza's National Guard were already in the country fighting alongside the Salvadorean army. Rather more attention, however, was paid to an incident that directly concerned the US operatives in El Salvador: the assassination on 4 January in the coffee shop of the San Salvador Sheraton of Rodolfo Viera, head of ISTA, and two US citizens working for AIFLD on the agrarian reform, Mark Pearlman and Michael Hammer. Since these men were central to the management of the reform it seemed highly likely that the culprits came from the extreme right. Within three months this proved to be the case when Ricardo Sol Meza, an owner of the hotel and member of the 'fourteen families', was arrested with his brother-in-law, Hans Krist.[38] Despite the fact that the AIFLD employees were in all probability working with the CIA and that the reform was nominally at the centre of the US strategy, the case drew a minimal response from Washington. The exigencies of the diplomatic offensive against Soviet interferences in Central America now precluded pressure being placed on the junta as a result of the deaths of US citizens. This was helped by the fact that the domestic outcry over these killings was markedly less than that over the deaths of the nuns, which may be partially explained by the fact that the victims were closely associated with US interests in the country.

The diplomatic offensive was put into action with great speed. Four weeks after Reagan had taken office, Edward Meese, the president's chief counsellor, declared that it was 'entirely possible' that the US would take direct action against Cuba if arms shipments to the FMLN did not stop. Secretary of State Alexander Haig supported this statement, reiterating that the US 'will not remain passive in the face of this Communist challenge . . . We consider what is happening is part of the global campaign coordinated by Havana and Moscow to support the Marxist guerrillas in El Salvador.'[39]

These statements were so bold that they could not be justified simply in terms of the ideological enthusiasms of the Reagan government. They were, in fact, made at a press conference to publicise the release of a State Department document entitled 'Communist Interference in El Salvador', which later became known as the 'White Paper'. This document, which had been leaked over the previous days to Juan de Onis of the *New York Times*, who ran its allegations as front page factual news, set out to substantiate three main charges:

(1) 'the central role played by Cuba and other Communist countries . . . in the political unification and arming of insurgent forces in El Salvador';
(2) that 'the insurgency in El Salvador had been progressively transformed into another case of indirect aggression against a small Third World country by Communist powers acting through Cuba'; and
(3) that 'Cuba, the Soviet Union and other Communist States . . . are carrying out what is clearly shown to be a well-coordinated, covert effort to bring about the overthrow of El Salvador's established government and to impose in its place a Communist regime with no popular support'.[40]

The White Paper contained proof positive of these serious charges in reproducing 19 of over 80 'captured documents' found by State Department officer Jon Glassman on a visit to El Salvador where, according to the *Washington Post*, he 'wandered around to various security force headquarters'.[41] The documents retrieved by Glassman were reproduced only in the form of short, highly selective quotes and condensed summaries in the printed version of the paper that was issued to the public. Only 100 copies of the full reproductions were handed out to journalists, and the State Department subsequently refused to issue any more or even accept payment for photocopies to be made.[42] This was a wise move, for close scrutiny of the 'proof' is not only an exceedingly laborious and painful task but also reveals such a plethora of non-sequiturs, contradictions, blithe and utterly improbable assertions on the part of the 'enemy' as well as factual errors and reams of inconsequential rambling that any curious reader who credited the FMLN with a modicum of efficiency would soon question the authenticity of many of the documents reproduced in the paper, let alone their capacity to substantiate the charges made by Washington. This is not the place to undertake a rigorous analysis: others have already done it with flair and precision.[43] It is, however, worth mentioning that the 'captured documents' maintain a remarkable consistency in openly naming Fidel Castro and other leading Cuban and Nicaraguan figures when the majority of people mentioned are given code-names; it is also a point of some curiosity that many of the documents have accents marked in by hand, suggesting that a typewriter with a Spanish face was not available to the Salvadorean guerrillas. One is further struck by the use of the term *'milicos'* to describe the military when in El Salvador the term in the vernacular is *'chafarotes'*, *'milicos'* being the slang used in the countries of the Southern Cone. Elementary logistical co-ordination on the part of either the FMLN or some over-hurried back-room boys from Langley is shown to be pitifully insufficient: the tonnages of weapons shipped from Nicaragua fail to square with their supposed arrival in El Salvador. Moreover, it is difficult even for somebody not well versed in logistics to comprehend how, if the guerrillas were swamped with weapons over the autumn of 1980, as the paper alleges, they continued to complain bitterly about lack of arms and munitions throughout this period and evidenced shortcomings with respect to firepower during the January offensive. One's confidence in the paper was unlikely to be enhanced by a photograph – reproduced in the printed pamphlet – of an extremely large lorry captured in Honduras with a cargo of arms. At a glance the vehicle appears as a veritable juggernaut, but on closer inspection the single photograph is found to be a composite of three separate images. In sum, much of the material bore signs of fabrication or presentation that was surprisingly slipshod given the experience of the US intelligence service in such work.

Even that material which appeared to be authentic was of little consequence, demonstrating merely that Cuba and Nicaragua took an active interest in the development of the guerrilla struggle and engaged in discussions with its leaders, Castro undeniably and thoroughly unsurprisingly counselling them to unify; that Shafik Handal had travelled to Moscow and talked with a number of secondary bureaucrats in the Soviet bloc was scarcely startling for the general secretary of a communist party. But at no point did the White Paper produce uncontrovertible and concrete evidence of the direct arming of the FMLN by the Soviet Union or its allies, a charge it had to substantiate if it was to have any semblance of credibility and diplomatic leverage. All this would be a revelation of some consequence were it not for one of those anomalous events that are so supremely North American: early in June 1981 the author of the paper, Jon Glassman, freely admitted to the *Wall Street Journal* that the document contained 'mistakes' and 'guessing' on the part of the State Department.[44] Although Glassman continued to defend its conclusions, he could produce no new evidence to support them. With the White Paper so comprehensively discredited, Washington's diplomatic campaign suffered the first of a string of setbacks, every one of them manifestly of its own making. Yet by June this campaign had built up such momentum and was so critical to the rest of the Reagan Cold War offensive that it could not be ditched; the paper was never formally withdrawn but simply passed over.

Washington had taken great pains to extract the maximum advantage from its 'revelations' by immediately dispatching two powerful diplomatic teams to persuade foreign governments to fall in behind it. General Vernon Walters was sent to the major Latin American states and Lawrence Eagleburger to Europe; both had a dismaying time, with most of the Southern Cone client states preferring to maintain their distance and the Europeans expressing serious doubts. Even the Thatcher government, enchanted by its ideological affinity with the Reagan administration, was held back from a precise and full endorsement of the document by the traditionally cautious assessment of the Foreign Office. Moreover, the member states of the EEC took great exception to Washington's efforts to stop them sending $900,000 worth of humanitarian aid to Salvadorean refugees – up to 300,000 of whom were living outside the country as well as an unknown but similar number housed in internal camps – on the grounds that this assistance would be used by the guerrillas.[45] This was a grave error since by mid-1981 the question of the refugees displaced by military operations, the appalling conditions of those in camps inside the country, and their very great vulnerability to raids by the armed forces, who executed hundreds as 'guerrillas', had become a major international issue with Washington signally failing to come to terms with the adverse propaganda effect. The impact of the massive US campaign over the Vietnamese 'Boat People' was still sufficiently fresh in the popular memory for US actions in El Salvador to appear not only comprehensively inhumane but also inconsistent and hypocritical.

None the less, the State Department did register some successes: by witholding development loans and making political and military threats to the Nicaraguan government it extracted a promise to put an end to any shipments of arms through its territory; through West Germany and Panama it exerted pressure on the FDR to embark on the 'negotiations' offered throughout 1981. But these were never a serious political initiative since they always contained the condition that the FMLN lay down its arms before any talks could begin; the offers were calculated to be rejected and in this they succeeded.[46] The FDR pointedly refused to rule out negotiations but insisted that these should be directly with the US since, according to Guillermo Ungo, 'there's no point in talking to the clowns if you can talk to the owner of the circus'. In the autumn the Nicaraguans acted on behalf of the FDR in proposing terms for negotiations of a ceasefire but because these included the maintenance of the FMLN on a war footing they were rejected out of hand by Washington, which was by this stage reorganising its diplomatic strategy around the holding of 'free and fair' elections in March 1982.

Throughout the spring of 1981 the FMLN insisted that it obtained its arms on the open market, through purchase from corrupt army officers (a practice that is common to almost every Latin American guerrilla war), or by capturing them from government forces. Journalists visiting their camps backed this up with reports of guerrillas possessing M–16 and Belgian FAL weapons but few if any arms of Soviet make, such as the AK47, the 'traditional' weapon of guerrilla warfare. This was answered by the claim that the US arms used by the FMLN were captured in Vietnam, but it added weight to the emphatic Soviet denials of interference in the region. From the liberal viewpoint this is reassuring, from a revolutionary stance quite the reverse. Whatever the case, it is extremely hard to avoid the conclusion that the USSR was intent upon nothing more than avoiding problems with the US over Central America.

As early as 15 February 1981 a Soviet Embassy official in Washington took the unusual step of going on North American television to refute the charges against his country.[47] This was followed by a more formal denial at the end of the month at a press conference to mark the opening of the 26th Congress of the CPSU, at which the PCS had no delegate.[48] In his opening speech to the Congress Brezhnev did not mention Central America once, referring only to 'mutually advantageous relations' with Latin American countries such as Brazil and Argentina, ruled by military dictatorships which had long since put a brutal end to the type of subversion supposedly nurtured by their Soviet trading partner. This point was further emphasised when Brezhnev held public meetings with leaders from Angola and Ethiopia but studiously refrained from seeing Carlos Nuñez, the Nicaraguan delegate. As if this was not sufficient indication that, in public at least, the Soviet Union was shying away from any confrontation, a senior member of the Foreign Ministry declared, 'If the Americans invaded Nicaragua, what would we do? What could we do? Nothing.'[49] The aims of Soviet foreign policy were outlined by the weekly *New Times*, which kept closely to the Pravda line when it stated that,

> the belief of the USSR lies not in the transformation of the third world into an object of confrontation between two opposing systems, but the guarantee of its peaceful and independent development, of an authentic equality and a just international economic order.[50]

So emphatic were these abdications of the essential Leninist task of building the world revolution and undertaking international proletarian solidarity that they obliged Fidel Castro to break the silence in a typically boisterous speech in which he denounced 'the aggressive projects aimed against the patriots of Guatemala and El Salvador', but called for nothing more than national liberation.[51] This indicated a degree of tactical difference within the Soviet bloc; while the USSR could best protect the interests of 'socialism in one country' by conceding that Central America was a US zone of influence, Cuba could afford no such luxury. The ultimate defence of Cuba rests with the Soviet Union but, as the Reagan administration has made clear on numerous occasions, should the region's liberation movements be defeated, the island workers' state would be the next target. While it has carefully desisted from sending large shipments of arms and soldiers to either Nicaragua or El Salvador in order to avoid immediate US reprisals, Cuba is obliged for its very survival to support these movements to a higher degree than its peers in the Soviet bloc. Yet even these limited measures of advice, training, gifts of medical and educational equipment, and public declarations of solidarity sufficed to excite that other major workers' state, China, to condemn it as a 'Trojan horse' for 'Moscow's intervention' in Central America.[52]

Of course, the fundamental flaw in the US denunciations of foreign intervention lay precisely and very publicly in its own intervention, which, however one construes the nature of its ends, was undeniably massive and constantly on the increase. The first aid package announced by the Reagan administration, five weeks after it came to power, consisted of $25 million in military equipment (including weaponry and munitions) and $63 million in economic aid.[53] This brought the level of all US-controlled aid to El Salvador to $523 million for 1981, compared with $183.9 million for 1980 and $79.3 million for 1979.[54] A country the size of Wales was now receiving one of the largest aid budgets made to any Latin American state. At the same time a further 20 military advisers and four Huey helicopters were dispatched, bringing the US military contingent in El Salvador to 54 men (the limit set by Congress is 55). While Colonel Vides Casanova of the National Guard happily declared, 'the new administration is giving us everything we need',[55] Duarte, still playing a threadbare diplomatic part, warned that 'Washington should not send too many advisers here. Otherwise this will soon be seen as America's war.'[56] Within a month he was requesting more equipment as the FMLN continued to destroy helicopters and vehicles.[57]

A large part of the March aid package had to be granted under Section 506(a) of the Foreign Assistance Act which precluded congressional approval. By this stage, there was growing concern on Capitol Hill as to the wisdom of the government's policy towards El Salvador. What united the misgivings of Congress was less a sense that the US was backing the wrong side than that it was doing it in the wrong way, inviting obvious comparisons with the early stages of the Vietnam War. For the liberal opposition this discontent was deepened when Robert White, now retired from the diplomatic service, launched a number of concerted attacks on the Reagan administration's policy and, after an extraordinarily rapid conversion, argued for a policy of negotiation with the FDR. Addressing the House Appropriations Committee on Foreign Operations on 25 February, White placed particular emphasis on the consequences of US military operations, from which he sought to disassociate himself:

> As the civilian responsible for the implementation of United States foreign policy in El Salvador over the past year, I would be at a loss as to how to define the mission of military advisers in El Salvador. You know, the security forces in El Salvador have been responsible for the deaths of thousands of young people, and they have executed them on the mere suspicion that they are leftists or sympathize with leftists. Are we really going to send military advisers in there to be part of that kind of machinery?[58]

Colonel Orlando Rodríguez, US military attaché in San Salvador, on the other hand, apparently entertained few doubts as to the correctness of this course of action. On retiring from the post late in June he told his Salvadorean colleagues,

> It is very difficult to say farewell when the blood of our brothers in arms stains red the fields of a nation that refuses to be subjugated by international communism. Made brothers by the cause, we defend the same ideals of democracy and struggle against a common enemy: communism... We say farewell to you with a military salute of profound admiration and respect.[59]

Of these two responses, that of Rodríguez was much closer to the thinking of the administration; Reagan had already stated on television that there were no dangers of counter-productive entanglements in the Salvadorean situation, but he allayed few fears when he followed this up by saying that the main lesson to be drawn from the experience of Vietnam was that if America did commit troops, which he would not rule out in this case, then 'we are going in to win'.[60]

The declaration of the Duarte government two days after the March aid package that it was freezing all the reforms proposed after October 1979, and the reappearance of Major D'Aubuissón, claiming that Reagan would support a coup d'etat, added further substance to the opinion in Washington that the US was entering an irretrievable position. Criticism of the government's policy centred on its complicity in gross violation of human rights, which drew the response from John Bushnell that the press was taking an excessive interest in the affairs of El Salvador and should direct its attentions to more productive subjects. The resulting outcry obliged the government to declare in less than convincing fashion that Bushnell had never been authorised to make such a statement.[62] Within eight weeks of coming to office the administration was made aware of the fact that if it wished to draw public attention to El Salvador it could not confine concentration to one single aspect – the international communist conspiracy – without people being informed of other events. The extent to which these had an impact was made impressively clear on 3 May, when Washington saw one of the largest demonstrations since the days of Vietnam in protest against intervention in El Salvador. Late in the year this found an echo in the legislature when the Senate passed a measure requiring the president to sign a statement confirming that the Salvadorean government was endeavouring to improve respect for human rights before it would sanction the release of further aid.[63] Reagan was eventually to do exactly this – on 28 January 1982 – stating that the Duarte regime had made a 'concerted and significant effort' to respect human rights. As a result, $25 million in military aid and $40 million in economic aid was disbursed. However, two days before the US president made this statement the press had published reliable reports that nearly 800 people had been slaughtered by troops in the village of Mozote, Morazán. The US Embassy in San Salvador immediately cast doubts on the reports but never denied them and later admitted that it was possible the massacre had taken place. Two days after Reagan had 'certified' the junta the bodies of 20 youths were found in the San Salvador *barrio* of San Antonio Abad; they had been taken out and shot by uniformed members of the National Guard the previous night in an 'anti-guerrilla' operation. There had been no fighting and the majority of the victims were in their early teens; one ten-year-old 'guerrilla' was said to have been raped ten times. This time, with the international press on the scene within a matter of hours, nobody challenged the veracity of the version of the raid given by the frightened *pobladores*.[64] Evidently the administration's conception of what constituted a human right approximated more closely to the right of Guardsmen to be given weapons by the US and employ them as they saw fit than the right of Salvadorean children to life.

Rising domestic opposition to the policy on El Salvador was matched with a hardening of the stance taken by the Second International and a discernible coolness from the major Latin American states except Venezuela and – after General Galtieri's subtle ousting of General Viola at the end of the year – Argentina; the position of most of these states was now clearly one of favouring a negotiated settlement of some sort.[65] One reason was the message from the Reagan government that a military intervention remained a possibility, and it seemed increasingly improbable that such action could be undertaken without complementary action against Cuba and Nicaragua. Such a course had distinctly frightening implications for many Latin American states but with constant talk of the possibilities of blockades and the high profile given to the training of right-wing paramilitary forces in Florida it could not sensibly be excluded. The tension caused by this belligerent line reached a peak in mid-November when for a number of days Haig's garbled but stentorian pronouncements appeared to presage direct action in the Caribbean. On 22 November the Secretary of State declared that 'the hours are growing rather short for Nicaragua', while the US reported 'an immense Soviet–Cuban-aided military buildup' in that country. The only impediment to direct action seemed for a while to be the Pentagon's reluctance to set in train measures which many of its senior staff obviously considered analogous to those that occurred in the early stages in Vietnam and conducive to a probable military disaster.

It is not difficult to appreciate the reservations of the military as to the logistical problems of a full operation in the region. Prior US experience had been restricted to operations in one country and had usually comprised the overthrow or destabilisation of a government. Under the existing circumstances they were faced with a scenario that called for the military defence of one manifestly unpopular regime in El Salvador combined with the destabilisation of another undeniably popular one in Nicaragua and measures against the strongest military power in the region, Cuba. On the State Department's own version of events no action could be taken in any one sector without complementary action in the others; the military problems were legion, the diplomatic impediments positively horrendous. The insistent refusal to rule out a 'military solution' quite naturally increased speculation and deep fears that it was in fact in the offing, but as it steered its erratic course the administration found it was bound as much by objective facts as it was impelled by its own voluntarism.

There was, perhaps, no more eloquent an indication of this in the international sphere than the removal of Giscard and the election of Mitterand to the French presidency, an event that subsequently saw the appointment of the dean of *foquismo*, Regis Debray, as counsellor on foreign relations, causing outbursts of apoplexy in almost every Latin American capital. By the summer this shift of power in Europe had registered firmly in Central American when the French government joined that of Mexico to give the FDR its most important international boost – the granting of belligerent rights. In September Duarte paid a fleeting and decidedly low-key trip to Washington and he used the occasion to denounce the Franco-Mexican declaration as 'intervention', which seemed finally to empty the term of any useful meaning.[66]

The dissident position taken by Mexico was of considerable importance since without its acquiescence any major initiative in the region was liable to encounter significant difficulties, jeopardising not only careful retrenchment of US interests in Guatemala and Honduras but also vital economic and political agreements with the US itself. Although the leadership of Mexico's all-embracing state bureaucracy is often very hard to 'read' politically because of the fine balance it must strike between maintaining the ideology of the revolution and overseeing the growth of an economy increasingly dependent on foreign capital, it represents a more dependable judge of shifts in the balance of forces in Central America than does the Reagan government. The decision to throw its weight behind a negotiated solution corresponded not only to an affinity with the social democratic strategy but also to a recognition that following the January offensive the FMLN had made sufficient advances to create a stalemate in the civil war.

Throughout the spring and early summer of 1981 this was evident in what the armed forces failed to achieve rather than in any extraordinary successes on the part of the guerrillas. Seven offensives against Guazapa followed by others in Chalatenango, Cabañas, Morazán and La Unión were all either beaten back or simply ran out of steam in failing to make contact. Although the military had recruited over 4,000 men in the two months following the January offensive and now numbered around 20,000 men to the FMLN's 6,000 regulars, this was nowhere near the ratio of 10:1 that was considered necessary to facilitate a victory. Moreover, many of the new recruits were youths up to four years under the official age limit of 18 for military service; a large number had been press-ganged into service and proved far less dependable in action than their bright uniforms and modern weapons suggested. The FMLN calculated that the regime's new US-trained shock-force, the Atlacatl Battalion, commanded by the young and energetic Colonel Domingo Monterrosa, could be kept in action for only three weeks at a time before it had to be rested and replenished. Furthermore, the guerrillas claimed to have killed or severely wounded 48 officers out of a total corps of 600 in the first six months of the year.[67] Whether one accepts the FMLN claim or not, it is hard to imagine that the military's morale would be high after the succession of failed operations it experienced during this period. The commander of Gotera was speaking for many of his colleagues when he declared at the end of April that 'if we go out the guerrillas attack us. In the last few days they have destroyed four jeeps and armoured vehicles. It is lucky that we have the helicopters provided by the United States.'[68] The local field hospital reported receiving up to 20 military casualties a day. A similar situation prevailed in Chalatenango, where by mid-June the town of Arcatao could only be supplied by air and few roads were reliably free from guerrilla attacks.

In July the FMLN moved to the offensive once again in a carefully planned campaign against economic targets. In ten days 62 electricity installations were destroyed, depriving the eastern provinces of power for two weeks and blacking the capital out for 48 hours. This was followed by the cutting of the country's communications network, a campaign that included the destruction of a number of bridges, including the important Puente de Oro over the Lempa river between Zacatecoluca and Usulután, impeding much commercial activity. In Morazán, the capture of Perquin led to the capture of 60 soldiers but the FMLN desisted from holding the town and establishing a static 'liberated zone', preferring to build on the advantages of its mobility and exhaust the armed forces through dispersal and constant harassment. By the end of the year the FMLN had indisputable operational control over at least a quarter of the national territory. Yet, while the guerrillas held the initiative, they still lacked the capacity for a final offensive. The military still controlled the capital, the major thoroughfares and cities, and possessed an apparently fathomless reserve of equipment as its stocks were progressively whittled down. The character of this stalemate was underlined when on 27 January 1982 the FMLN scored a major victory in a lightning raid on the country's main airbase at Ilopango. Using mortars and armour-piercing rockets the guerrillas destroyed eleven aeroplanes and six of the military's fourteen Huey helicopters; the regime's airpower was halved in one blow. A week later Haig announced that the US 'would do whatever is necessary to prevent a guerrilla victory' and $55 million was set aside to make good the losses of the Salvadorean airforce.[69] Total US aid for 1982 had now reached $388,278,000, while that projected for 1983 already stood at $389,221,000. One of the more disturbing aspects of this incident was the fact that soon afterwards the high command ordered the arrest of a number of airforce NCOs for complicity in the attack. The FMLN had made no secret of its advice to youths not to avoid military conscription but to join up, acquire basic skills and then join the guerrillas with their weapons; now it appeared that its sympathisers inside the armed forces were engaged in more positive activity.

'Diplomacy' and Elections

1982 opened with Washington returning to the offensive on all fronts but quickly finding itself undermined by the fact that whilst its accusations of foreign intervention became ever more vociferous, it could not provide them with convincing proof. This assisted the tangible collapse of domestic and international acceptance of the administration's policy in Central America. As a result, the Reagan government did not conduct a measured retreat or adopt a more flexible form of implementing its line but maintained its stridency, adding hasty caveats and a string of ingenuous 'no comments' that only served to heighten the sense of confusion and apprehension. This soon had an effect on the public statements of the State Department but did not diminish by one iota the attachment of the government to its rude domino theory.

Early in February Assistant Secretary of State Thomas Enders produced the most widely-quoted and cogent presentation of this position:

> The decisive battle for Central America is under way in El Salvador. If, after Nicaragua, El Salvador is captured by a violent majority, who in Central America would not live in fear? How long would it be before major strategic interests – the Panama canal, sea lanes, oil supplies – were at risk? . . . [In Nicaragua] Soviet, East European and 2,000 Cuban military advisers are building Central America's largest military establishment with Soviet arms. Outside Nicaragua, the clandestine infiltration of arms and munitions into El Salvador is again approaching the high levels recorded just before last year's 'final offensive'.[70]

Statements such as this openly suggested the direct use of US military forces, but a week after Enders' statement Haig moved to head off such fears while simultaneously reinforcing the substance of his inferior officer's speech: 'There are no current plans for the use of American forces, [but] the sterility of drawing lines around America's potential options constitutes the promulgation of roadways for those who are seeking to move against America's vital interests' [sic].[71] This clarified nothing at all. Moreover, the feeling that it was a safe form of words designed to leave all possibilities open received some support from the administration's undisguised efforts to deepen its commitment to funding military activity in the region. Several days after Haig delivered his statement the government went to Congress to ask for the release of $250,000 in military aid to Guatemala, pending improvements in the dictatorship's handling of human rights.[72] This was Reagan's first concerted attempt to reverse the Carter administration's freezing of aid in 1977, and it reflected a certain desperation since the Guatemalan regime was uncommonly unpopular in Congress for its historic proclivity for violence and refusal to comply with Washington's desires as to its outward comportment. The administration's pacific and non-interventionist intentions came under even more suspicion two days later when the press carried reports that Reagan had approved a $19 million CIA plan for the active internal destabilisation of Nicaragua, including the use of a 500-man force comprised of the much-publicised and pointedly undiscouraged rightist emigré paramilitaries training in Florida.[73] There was some confusion over the details of the plan but the only response of the government to insistent questioning was a refusal to comment, further increasing fears of a new Bay of Pigs.

This tight-lipped bellicosity soon found a response. On 21 February, President López Portillo of Mexico stepped in to halt the escalation and produce an alternative strategy designed to reduce regional polarisation. Speaking in Managua, he offered a new initiative centred around a categorical renunciation of further threats of the use of force by Washington, negotiations between Cuba, Nicaragua and the US, a mutual non-agression pact between the US, Nicaragua and Nicaragua's neighbours, and a commitment by Managua to begin to reduce its forces.[74] The immediate response from Washington was minimal, Haig later stating that while there was 'some convergence of views' with Mexico, López Portillo's 'Managua Appeal' did not address the key issue of Nicaraguan military assistance to the Salvadorean rebels.[75]

Reagan's next step was the unveiling of the long-promised 'Caribbean Basin' development plan, announced with a great fanfare on 24 February. The plan was touted as a major initiative and expected to herald a new phase in the administration's Central American policy. The rhetoric far outstripped the substance. Reagan's mini Alliance for Progress comprised not the massive economic programme of some

$10 billion originally spoken of but a distinctly tatty $350 million aid package combined with some discrete tariff concessions. A substantial portion of the funds (34 per cent) was directed towards keeping the depleted Salvadorean industrial sector above water and a similar (unsolicited) amount was marked to bail Costa Rica out of part of its crippling $3 billion foreign debt; the amounts earmarked for these states were out of all proportion to their importance in the regional economy. The tariff concessions hailed as a triumph for the policies of free trade and a long-term panacea for regional underdevelopment were quickly identified as irrelevant: 87 per cent of the $10 billion US imports from the region were already free of tariffs.[76] The plan disappeared very quickly from the news to be overtaken by a matter that was clearly of greater import to Washington.

This was the diplomatic offensive against Nicaragua which had reached such a pitch by early January that even ousted junta-member Alfonso Robelo was obliged to protest on behalf of domestic capitalists that 'all this verbal agressiveness doesn't help our case at all'.[77] Indeed, the panic sown by Haig's statements in November had obliged the private sector to seek some form of *rapprochement* with the FSLN, which, with a good deal more perspicacity than the State Department, it viewed as being both strengthened and radicalised by US threats. On 28 February William Casey, the director of the CIA whose appointment had caused considerable alarm in July 1981, produced a typically brusque statement that bore few signs of political finesse: 'This whole El Salvador insurgency is run out of Managua by professionals experienced in directing guerrilla wars.'[78] Defense Secretary Caspar Weinberger immediately backed this up to demonstrate that Casey's impromptu remark was not out of line and that Managua was still the prime target.

In order to register this point, Haig promised Congress that he would prove the charges by identifying and presenting a Nicaraguan sent to El Salvador 'by the Nicaraguan government to assist the revolution'.[79] However, the next day it transpired that this 'guerrilla' had beguiled the Salvadorean police into taking him to the Mexican Embassy in order to identify his contact there, whereupon he nimbly skipped inside the door and claimed political asylum. The Mexican government soon confirmed Managua's claims that the man was a student foolishly making his way to his university in Mexico City via El Salvador. To deny this without any further evidence would have greatly prejudiced Washington's relations with its largest local ally, and unfortunately the Mexican version was true. However, undeterred by this experience, Haig went ahead without White House permission with the presentation a week later of another Nicaraguan to the press in Washington. 19-year-old Ernesto Tardencillas was expected to confirm his story to the National Guard that he had been trained in Ethiopia and Cuba and specially sent to El Salvador by the Nicaraguan regime. The fact that he had been transported to the US capital without a visa or the slightest observance of international law aroused nobody's interest until the young man showed the fortitude to deny the whole story, which, he plausibly claimed, he had concocted in order to avoid further torture and death at the hands of his captors. That he could show the signs of this torture and come across as a candid and committed volunteer inside the very portals of the State Department only increased the embarrassment of the administration, which was eagerly awaiting its first propaganda victory.[80]

These blunders were expected to be offset by a more carefully planned demonstration of Managua's belligerent intentions in a presentation of aerial photographs taken of Nicaraguan military installations, of which the great majority were marked as 'Soviet-style'. However, the detailed pictures only succeeded in proving that Managua was increasing its national defences; there was no pictorial evidence of shipments being made to El Salvador and no indication of any preparations for invasion of neighbouring states, unless one imagined that this could be undertaken by two Soviet helicopters. Moreover, the preparation of the evidence manifested some of the same traits as that of the previous February's White Paper: not only was there shown to be quite insufficient housing for the number of troops claimed to be under arms, but Washington's planners failed to ascertain in advance that the much-discussed extension of the landing strip at the country's main airbase had not, in fact, been planned and financed by the USSR or Cuba but by a US consortium and at the cost of $1 million to the US taxpayer.[81] The Nicaraguan government did not hesitate to point this out or to denounce the overflying of its territory for the purposes of espionage or to question how any of the findings proved that they were aiding the FMLN and doing anything other than preparing for an invasion and internal destabilisation that in terms of both history and the Reagan administration's statements it had every reason to believe would be forthcoming.[82] The blowing up of two bridges on the Honduran border so convinced them of the imminence of this danger that a state of emergency was declared.

Inside the US the anti-Nicaragua campaign served to revive and increase opposition to the government's actions in Central America. This was made all the more acute by the effects of Reagan's budget for fiscal year 1983 which was $32 billion dollars up on that for 1982, with cuts in social security entitlements of $2 billion, an increase in military spending of $34 billion, and an overall projected deficit rising to $91.5 billion – despite Reagan's election campaign promise to obtain a balanced budget. The budget increased the rift with Congress, which had previously been extraordinarily docile in its response to the harsh deflationary and explicitly anti-working-class economic policies of the administration. This contributed to the hardening of the challenge to the government's foreign policy. In a series of articles the eminently conservative *New York Times* attempted to apprise both the administration and the public of the fact that the FSLN still enjoyed considerable popularity and that an all-out offensive against Nicaragua would achieve the exact opposite of its objectives. Both houses of Congress sent off commissions to El Salvador to provide themselves with an independent view on developments there and a basis on which to challenge the version of events put out by the administration. Both teams returned to make highly critical reports of the armed forces, casting doubt on Duarte's ability to control them, and predicting adverse consequences of an escalation of US military aid. When a number of US advisers were filmed carrying rifles in a combat zone near San Miguel the image of Vietnam acquired much wider currency, forcing Reagan to order the commander home.[83]

By mid-February, mail to the government was running 20:1 against further involvement in El Salvador. A *Newsweek* poll in the same month found that 74 per cent of those questioned believed that US involvement could turn El Salvador into the Vietnam of the 1980s; 49 per cent disapproved of the Reagan policy towards the country; 60 per cent were against sending military aid to the Salvadorean regime, and 89 per cent against sending troops.[84] A CBS–*New York Times* poll later in the month broadly confirmed these findings but added a number of disturbing features: 50 per cent of its respondents thought Soviet and Cuban troops were fighting in El Salvador and 41 per cent considered that whatever happened the marines were likely to be sent in.[85] From this it can be deduced not only that sections of the US public remained profoundly ignorant of developments in Central America but also that the government's propaganda campaign had had a major impact, with opposition to it being based not on an informed appreciation of the character of the struggle in El Salvador but a fundamental fear and expectation of costly and dangerous foreign adventures. The government's actions over Central America had sharpened the memory of Vietnam to reawaken the isolationist reflexes of the American public. Early in March a hundred members of Congress wrote to the president urging him to change his Salvadorean policy, accept the López Portillo plan and begin negotiations with the FDR. On 2 March the House of Representatives voted 393 to 3 to call on Reagan to press for conditions in the elections that would enable the participation of all political sectors.

Obliged to respond to this pressure, Reagan allowed it to be leaked that the sending of combat troops to El Salvador had been ruled out– as opposed to the fact that no plans existed for this eventuality – but no formal statement was made to this effect.[86] On the diplomatic front Haig changed tack by referring to a 'global approach', speaking of the Mexican plan in more favourable terms, and even hinting at the possibility of talks with Cuba. However, a day later he denied that US policy had softened and insisted that the only basis for a negotiated settlement was for Nicaragua to 'get out of El Salvador'.[87] The press complained of confusion and vagueness but if the Reagan government was indeed boxed in a corner, it gave no hint of halting the escalation of military aid to the Duarte regime or of seeking any solution other than a military one.

As had been borne out by the signal lack of success on the part of the armed forces since the January 1981 offensive, the entire US strategy in the region depended on a provincial military apparatus that lacked the capacity to defeat a major insurgency. Although by early 1982 the armed forces had been increased in size to 22,000 men, it was apparent that the US advisers in the country were not able to transform the young and unsteady recruits into a dependable force, and it was politically unacceptable to send in more advisers. As a result, Washington decided to bring the Salvadoreans to the US. In mid-January 1,000 troopers were shipped to Fort Bragg, North Carolina, to undergo a four-month intensive course in basic infantry skills. At the same time nearly 500 officer cadets, the whole of the rapidly expanded military academy, were sent on a 14-week course in leadership at Fort Benning, Georgia. According to a military observer in San Salvador, 'The left is running circles around the army, and the army is getting dizzier and dizzier',[88] and even Duarte admitted, 'We are losing the war with the guerrillas in the countryside.'[89] Clearly some major initiative such as this had to be taken on the military front if the FMLN was to be stopped from gaining an irreversible advantage.

Garcia, who had now promoted himself, Gutiérrez and Vides Casanova to the rank of general and quietly taken over as army commander, responded to the military crisis by telling a congressional commission in mid-February that in order to win the war he needed not more US troops but more equipment, including ten jet fighters, patrol boats, electronic surveillance equipment and enough helicopters simultaneously to transport two battalions, requiring at least 180 craft.[90] The estimated cost of such a consignment would have been, according to one congressman, half a billion dollars. However, the Salvadorean armed forces could not possibly absorb such an influx of equipment: they possessed only 20 helicopter pilots and manpower reserves had reached their limits. This point was confirmed by General Wallace Nutting, the US commander in the Canal Zone, who made a visit to reassess the military position. It was becoming ever more apparent that if Washington wished to obtain a decisive superiority in manpower, which was estimated to mean at least a doubling of the size of the armed forces, it would have look elsewhere.

The most obvious source was Argentina, which had been to the fore in the planning and execution of the Bolivian coup of July 1980, was playing a major role in improving the efficiency of the Guatemalan intelligence service, and early in February announced its intention of sending 50 advisers to help train exiled Nicaraguan paramilitary forces. Rumours in Buenos Aires had a special anti-guerrilla unit training in countryside similar to the Salvadorean *campo*, and Garcia made no secret of the possibility that General Galtieri would send him troops.[91] By the end of the month this possibility seemed to have hardened when Flores Lima travelled to Argentina and was accorded with full honours before moving on to discuss the details of assistance. On 10 March the government in Buenos Aires announced that it intended to sell arms and give 'all possible aid' to the Salvadorean regime.[92] This step gave greater substance to the plans for a 'Pan American Army of Peace' to be sent to El Salvador under the leadership of the Argentines and with contingents from the major dictatorships and possibly Colombian and local troops. Such as endeavour could be justified with reference to the 1947 Rio treaty, which allowed for mutual defence against communist agression to be undertaken under the aegis of the Inter-American Defence Board, the military wing of the OAS. Washington was quick to play down speculation about this plan, which unless it was very carefully orchestrated stood to prejudice the already slim chances of obtaining full support for military intervention from the OAS. Although Argentina, Chile, Bolivia, Paraguay and, to a lesser extent, Colombia and Venezuela might ultimately desire such a move and could feasibly mount support for it, they would without doubt face insuperable domestic problems as a result. Brazil and Mexico were amongst those countries which made it clear that they would not support such action, and the Central American states were so hard-pressed that their contribution would involve great risks. Nevertheless, Washington had taken some steps towards providing greater unity between them in sponsoring the Central American Democratic Community (CDC) as a complement to the now disorganised CONDECA and the effectively moribund CACM. Under the circumstances prevailing in the region the CDC could not only realistically constitute an *ad hoc* political grouping designed to improve co-ordination and provide a forum for strategic debate. But even this seemed to be a belated and insignificant bureaucratic manoeuvre since by mid-March the tempo of political crisis had reached such a point that it was plain that none of the states could undertake meaningful action without massive assistance from the US. This also applied to the various scenarios for military intervention, which promised to be of such a dimension that, whatever the nationality of the troops used, US participation and supervision would be necessary to ensure any possibility of success.

This was apparent from the balance of forces within El Salvador as well as throughout Central America as a whole. In the first three months of 1982 the FMLN demonstrated that it had built on the steadily developed advances of the previous year. The Ilopango attack was the single most incisive incident but an equally high level of co-ordination was manifest in the New Year's Day operation against electricity installations, blacking out the entire country and demonstrating that the guerrillas had moved beyond their strongholds in the north and east and were capable of undertaking operations in regions where they had not previously had a presence. This fact was confirmed in mid-February, when the garrisons of Usulután, San Miguel and San Vicente found themselves hard-pressed to ward off attacks in these central towns, which had not suffered direct and extended offensives since January 1981. At the beginning of March FMLN units went into action in the capital itself for the first time in a year. The working-class *barrios* were the scene of extended skirmishes with small guerrilla groups, but it soon became clear that this was a probing action not intended to develop into a major offensive. Such an advance was planned to escalate into a complete disruption of the elections of 28 March, but there was no early push, the FMLN having inculcated the errors of the 'final offensive'. It is not impossible that this caution also reflected the advice of Cuba and Nicaragua, both of which made little secret of their fear that an emphatic advance might not lead to a defeat but to a decisive victory, which they perceived as highly likely to compel direct US intervention.[93] In all events, the FMLN offensive was carefully measured and not publicly proclaimed until 9 March – over *Radio Venceremos* – with the following days seeing no qualitative increase in operations although the election campaign was well under way.

As a result of both pre-ordained election calendars and Washington's keenness to preserve a democratic facade for its counter-offensive, this was a period full of elections in Central America. For some time the US had been endeavouring to stabilise Honduras by encouraging a gradual withdrawal by the army from open political power. In 1980 General Policarpo Paz García was persuaded to hold congressional elections, which the opposition Liberal Party won by a narrow margin and without threatening any basic changes to the political system or the balance of power, Paz and the army remaining firmly in control. On 29 November 1981 presidential elections led to the victory of the Liberal leader Dr Roberto Suazo Córdova, whose political inexperience and stolid conservatism guaranteed the permanence of the military as the power behind the throne although the country was now officially ruled exclusively by civilians. Having re-established democracy without a whimper, the major outstanding concern of the State Department and the Pentagon was to preserve the unity of the armed forces, which have been plagued over the last decade by the recurrent appearance of strong reformist tendencies amongst the junior officer corps. Highly reliant upon its airforce rather than the doubtful efficiency of its ground forces, which number only 7,000 men, the Honduran military apparatus is over-stretched in the extreme under the current conditions and any split might severely undercut the value of the increased stocks of weapons being syphoned in by Washington since mid-1981.

In Costa Rica, the economic crisis of the last five years produced a substantial victory in the poll of 7 February 1982 for the opposition PLN, a social democratic party led by Luis Alberto Monge. Of all the elections, this was the cleanest, most enthusiastic, and most free of US interference, since Costa Rica possesses a relatively well-established electoral tradition following the civil war of 1948. Monge's victory did not, however, promise any major alteration in either domestic or regional political conditions; he began to prepare for negotiations with the IMF over the foreign debt, limited himself to reiterating the Second International's desire for negotiations in El Salvador, and reconfirmed Costa Rica's membership of the CDC alongside the Duarte regime.[94] There would be no attempted intervention or arbitration as in Nicaragua in 1979; Costa Rica would endeavour to evade all but the inevitable consequences of the Salvadorean conflict.

The Guatemalan poll of 7 March 1982 developed in an altogether different manner. For the fourth time in a row the official candidate was the incumbent Minister of Defence, this time General Anibal Guevara, chosen to continue the extreme right-wing policies of the military regime led by General Romeo Lucas García. As in 1978, the main challenge to the official candidate came not from the left, which had long since embarked on armed struggle and urged a boycott of the poll, or even the Christian Democrats, large numbers of whom had been executed by the death squads in an apparent effort by the military to avoid a 'Salvadorean situation' of being foisted with dangerously ambitious civilian politicians, but from the extreme rightist MLN, headed by Mario Sandoval Alarcón, whose position was close to that of D'Aubuissón in his desire for a rapid and uninhibited war of extermination against the guerrillas. Although the newly unified military front of the left – the *Unión Revolucionaria Nacional Guatemalteca* (URNG) comprised of the EGP, FAR, PGT and ORPA – launched a number of operations to thwart the poll, voting took place in most areas and Guevara was soon declared the victor by an overwhelming majority following the traditional fraud. This drew an unprecedented show of unity on the part of the opposition candidates, whose demonstrations of protest were repressed without hesitation; for the first time in decades, elegant upper-class ladies were subjected to beatings and tear-gassing by a police force they employed to keep the lower classes in check.

Guevara appeared to have survived the crisis inside the ruling class, which was this time much more acute than usual at election time, when, on 23 March the Lucas García regime was overthrown by a remarkably bloodless and efficient coup d'etat, the first in nearly 20 years. The authors of the coup were largely junior officers but although their initial manifesto inveighed against electoral fraud, government corruption and the violation of human rights, they stopped well short of the

pronouncements of their Salvadorean colleagues after 15 October
1979. The junta set up by the rebels was headed by General Efraín Ríos
Montt, who had been deprived of victory by fraud in the 1974 elections,
when he stood for the Christian Democrats. He had since retired from
military life and acquired a formidable reputation as a 'born-again'
Christian, being obliged by the rebel captains to leave a prayer meeting
to take over from Lucas García. Nevertheless, he still possessed
considerable prestige inside the armed forces for his efficiency in
directing anti-guerrilla operations as chief of staff, and his manifest
antipathy to the *continuismo* of the government party made him one of
the very few obvious choices for a 'clean' military figurehead. However,
the general immediately proved to be highly independent and
distinctly erratic in his public pronouncements, which were peppered
with biblical allusions. The junior officers who had staged the coup and
the MLN, which had given it backing, were edged aside, no mention
made of a date for new elections or plans for reform, and no political
initiatives promised. It appeared as if nothing had happened beyond a
settling of old scores within the dominant bloc. The situation remained
unstable. It is hard to read a clear US role into this. Although it was
aware of discontent, the US Embassy was obviously taken by surprise,
and the coup by no means necessarily ameliorated Washington's
position, since it introduced yet a further element of instability into
Central American politics. There certainly now existed greater
possibilities for arming and aiding a Guatemalan government but the
country's ruling class was thrown into even greater disunity
in the face of the growing guerrilla menace.

The Guatemalan coup provided a sharp and sobering distraction
from the campaign for the most critical election of all, the vote in El
Salvador on 28 March. This poll had been announced in the summer of
1981 and was perceived by Washington as crucial in lending legitimacy
to its presence and operations in the country. Without a popularly
elected government it could only refer to the 'established government',
which possessed an authoritative ring but lacked sufficient democratic
credentials to serve as an adequate victim for international
communism. Duarte himself was not averse to such a step since it
promised to fulfil his long-held ambition to be the elected president of
El Salvador, while the right, now championed by D'Aubuissón and his
ARENA party, eagerly seized the opportunity to reverse the changes
effected after October 1979.

The elections were for a constituent assembly which would itself elect a president until full congressional and presidential polls were held in 1983. Campaigning began in earnest in February but from the very start the legitimacy of the poll was challenged both inside the country and internationally. US Ambassador Deane Hinton proclaimed that the vote was the 'first free election in fifty years', and this same opinion was voiced by a BBC television reporter.[95] However, such a position was dimissed as absurd by those who pointed to the history of elections in El Salvador, which no self-respecting psephologist would grace with serious study. There was no electoral register, and the poll was being boycotted by all parties to the left of the rightist Christian Democratic rump of Duarte because, amongst a multitude of other reasons, the names of all their leaders had for over a year been at the top of the death lists drawn up by the rightist terror squads. This point registered very firmly on foreign opinion when four Dutch journalists were killed in Chalatenango under circumstances that pointed to the traditional executions of the security forces. More important than these factors, however, was the fact that the elections were being held in the midst of a civil war. Voters were presented with a choice of casting their ballots, which was compulsory, or being sought out and dealt with as 'subversives' by the armed forces with the customary bloody result. This was scarcely the optimum means of organising a demonstration of the popular will but it could be guaranteed to coerce large numbers of people to present themselves at the booths, where they could either choose between various shades of right-wing politics or deface their ballot. These mechanisms were, unsurprisingly, given little publicity by those in favour of the election but once they became known more broadly a large turnout was expected even despite the FMLN's boycott campaign.

Jorge Bustamante, the president of the electoral commission, ruefully admitted that he had never voted before but expressed every confidence that the freedom for people to vote anywhere in the republic that they wished would avoid intimidation by the FMLN and not be an extra incentive for time-honoured fraud, which would for the first time be absent under these auspicious circumstances.[96] This failed to convince 40 out of the 60 nations invited to send observers and give the final stamp of approval to the vote. Eventually, only the US, the obvious client states such as Egypt, Taiwan and Israel, most Latin American countries, many of them ruled by soldiers whose only knowledge of democracy was overseeing its eradication, and Great Britain, alone of the EEC countries, accepted this invitation. The British position had never been in doubt; in the words of the former Secretary of State at the Foreign Office, Nicholas Ridley, 'It is understandable that the US government feels the need to resume military assistance to the government of El Salvador. Their interest in countering Soviet and Cuban subversion in Central America is one we share.'[97]

When the Conservatives finally found two dignatories prepared to act as its 'independent' observers their conduct matched the farcical nature of the elections as a whole. Bottled up in their hotel 'consulting with themselves', refusing to speak with the press or accept the offer of British journalists to take them on a genuinely independent trip into the *campo*, they relied on lighting visits in their bullet-proof limousine under the organisation and control of the military to reach their informed and impartial verdict on the context, conditions and cleanness of the poll.[98] The arrival a day before the vote – which one can assume would concentrate attention on the mechanisms of actually casting votes rather than the conditions under which this took place – of a plethora of voluble US observers predictably did little to alter the widespread conviction that what was underway was nothing less than a 'macabre farce', in the words of Dennis Healey.

The contest was between six parties: ARENA, the PDC, the PCN, the rapidly revived PAR, Medrano's new vehicle, *Partido de Orientación Popular*, the PPS and the small Acción Democrática party, which, despite its name, shared with all the other parties the property of being to the right of the Christian Democrats and seeking the annulment of the agrarian reform. This was an abnormally wide field, but it soon became clear that only three forces were leading contestants: the PDC, ARENA and the PCN. Of these, the PCN played by far the most subdued role in the campaign, relying less on its visibility at the hustings than the still intact network built up over the 18 years of its rule; if the PCN was no longer the principal standard-bearer of the right, it could certainly expect to contribute towards an oligarchic bloc against the PDC in the assembly.

Neither Duarte nor the PDC showed excessive optimism throughout the campaign, Duarte himself freely admitting that he might not be able to obtain an overall majority. In this he showed his recognition of the isolation of the PDC from all other political parties and the enormous damage done both to its prestige and to the party machine by the violence of the last two years. It was something of an irony that the PDC's campaign should include claims to have borne a substantial part of the repression unleashed by their partners in government. The campaign was more lacklustre than many expected from Duarte, who relied heavily on his past populist reputation, his authority as president, the promise of implementing the post-October 1979 reform programme, and, far from least, the critical papal injunction given to the people to participate in the poll.

On the other hand, D'Aubuisson's offensive at the head of ARENA was positively bombastic and reflected considerable funding from the landlords now ensconced in Florida. Employing North American electioneering techniques to great effect, the unrepentant fascist whom Robert White had dubbed a 'pathological killer' toured the country assiduously to build up a following that took observers by surprise and within a week of the vote put the PDC's chances of obtaining a majority in the assembly in grave doubt. D'Aubuisson had lost none of his personal charisma or political radicalism. According to Duarte, the peace offered by ARENA was 'the peace of death', and little that 'Major Bob' or his henchmen said refuted this. The party's campaign song entoned far from pacifically that 'El Salvador will be the tomb where the Reds end up'; given that D'Aubuisson considered the PDC 'crypto-communists', it was far from clear where this sentence of death would begin or end. D'Aubuisson proclaimed in uncompromising terms that 'with the people and the armed forces united in a strong government the country can be pacified in three months'. As if this required further elaboration, ARENA's general secretary, Mario Redaelli, told the press that, 'We don't believe the army needs controlling. We are fighting a war, and civilians will be killed. They always have been. It's got to be that way.'[99] Later in the campaign, after D'Aubuisson had suffered a minor bullet wound in an assassination attempt which he blamed on the PDC, one of his spokesmen revealed that 'napalm will, of course, be indispensable' in order to 'exterminate' the guerrillas in a war 'without limitations'.[100] The wealth, energy and unambiguously extremist nature of ARENA's campaign made the party the champion of the right and the clear favourite of many in the armed forces. The landed bourgeoisie quite patently no longer had confidence in the corrupt formations of the old dictatorship; it had thrown its weight behind a party of a thoroughly fascist character. The constituent assembly looked set to become D'Aubuisson's Reichstag; his constituency reflected very faithfully the historical properties of fascism in financial and political backing from large capitalists and the support of a desperate and confused mass of petty bourgeois and peasants.

At the end of the last week of campaigning Ambassador Hinton bowed to the obvious in acknowledging that although D'Aubuissón had been 'amongst the rough stuff', he would get Washington's backing if he won.[101] Although it seemed improbable that ARENA would receive a vote that would enable it to do anything more than hold the balance of power, the US had to weigh the embarrassment of supporting a figure such as D'Aubuissón against the inevitable disaster if it repudiated one of the leaders thrown up by an election that stood right at the fulcrum of its Central American policy; it had no other choice. The US position had undergone the quiet metamorphosis from backing Duarte, to backing the elections in themselves, to offering backing to anybody who might win. Duarte still remained their favourite but his monopoly on favours now had to be withdrawn.

The FMLN's response to the elections did not get fully underway until the day before the poll. While this may have made sense in terms of concentrating forces and reserving the maximum impact for the last moment, it was not successful nor did it reach the expected proportions. There were a number of fierce battles, particularly in Morazán, Usulután, San Vicente and the outskirts of the capital but although the fighting continued through the day of the poll, this impeded rather than halted the election except in Usulután, which was cut off amidst unprecedentedly fierce fighting. Outside the areas under FMLN control voting was high; it was clear that implementing the boycott was extraordinarily difficult in tactical terms. While the boycott was a perfectly logical political position to take, in itself it was an inadequate answer for the many thousands of voters who lived outside the protection of the guerrillas and were therefore highly vulnerable if they did not present themselves at the booths. Moreover, military interruption at the place of voting proved highly problematic: these could not be attacked as military targets because of the large congregation of civilians there. In the end retribution from the FMLN was feared less than that from the military since the turnout was high enough for it immediately to be accounted by Haig as a categorical defeat for the guerrillas. It may be that the FMLN would have been better advised to have taken that course followed by an appreciable number of voters, calling for either a blank or spoiled vote as the best way to register repudiation of the elections.

After a number of days counting, which was held up both by disorganisation and continued fighting in many areas, it became plain that while the PDC led the field, it had not polled enough votes to secure control of the assembly or claim a decisive show of popular approval.

The possibility of the vote giving Duarte a mandate to continue as before was further and critically diminished when the five parties opposing the PDC declared that they were forming an alliance to deny it victory. The united opposition of these parties to the agrarian reform and nationalisation of the banks was the key element in this agreement, which effectively removed the Christian Democrats as the leading partners of the military. The isolation of the PDC and the substantial support given to the formations of the extreme right, especially ARENA, ensured that the 'reform' programme would be blocked if, indeed, it was ever reactivated. At the same time, it seemed increasingly improbable that the US would take the risk of enforcing its revival.

In this sense the election conformed to the logic of the absolute retrenchment of the ruling class; under the conditions of civil war it was the likes of D'Aubuissón not Duarte that held the initiative. The hardliners had secured a formal representation of their already existing influence inside the armed forces, and marginal movements in the tally of votes were not going to unseat them. The emergence of D'Aubuissón may well have attracted considerable international attention, but inside the country the effects of his politics were already very well known; there would be no fundamental change.

The fact that the tempo of the war continued to increase and that, despite its failure to stop the vote, the FMLN exercised virtual control over El Salvador's two main highways and had almost completely isolated Usulután throughout the week following the poll gave the lie to the notion that the election had either defeated the guerrillas or altered the terms of the real conflict in the country. The war carried on and would continue to do so.

CONCLUSION

> Our programme is for a democratic, revolutionary government, not for a
> Socialist government. The programme for the democratic government is
> very broad – broader than that of many of the democratic governments in
> Europe.
>
> As part of the effort to achieve dignity and national sovereignty in El
> Salvador, there is room for everybody's contribution, from large
> businessmen to small farmers and merchants – for anyone who supports
> the independent development of the country, opposes fascism and wants
> democracy. We don't believe that this broad programme has anything to do
> with Socialism or a Socialist government.
>
> Salvador Cayetano Carpio, February 1982[1]

It is no anomaly that the crisis in El Salvador should be a crisis for the
US, impinging on the very fabric of domestic political life and
progressively eroding the credibility and space for manoeuvre of the
Reagan government. While many in the FDR, and many more outside
it, say that they seek only peace, democracy and good relations with
Washington, they do not recognise, at least not explicitly, that a victory
for the FMLN would represent a defeat for the US locally, regionally
and internationally. This, as Rubén Zamora points out, would be most
unlikely to presage an entente and would indeed diminish any
possibility of establishing the pluralist democracy and mixed economy
that he desires. In this he is at one with the domino theorists of the State
Department, and both are correct.

Zamora and his reformist confrères in the FDR believe that they can
obtain these objectives through negotiation. However restricted their
options have become, the managers of US foreign policy recognise that
in the last resort US interests can only be secured by a military solution.
They differ with the Salvadorean liberal oppositionists on this point

because they understand that any substantial erosion of the dictatorship, whether by negotiations or a guerrilla victory, can by no means be guaranteed to halt at the point desired by the advocates of bourgeois democracy. Moreover, Washington's current fixation with domino theories is conducive in the context of Central America to a comprehension of the broader facets of the conflict, however base and ill-considered the fundamental tenets of such theories may be. The addition of El Salvador to Nicaragua and Cuba would have a qualitative as well as quantitative effect upon anti-imperialist mobilisation in the Americas. Although Alexander Haig is incapable of organising his tongue to express this in English, he clearly understands that such an outcome would compound the already serious damage inflicted upon US power and prestige in South Asia, Iran and Southern Africa. It is for this reason that Soviet complicity must be proved; the Soviet bloc is perceived as the most immediate beneficiary on a world scale of any setback to Washington. Hitherto the response to this line has concentrated on the fact that there is a staggering paucity of evidence for such 'intervention' and that the obsession with it has led the US seriously to misunderstand the indigenous roots of the conflict, thereby debilitating its capacity to resolve it. Nobody could argue with this, but such a response ignores the very real and increasingly critical international dimensions of the conflict, which is now irretrievably situated in the new Cold War.

Sandino once said that his aim was to expel the US marines from Nicaragua, not to defeat the US; he was scarcely going to lead his band of illiterate *guerrilleros* on an offensive up the Potomac. Today, the accomplished diplomats of the FDR say much the same thing; their aims are circumscribed both politically and geographically. In this they are battling against history. The gains of the FMLN build on those already made by the FSLN and the Cuban guerrillas of the Sierra Maestra to force the Reagan government – the most unashamedly pugnacious and reactionary US administration for decades – into an apparently insoluble domestic dilemma that leaves it stranded between 'losing Central America to the communists' and overriding the majority opinion for withdrawal and isolation. A guerrilla attack on Perquín or Suchitoto registers in a different form but ultimately with little less decision in St Louis or New Orleans. Needless to say, its impact in Tegucigalpa or the insurgent Guatemalan provinces of Huehuetenango and Quiché is even more pronounced. The Salvadorean revolution is inescapably part of an international offensive against the US empire, although this offensive is taking place in spite of rather than because of the actions of the USSR.

It is as much for this reason as for its insistent and highly public incompetence that the Reagan government has been driven into a corner. This also extends in part to the Thatcher government – Washington's only firm European ally on the Salvadorean question – which has perceived an issue that is too distant from itself and yet too critical to the US to compel it to suggest the adoption of a Zimbabwe-style resolution and the ditching of Duarte as it did Muzorewa. This, it is true, was abnormally dexterous when compared with the rest of its policies and may in any case be irrelevant in El Salvador but it is an option that has been significantly withheld for some considerable time in the face of growing pressure in both the US and Europe.

The US lobby for non-intervention and negotiations appears more flexible and perspicacious than the sabre-rattling to which it is a response. It offers Washington a defensible retreat and space for manoeuvre; for Salvadoreans its great promise is a halt to the carnage. Yet its success is entirely predicated upon the understanding that negotiations could yield a workable solution in El Salvador and safeguard US interests. As has been argued, nothing in the last two years suggests that this is realistic either in terms of the balance of power in El Salvador or for the defence of US hegemony in the Americas.

None the less, the US opposition has continued to acquire support and authority at least partly because it has much in common with the proposals made by European social democracy, which has consistently registered its disagreement with a military solution. The strength with which this dissenting position has been sustained has contributed to a discernible fissure in the metropolitan bloc, comparable perhaps only with Suez in the post-war era. Here again, there are perceptible domestic factors. The depth of the economic crisis and unexpectedly strong impact of the anti-war movement in Europe have compelled the social democratic parties to look to their left flank by scrambling to increase the distance between themselves and Washington. Even the SPD has gone some way down this road in an effort to close the dangerously wide gap with the increasingly popular, radical and anti-American current that is growing in Germany and beginning to gnaw at the fringes of the parliamentary party. In Britain, Dennis Healey, noted more for his connections with the IMF than his espousal of the cause of anti-imperialism, was moved to pen an attack on the elections and Reagan's policy which, while far from radical, was unequivocal in its rejection of a military solution. The stronger profile of the Mitterand government is less anomalous and conforms to long-standing differences with the US but nevertheless coheres with the general pattern.

That such political space should be available to social democracy is not only explained by rising domestic pressures; it is also facilitated by the simple fact that El Salvador is very distant and no European power possesses important interests there, making it optimum terrain on which to express discontent with the US. It would be inconceivable for the SPD to take a similar stand in Brazil, where German capital has extensive interests, or that the roseate influence of Debray should compel Mitterand to realise in Mali or Upper Volta, neo-colonial states under French tutelage, the programme he advances for El Salvador. This factor is further emphasised by the appearance of tensions inside the social democratic movement itself at the beginning of 1982, when the Latin American parties began to voice their objections to the enthusiasm of the Europeans for guerrilla-based national liberation movements and made a much harsher assessment of the FSLN, accusing it of deliberately holding back from the introduction of a pluralist system. Only the Mexican PRI, for which a full reversal of the Nicaraguan revolution would result in serious damage to the democratic revolutionary ideology that has sustained it for four decades, endorsed the European strategy with conviction.

This being said, the social democratic project of Central America is far from being simple international horse-trading. In arguing for negotiation, the Second International is following a distinct strategy for the defeat of revolutionary socialism in El Salvador. This is by no means immediately obvious if only because social democracy recognises and gives support to the FDR–FMLN and clearly seeks to avoid its military defeat. However, this support is a two-edged sword. While it gives the opposition diplomatic and political assistance, which the left obviously accepts in confronting its immediate and most dangerous enemy, social democracy is simultaneously attempting to use the leverage this gives it to oblige the opposition to halt its programme and mobilisation at the bourgeois democratic stage and hold back any drive to the full expropriation of capital and establishment of a workers' and peasants' government. We have already seen that such a course is entirely possible within the context of the FDR's Programmatic Platform even if it may prove difficult to achieve in practice.

The national liberation movement in El Salvador is similar to all other post-war anti-imperialist mobilisations in that it incubates two revolutions: the bourgeois democratic and the socialist. In a recent highly suggestive book Michael Löwy has concentrated on exploring the relationship between these, identifying the essence of the bourgeois democratic revolution in three major points: (a) a solution to the agrarian problem through the abolition of pre-capitalist modes of exploitation; (b) national liberation in 'unification of the nation and its economic emancipation from foreign domination'; and (c) democracy 'in a secular republic based on democratic freedoms'.[2] All the opposition is agreed on these issues, which are the cornerstone of the Programmatic Platform. Indeed, the level of agreement between the left and the bourgeois opposition is in many respects greater than that which might be expected to obtain in the states of the capitalist metropolis precisely because of the importance of democratic demands in countries deprived of all vestige of democratic rights from the day they became politically independent. There is, then, no disagreement over the priority of these objectives. However, substantial differences do exist over their adequacy in themselves to develop El Salvador or, indeed, be sustained at all within the capitalist mode of production.

As Löwy demonstrates, even in the states of the capitalist metropolis the ideals of bourgeois democracy obtain in less than perfect manner. and in some countries (Japan, West Germany, Italy) their realisation has only been approximated to in the recent period and as the result of defeat in a world war. Equally, only a completely unreconstructed Stalinist would maintain that these aims have been fully met in those countries where capitalism has been overthrown and a full break made with the metropolis. However, in all such cases there has been a qualitatively greater advance in that direction than in those neo-colonial states (Mexico, Egypt, Algeria, India, Syria, Iraq, Iran and others) where political movements adhering to the fundamental aims of national liberation have been stopped in their tracks at the bourgeois democratic 'stage' and their gains progressively rolled back in each of the three basic areas. This, of course, does not take account of those cases – Chile, Argentina, Bolivia, Indonesia, Guatemala, Turkey – where such advances, however timid and tenuous they may have been, have been brutally and decisively reversed by counter-revolution, a prospect that is far from remote in contemporary Central America. In either case the one irrefutable lesson of history is that there do not exist in backward capitalist states the social conditions for the full realisation of a bourgeois democratic programme. This can only be sustained in a partial and uneven manner in the metropolis precisely by exploitation of the periphery in such a manner that the basis for such advances is absent and any effort to realise them consistently isolated, boycotted and, in the last instance, reversed by violence.

Yet, neither the reformist wing of the FDR nor its social democratic patrons advocate a purely parliamentary model; their aim is one of a strong reforming state capitalism that will take over the bulk of the economic infrastructure and mediate competition between capitals in an economically and socially more rational manner than has hitherto obtained. This project is far from alien to the European powers, which have appreciable experience of patronising such regimes. In many cases these represent very reliable partners for foreign capital and efficient buffers against popular mobilisation, whether it be by state-controlled populist ideology derived from the struggle for political liberation and enforced by a centralised bureaucratic regime of the petty bourgeoisie (Algeria/Zimbabwe) or a more directly coercive variant of this (Syria/Egypt). Obviously the precise characteristics of these regimes vary from case to case but the crucial factor in their development is the progressive limitation of the political independence of the working class, expressed in workers' and peasants' councils, and the imposition of the political leadership of the bourgeois or, more frequently, petty bourgeois parties.

Under the probable conditions following a guerrilla military victory in El Salvador such a strategy will be highly precarious. The weakness of the liberal reformist parties, the high level of popular mobilisation, the extremes of the war, and the strength of the radical parties on the left must place its future in serious doubt. On the other hand, it possesses certain ready-made advantages. It is clearly differentiated from Washington's blueprint for the total eradication of the left and reliance upon the existing repressive apparatus which makes a mockery of the proposed 'reforms'. Additionally, the bourgeois opposition derives considerable popularity from its alliance with the left inside the FDR and will continue to be viewed by the Salvadorean masses as their own and in consonance with their interests until it is obliged to enter into open conflict with the forces that comprise the CRM and FMLN. This is a recurrent feature of popular fronts, where workers' parties enter into alliance with liberal bourgeois parties on the basis of the minimum programme and an abdication of the right to argue and fight for a full revolutionary programme.

Equally, it can by no means be supposed that the left itself is either clear about this position or unambiguously set against it. The left's lack of a coherent and independent direction is evident in the steps it has already taken towards a common acceptance of a finite democratic stage in the Salvadorean revolution although it is far from clear, and is unlikely to be otherwise until after a victory, what this stage constitutes and for how long it will last in the eyes of forces such as the FPL and BPR. While it would be overly innocent to imagine that Salvador Cayetano's statement at the beginning of this chapter was not partly phrased to woo the press of the metropolis to which it was directed, it would be equally ingenuous to suppose that it does not contain a certain authenticity and is purely and simply a deceit.

It is clear that the USSR and Cuba would like Cayetano and the forces of the left to establish a lasting *rapprochement* with the reformist opposition; nothing in their activities or statements over the last two years suggests otherwise. The Soviet Union has steadfastly desisted from lending the FMLN any but the most minimal assistance while Cuban aid has been limited to little more than advice and verbal support, just as in the case of Nicaragua before July 1979. There is little likelihood of a break to the left being compelled by these forces, which believe that a simple emulation of Nicaragua would be an optimum resolution, placing pressure on the US but not jeopardising the possibilities for international detente in itself.

Inside the Salvadorean left the example of Nicaragua has had a substantial influence although it would appear to have greater currency in external affairs than internally, if only because in El Salvador the liberal opposition is bourgeois in its ideology and programme rather than its social base; there are no Salvadorean counterparts to Robelo and Chamorro, who have in any case long since made their departure from the Nicaraguan junta. Furthermore, the CRM and FMLN have had time to consider the FSLN's failure to placate Washington by breaking popular radicalisation and reiterating guarantees to domestic entrepreneurs, a process that would be considerably harder to effect in El Salvador where both the left and the masses have been radicalised to a higher degree for historical as well as conjunctural reasons.

This conjecture might tend to suggest that from a socialist perspective the Salvadorean revolution can only be safeguarded by a return to the pre-April 1980 period and the expulsion of the non-socialist parties from the FDR. Under the circumstances of the present war this would in all probability be disastrous. The absence of a national bourgeoisie and the insufficiency of a bourgeois democratic programme in no sense erase the possibilities of success for an anti-imperialist united front. El Salvador is an oppressed nation as a whole and the task of national liberation is manifestly first on the agenda. Moreover, as is evident from the formation of the FDR, substantial sectors of the professional middle classes and petty bourgeoisie, while they derive their being from the exploitation of the masses, are themselves exploited by imperialism to a significantly higher degree than occurs in comparable layers in the metropolis and will at times enter into fierce conflict with it. Their support is vital to the national liberation movement, as has been shown by the important role played by the students and middle-class Christian radicals. If substantial numbers of these sectors are not won to a socialist programme the opportunities for revolutionary change will be gravely reduced.

Finally, it is inconceivable that the Salvadorean revolution might develop into a genuinely radical, anti-capitalist movement without the full support of the peasants and rural workers, who greatly outnumber the industrial proletariat and have played a major part in popular mobilisation, refuting the notion that they possess the political characteristics of a sack of potatoes or any more modern sociological variant thereof. The battle for the allegiance of the peasantry and rural proletariat is not only central to the outcome of the civil war but also highly likely to be the decisive factor in the political resolution of victory by the FDR–FMLN. Although the rural labour force was been significantly radicalised by the process of dispossession of lands, proletarianisation and unemployment over the last decades, and will not be satisfied with any agrarian reform that does not completely overhaul relations of production in the *campo*, it remains highly vulnerable to the current high levels of attrition and may become physically exhausted and politically atomised. Under such conditions it will be very hard for the left to consolidate and deepen the worker–peasant alliance around a socialist programme and correspondingly easier for a populist petty bourgeois regime to capture the leadership of the rural masses.

Discussion of these factors may appear precipitate but, in fact, all are critical to the outcome of the present war. The notion that there exist two homogeneous forces engaged in a purely military encounter is thoroughly erroneous, as demonstrated by the conflicts within the ruling bloc and the temporarily submerged but identifiable divisions within the opposition. Nicaragua has provided a lucid illustration of this, remaining in political limbo three years after the overthrow of Somoza. The extreme vulnerability of the Nicaraguan revolution both to full counter-revolution and to piecemeal ossification of the gains already made also highlights the limitations of national liberation in Central America: while it is manifestly contagious in terms of subverting the existing form of domination, it is only a partial and insufficient step to the liberation of the region as a whole and the establishment of a planned Central American economy. While Washington has insisted on Nicaraguan 'intervention' in El Salvador, Managua's role in the Salvadorean conflict has been markedly less than that expected even by many of the FSLN's most fervent supporters. In the cause of defending its own revolution, the FSLN has been at pains to meet US accusations in their own terms, but without a popular victory in El Salvador the Nicaraguan and Cuban revolutions will themselves be significantly weakened and the growing insurgency in Guatemala, which promises to determine the balance of powers in the region as a whole, gravely prejudiced. This is most obviously the case in immediate military and political terms but it is no less true for the longer-term economic survival of these extraordinarily small and impoverished states which cannot develop on their individual resources beyond very tight limits. Central America vies perhaps only with West Africa for the rank irrationality of its current political divisions, which correspond to the administrative and ecclesiastical boundaries of the Spanish empire; the supercession of the economic backwardness and political oppression inherited from those days can only be viably construed in terms of the federal united states of Central America.

Such a conclusion might be passed off as a pure flight of fancy were it not for the fact that the struggle in El Salvador has already made a political earthquake of Central America and sorely wounded the US. At the time of writing the overbearing task is the defeat of a sordid cabal of butcherous colonels and bankrupt politicians, but the intensity of this battle has altered the field on which it is being fought and increased the stakes immeasurably. So many valiant people have not died in order that their tiny country might be cordoned off, besieged and maintained for perpetuity in the rubble of poverty it has historically always been. For Washington this is the only real option. For the people of El Salvador it continues to be the object of a terrifying daily struggle which they cannot afford to lose.

NOTES

Chapter 1

1. The best survey of the early development of the republics is Edelberto Torres Rivas, 'Sintesis Histórica del Proceso Politico' in *Centroamérica Hoy* (Mexico 1976) pp. 9–118.
2. David Alejandro Luna, *Manual de Historia Económica de El Salvador* (San Salvador 1971) pp. 202-3. See also Eduardo Colindres, 'Periodos de la historia económica de El Salvador' (*Estudios Centroamericanos*, XXXI, no. 329, March 1976).
3. *'Acuerdo Legislativo'*, *Diario Oficial*, 26 Feb. 1881, quoted in David Browning, *El Salvador: Landscape and Society* (Oxford 1971) p. 205; Luna, pp. 182 ff. reprints the major laws of expropriation.
4. Quoted in Torres Rivas, p. 91.
5. United States, National Archive, 'Dispatches from US Ministers to Central America, 1824–1903', quoted in Robert B. Elam, 'Appeal to Arms: The Army and Politics in El Salvador, 1931–64' (unpublished PhD, University of New Mexico 1968) p. 8.
6. Everett Alan Wilson, 'The Crisis of National Integration in El Salvador, 1919–35' (unpublished PhD, Stanford University 1970) p. 38.
7. *La Patria*, 30 Sept. 1929, quoted in Wilson, p. 187.

Chapter 2

1. Quoted in Thomas P. Anderson, *Matanza. El Salvador's Communist Revolt of 1932* (Lincoln, Nebraska 1971) p. 17, from interviews contained in Joaquin Méndez, *Los Sucesos Comunistas en El Salvador* (San Salvador 1932).
2. Quoted in Arthur Ruhl, *The Central Americans* (New York 1927) p. 189.
3. Quoted in Wilson, pp. 225-6.
4. Ciro F. Cardoso and Héctor Pérez Brignoli, *Centro América y la Economia Occidental (1520–1930)* (San José 1977) p. 294; Ralph Lee Woodward Jnr, *Central America: A Nation Divided* (New York 1976) pp. 185-6.
5. NACLA, *Yanqui Dollar* (Berkeley 1972) pp. 3-10.
6. Chester Lloyd Jones, *Costa Rica and Civilization in the Caribbean* (Madison 1935) p. 159.
7. For various examples see Scott Nearing and Joseph Freeman, *Dollar*

Diplomacy. A Study in American Imperialism (New York 1925, reprinted 1966). A full account of US relations with Central America is given by ex-diplomat Dana Munro, *Intervention and Dollar Diplomacy in the Caribbean 1900-1921* (Princeton 1964)

8.   Confidential Memorandum, Robert Olds, 2 January, National Archive, RG 59, 817.00/4350, quoted in Richard Millett, *Guardians of the Dynasty. A History of the US-created Guardia Nacional de Nicaragua and the Somoza Family* (Maryknoll 1977) p. 52.

9.   Report to Secretary of State Kellogg, quoted in Millett, p. 88.

10.   Quoted in ibid., p. 134.

11.   For Costa Rica see Samuel Stone, *Los Cafetaleros* (San José 1971) and John Patrick Bell, *Crisis in Costa Rica: the Revolution of 1948* (Austin 1971)

12.   John Gunther, *Inside Latin America* (London 1940) p. 102.

13.   Roque Dalton, *Miguel Mármol* (San José 1972).

14.   Mario Salazar Valiente, 'Esbozo histórico de la dominación en El Salvador: 1920-1974' (*Avances de Investigación*, Universidad Nacional Autónoma de México 1976) p. 5; Anderson, p. 12.

15.   *La Patria*, 3 July 1930, quoted in Wilson, p. 187.

16.   *La Patria,* 5 Nov. 1930, quoted in ibid., p. 214.

17.   Elam, pp. 20-6.

18.   Quoted in Anderson, p. 26.

19.   Cited in Mauricio de la Selva, 'El Salvador: Tres Decadas de Lucha' (*Cuadernos Americanos*, no. 21, Jan.–Feb. 1962) p. 202. The standard biography of Marti is Jorge Arias Gómez, *Farabundo Martí* (San José 1972).

20.   For discussion around this point see David Alejandro Luna, 'Un Heroico y Trágico Suceso de Nuestra Historia' in *El Proceso Político Centroamericano* (San Salvador 1964) pp. 49 ff.; Dalton, pp. 244; 248; 268.

21.   Dalton, p. 248.

22.   Ibid., pp. 274-5.

23.   The fullest description of the revolt is contained in Anderson, pp. 98-123.

24.   The figures are discussed by Anderson, pp. 135; 145.

25.   Cited in ibid., p. 148.

26.   Quoted in Wilson, p. 262.

27.   *Prensa Gráfica,* 27 Jan. 1932, quoted in Elam, p. 42.

28.   Anderson, p. 136.

29.   Jorge Schlesinger, *Revolución Comunista* (Guatemala 1946) p. 198.

30.   Quoted in Wilson, p. 263.

31.   Alastair White, *El Salvador* (London 1973) pp. 113-14; Kenneth J. Grieb, 'The United States and the Rise of General Maximiliano Hernández Martínez (*Journal of Latin American Studies,* vol. 3, no. 2, 1979) p. 163.

32.   *Communist*, March 1932, quoted in Anderson, p. 146.

33.   See, for example, A. Gualán, 'Years of Valiant Struggle: 35 Years of the

Communist Party of El Salvador' (*World Marxist Review*, vol. 8, no. 6, June 1965) p. 46. For a concise critique of the role of the PCS in 1932 see Benedicto Juárez, 'Weaknesses of the Revolutionary Movement of 1932' in Tricontinental Society, *Revolutionary Strategy in El Salvador* (London 1981) pp. 29-32.

Chapter 3

1. Quoted in John Martz, *Central America: The Crisis and the Challenge* (Chapel Hill 1959) p. 94.
2. Paul P. Kennedy, *The Middle Beat. A Correspondent's View of Mexico, Guatemala and El Salvador* (New York 1971) p. 177.
3. The fullest survey of the regime to date is David Alejandro Luna, 'Análisis de una Dictadura Fascista Latinoamericana. Maximiliano Hernández Martinez, 1931 – 1944' (*La Universidad*, San Salvador, año 94, no. 5, Sept.–Oct. 1969).
4. Quoted in *Time*, 15 May 1944.
5. Quoted in Woodward, p. 229.
6. NACLA, *Guatemala* (Berkeley 1974) p. 47.
7. Quoted in Frank Parkinson, *Latin America, the Cold War, and the World Powers, 1945–1973* (Beverly Hills 1974) p. 40.
8. Adolf A. Berle, *Navigating the Rapids* (New York 1973) pp. 617-18.
9. Quoted in NACLA, *Guatemala*, p. 68.
10. *Time*, 26 July 1954.
11. Stephen Webre, *José Napoleón Duarte and the Christian Democratic Party in Salvadorean Politics, 1960–1972* (Baton Rouge 1979) pp. 24-5.
12. Martz, p. 100.
13. *Diario de Hoy*, 22 Sept. 1960, quoted in Webre, p. 29.
14. *Newsweek*, 7 Nov. 1960, quoted in ibid., p. 31.
15. Kennedy, p. 179.

Chapter 4

1. Quoted in Parkinson, p. 69.
2. Quoted in Jerome Levinson and Juan de Onis, *The Alliance that Lost its Way* (Chicago 1970) p. 334.
3. Pablo González Casanova, *Imperialismo y Liberación en América Latina* (Mexico 1978) p. 38.
4. Webre, p. 37.
5. *Diario de Hoy*, 20 June 1961, quoted in ibid., p. 39.
6. Quoted in ibid., p. 39.
7. Quoted in Kennedy, p. 185.
8. Ibid., pp.190-1.
9. G.E. Karush, 'Plantations, Population, and Poverty: The Roots of the

Demographic Crisis in El Salvador' (*Studies in Comparative International Development*, vol. 13, no. 3, 1978) pp. 67 ff.

10.   Rafael Menjívar, *Crisis del Desarrollismo: Caso El Salvador* (San José 1977) p. 30; Oscar Bravo, 'Modernización, Industrialización y Política en América Central: El Salvador, Guatemala y Honduras' (Occasional Paper, Institute of Latin American Studies, Stockholm, August 1980) p. 36.

11.   The source for Tables 1 and 2 is T.J. Downing, 'Agricultural Modernization in El Salvador, Central America' (Working Paper 32, Centre for Latin American Studies, University of Cambridge 1978). The original sources are: Conaplan, *Plan de Desarrollo Económico y Social 1968–72* (San Salvador 1972); Ministerio de Planificación, *Indicadores Económicos y Sociales* (San Salvador 1975); Banco Central, *Informe* (San Salvador 1977).

12.   Gert Rosendthal, 'El Papel de la Inversión Extranjera Directa en el Proceso de Integración', in *Centroamérica Hoy*, p. 125.

13.   Bravo, p. 53.

14.   Jacobo Waiselfisz, 'El Comercio Exterior, el Mercado Común y la Industrialización en Relación al Conflicto' in *Contribución al Estudio del Conflicto Hondureño-Salvadoreño* (San Salvador 1969) pp. 22; 73, quoted in White, p. 228.

15.   White, p. 228; Menjívar, *Crisis*, p. 78.

16.   Susanne Jonas Bodenheimer, 'El Mercomún y la Ayuda Norteamericana' in *La Inversión Extranjera en Centroamérica* (San José 1975) p. 99.

17.   Ibid., p. 98.

18.   Downing, Table 6, p. 35.

19.   Menjívar, *Crisis*, p. 34.

20.   Ibid., p. 30.

21.   Downing, pp. 7; 35.

22.   Mauricio Domenech *et al.*, 'The Basis of Wealth and Reaction in El Salvador' (mimeo, San Salvador 1976).

23.   Downing, p.7.

24.   International Labour Office (ILO), *Year Book of Labour Statistics* (Geneva 1980).

25.   ILO, ibid. The ILO figures are in general less reliable than the sources used by Downing, who gives no statistics for the urban labour force. Harald Jung uses the ILO figures extensively in his cogent essay, 'Class Struggles in El Salvador' (*New Left Review*, no. 122, July–Aug. 1980, pp. 3-26), which leads him to underestimate developments in the industrial labour force.

26.   CEPAL, *Estudio Económico de América Latina* (Santiago, various years).

27.   *El Salvador: A Review of the Commercial Conditions* (HMSO, London 1948) p. 4; *Statistical Abstract of Latin America*, vol. XX, ed. James W. Wilkie and

Peter Reich (Los Angeles 1980) p. 69.

28. Melvin Burke, 'The Proletarianization of Agricultural Labour in Latin America: The Case of El Salvador' (mimeo 1976), quoted in Jung, p. 9.

29. See, for example, Alastair White, 'Squatter Settlements, Politics and Class Conflict' (Occasional Paper 17, Institute of Latin American Studies, University of Glasgow, 1975).

30. J. Sánchez, 'Social Developments in El Salvador and the Policy of the Communist Party' (*World Marxist Review*, vol. 8, no. 8, Aug. 1965) pp. 9-10.

31. For brief surveys, see Latin America Bureau, *Unity is Strength. Trade Unions in Latin America – A Case for Solidarity* (London 1980) pp. 94-7; CIDAMO, *El Movimiento Obrero en El Salvador* (Mexico 1979).

32. Menjívar, *Crisis*, p. 18.

33. Ibid., p. 22.

34. Karush, pp. 67 ff.

35. Bravo, p. 20.

36. Downing, p. 41.

37. Santiago Ruíz, 'La Modernización Agrícola en El Salvador' (*Estudios Centroamericanos*, XXXI, no. 330, April 1976) p. 154.

38. Roger Burbach and Patricia Flynn, *Agribusiness in the Americas* (New York 1980) p. 99.

39. *Censos Nacionales de 1971, Censo Agropecuario* (San Salvador 1971) p. 22; Naciones Unidas, *La Transformación del Campo y la Situación Económica y Social de las Familias Rurales en El Salvador* (New York 1976) tables 12 and 18; Peter Dorner and R. Quiros, 'Institutional Dualism in Central America's Agricultural Development' (*Journal of Latin American Studies*, vol. 6, 1973).

40. Burbach and Flynn, p. 147.

41. Downing, p. 16. Official figures unambiguously confirm the fall in real rural wages despite the introduction of minimum wage rates, Ministerio de Planificación, *Diagnóstico Global y Sectorial del Cuarto Quinquenal de Desarrollo Económico y Social de El Salvador* (San Salvador 1977). For a summary of these findings, see *El Salvador under General Romero* (London 1979).

42. Menjívar, *Crisis*, p. 73.

43. Mario Menéndez Rodríguez, *El Salvador: Una Auténtica Guerra Civil* (San José 1980) p. 14.

44. Details of the 1976 agrarian reform are given in Downing, p. 19; Webre, pp. 122; 144; 157; Bravo, pp. 27-8; Rubén Zamora, Guillermo Ungo, Luis de Sebastián in *Estudios Centroamericanos*, XXXI, no. 335, Sept. 1976; Ruíz; Latin America Bureau, *Violence and Fraud in El Salvador* (London 1978) p. 6.

45. Menjívar, *Crisis*, p. 76.

46. Conaplan, *Indicadores* (San Salvador, Jan.–March 1971).

47.   *Statistical Abstract 1980*, p. 144.
48.   Roberto Badia. 'Consideraciones Básicas para una Politica de Población en El Salvador. Aspectos de Salud' (*Estudios Centroamericanos*, XXXI, no. 329, March 1976) p. 107.
49.   *Statistical Abstract 1980*, p. 87; Audrey Bronstein, *The Triple Struggle. Latin American Peasant Womer* (London 1982) p. 190.
50.   Quoted in C. Alegria and D.J. Flakoll, *La Encrucijada Salvadoreña* (Barcelona 1980) p. 18.
51.   *Statistical Abstract 1980,* p. 104.
52.   Badia, p. 110.
53.   Bravo, p. 127.
54.   White, p. 233.
55.   *Statistical Abstract 1980*, p. 80.
56.   *El Mundo*, 15 Dec. 1970, quoted in White. p. 213.

Chapter 5

1.   *Diario de Hoy*, 16 April 1962, quoted in Webre, p. 47.
2.   Quoted in Webre, p. 143.
3.   Quoted in John Saxe-Fernandez, 'The Central American Defence Council and Pax Americana' in Irving Louis Horowitz, Josué de Castro and John Gerassi (eds), *Latin American Radicalism* (New York 1969) p. 82. The best survey of US–Latin American military relations to the mid-1960s is Willard F. Barber and C. Neale Ronning, *Internal Security and Military Power* (Columbus 1966).
4.   US Department of Defence, Tables (Washington 1975), quoted in NACLA, *The Pentagon's Proteges* (New York 1976) p. 28.
5.   US Department of Defense, *Foreign Military Sales and Military Assistance Facts* (Washington 1979), quoted in Cynthia Arson, 'Background Information on the Security Forces in El Salvador and US Military Assistance' (Institute for Policy Studies, Washington, March 1980) p. 12.
6.   US Department of Defense, *Congressional Presentation Document: Security Assistance Fiscal Year 1978* (Washington 1977) p. 323, quoted in Arnson, p. 7.
7.   McNamara to Senate Foreign Relations Committee, 20 April 1966, cited in Saxe-Fernandez, p. 94.
8.   On CONDECA see Saxe-Fernandez; NACLA, *Guatemala*, pp. 204-7.
9.   Roque Dalton Garcia, 'Lo que el pueblo debe saber sobre ORDEN' (*Polémica Internacional,* segunda epoca, no. 1, San Salvador, Feb. 1980).
10.   Webre, pp. 58-64.
11.   *Diario de Hoy*, 9 June 1969, quoted in Webre, p. 57.
12.   Jorge Shafik Handal, 'El Salvador: A Precarious Balance' (*World Marxist Review,* vol. 6, no. 6, June 1973) p. 15.

13. White, pp. 184-5.
14. Bodenheimer, p. 111; Vincent Cable, 'The "Football War" and the Central American Common Market' (*International Affairs*, vol. XLV, 1969) pp. 658-71.
15. Shafik Handal, p. 16.
16. Quoted in Facts on File, *Latin America 1972* (New York 1973) p. 160.

Chapter 6

1. Mendéndez, pp. 150-1.
2. *El PCS celebró su Séptimo Congreso* (San Salvador 1979) p. 3.
3. Partido Comunista de El Salvador, *Fundamentos y Perspectivas* (San Salvador 1979) p. 21.
4. Regis Debray, *Revolution in the Revolution* (London 1967); *Strategy for Revolution* (London 1973). For his later work, which evidences elements of self-criticism, see *La Critique des Armes*, 2 vols (Paris 1974).
5. For the self-criticism of the United Secretariat of the Fourth International, see Joseph Hansen (ed), *The Leninist Strategy of Party Building* (New York 1979), which contains the resolutions of the 1969 and 1974 world congresses. For a critique by that current of orthodox Trotskyism that consistently rejected *foquismo*, see Guillermo Lora, *Foquismo y Revolución* (La Paz 1971). The Maoist position is given in Antoine Petit, *Castro, Debray contre le Marxisme-Leninisme* (Paris 1968). The 'traditional' critique of *foquismo* is best represented by the muddled but interesting collection edited by Leo Huberman and Paul Sweezy, *Regis Debray and the Latin American Revolution* (New York 1968).
6. For a survey of these movements, Richard Gott, *Rural Guerrillas in Latin America* (London 1973). The best insight into their character and problems is gained by reading the diaries of participants, for example, Daniel James (ed), *The Complete Bolivian Diaries of Che Guevara and Other Captured Documents* (London 1968) and Ricardo Ramírez, *Lettres du Front Guatemalteque* (Paris 1970). For Nicaragua, see George Black, *The Triumph of the People. The Sandinista Revolution in Nicaragua* (London 1982) pp. 75-86.
7. FPL, 'Nine Years of Prolonged People's War' in Tricontinental Society, *El Salvador: The Development of the People's Struggle* (London 1980) p. 9.
8. 'Elements of the Strategy of the "Farabundo Marti" Popular Liberation Forces (FPL)' in Tricontinental Society, *Revolutionary Strategy in El Salvador* (London 1981) p. 12.
9. *Development of the People's Struggle*, p. 5.
10. Menéndez, p. 42.
11. *Revolutionary Strategy*, pp. 17-18.
12. Ibid., p. 16.
13. Ibid., p. 21.

14. Resistencia Nacional, *Por la Causa Proletaria* (San José 1977) pp. 6-9.
15. Ibid., p. 13.
16. Ibid., pp. 18-22.
17. Inforpress, no. 230, 17 Feb. 1977.
18. Ibid., no. 235, 23 March 1977.
19. Menéndez, pp. 125; 127.
20. Parti de la Revolution Salvadorienne, *El Salvador: Une Perspective Revolutionaire* (Algiers 1977).
21. Lateinamerika Nachrichten, *El Salvador. Ein Land im Kampf um seine Befreiung* (Berlin 1980) p. 158.
22. Menéndez, p. 126.
23. *Pueblo Internacional*, no. 7, June 1980.
24. See *Polémica Internacional*, no. 3, June 1980.
24. *Por la Causa Proletaria*, p. 29.
26. Ibid., p. 71.
27. Ibid., p. 34.
28. Ibid., p. 55.
29. Ibid., pp. 38; 54; 63; 89.
30. Ibid., pp. 29; 32.
31. Menéndez, p. 182.
32. Carolyn Forché and Philip Wheaton, *History and Motivations of US Involvement in the Control of the Peasant Movement in El Salvador. The Role of AIFLD in the Agrarian Reform Process, 1970-80* (New York 1980).
33. *Pueblo Internacional*, no. 3, July 1979, pp. 1-2; ibid., no. 9, March 1980, pp. 20-1.
34. Ibid., no. 3, pp. 3-4.
35. Ibid., p. 2.
36. Webre, pp. 185; 189; 190; *Violence and Fraud*, p. 12.
37. *Combate Popular*, no. 3, July 1977, p. 5.
38. Ibid.
39. BPR, 'The People's Alternative' in *Development of the People's Struggle*, p. 15.
40. FECCAS–UTC, 'Historical Perspective of the Revolutionary Peasant Movement in El Salvador' in *Revolutionary Strategy*, p. 37; *Development of the People's Struggle*, pp. 17-18.
41. *El Salvador. Ein Land im Kampf*, pp. 158-61.

Chapter 7

1. This is, of course, nowhere admitted by the UNO leadership as it would endanger their democratic bona fides. None the less, two such different

sources as Rafael Menjívar, *El Salvador: El Eslabón más Pequeño* (San José 1980) p. 77, and the PRS, *Perspective Revolutionaire*, p. 54, share this interpretation, which seems to me to be correct.

2.   Menjívar, *Eslabón* p. 18.

3.   Inforpress, no. 220, 2 Dec. 1976; ibid., no. 226, 20 Jan. 1977.

4.   Ibid., no. 231, 24 Feb. 1977.

5.   Details of the 1977 poll may be found in *Violence and Fraud*, p. 29; *Latin American Political Report* (henceforth referred to as LAPR), XI, no. 7, 18 Feb. 1977; ibid., no. 8, 25 Feb. 1977; Lee Calvo, 'El Salvador Elections of an Elite' (mimeo, Washington 1978); Webre, p. 197; *Facts on File 1977*, p. 139.

6.   *Facts on File 1977*, p. 139.

7.   Ibid.; *Violence and Fraud*, p. 30; LAPR, 3 March 1977.

8.   *Facts on File 1977*, p. 139.

9.   *Por la Causa Proletaria*, p. 57.

10.   Menéndez, pp. 124; 154.

11.   Italo López Vallecillos and Victor Antonio Orellana, 'La Unidad Popular y el Surgimiento del Frente Democrático Revolucionario' (*Estudios Centroamericanos*, XXXV, March-April 1980) p. 187.

12.   Quoted in Menjívar, *Eslabón*, pp. 39-40.

13.   *El Salvador under Romero*, p. 179.

14.   Alegría and Flakoll, p. 33.

15.   LAPR, 29 July 1977.

16.   Noam Chomsky and Edward S. Herman, *The Political Economy of Human Rights*, 2 vols (Nottingham 1979); Jenny Pearce, *Under the Eagle. US Intervention in Central America and the Caribbean* (London 1981).

17.   Pearce, pp. 101-6. For an excellent survey of the economic conditions of this period, see Riccardo Parboni, *The Dollar and its Rivals* (London 1981) pp. 7-24.

18.   A position eloquently espoused by Richard Feinberg, head of political planning for Latin America and the Caribbean at the State Department from May 1979 to January 1980, interview with Gino Lofredo, *Sin Censura* (Washington, May 1980).

19.   Quoted in Menjívar, *Eslabón*, p. 14.

20.   Ibid., p. 23.

21.   *El Salvador under Romero*, p. 60.

22.   Quoted in Pearce, p. 219.

23.   *El Salvador under Romero*, p. 27.

24.   *Diario de Hoy*, 7 Jan. 1978, quoted in ibid., p. 195.

25.   *Diario Latino*, 5 Oct. 1977, quoted in ibid., p. 79.

26.   *Diario Latino*, 16 Nov. 1977, quoted in ibid., p. 91.

27.   *Diario Latino*, 24 Nov. 1977, quopted in ibid., p. 100.

28.   *Diario de Hoy*, 5 Oct. 1977, quoted in ibid., p. 74.

29.   *El Mundo*, 15 Nov. 1977, quoted in ibid., p. 102.

30.   *Diario Latino*, 15 Nov. 1977, quoted in ibid., p. 100.
31.   Ibid., pp. 40-1.
32.   The full text is given in ibid., pp. 115-23.
33.   *Guardian* (henceforth referred to as Gdn), 23 Oct. 1978.
34.   Ibid., 24 April 1979.
35.   *New York Times*, 26 February 1978.

Chapter 8

1.   Pearce, pp. 123-5.
2.   Ibid., pp. 126-7; Latin America Bureau, *Nicaragua: Dictatorship and Revolution* (London 1979) pp. 28-9.
3.   Pearce, p. 135.
4.   Quoted in ibid., p. 134.
5.   Henri Weber, *Nicaragua. The Sandinist Revolution* (London 1981) pp. 21-2; 53-4.
6.   For example, the journal of the GPP faction, *Lucha Sandinista* (1978), talked only of national liberation and anti-dictatorial struggles without elaborating on their social or class content.
7.   While the unification agreement of the FSLN mentions socialism twice it makes no consideration of social classes and concentrates entirely on the anti-dictatorial struggle, Empar Pineda (ed), *La Revolución Nicaragüense* (Madrid 1980) pp. 105-17. Weber objects to the description of the *terceristas* as social democrats (p. 55). However, his rebuttal of this characterisation by James Petras is limited to expressing surprise that social democrats should engage in revolutionary war and an insurrectional general strike. This is ingenuous in the extreme; it is the political content of such actions rather than the actions themselves that matters. As Weber himself shows, significant elements of the bourgeoisie supported strikes during this period. Does this make them Marxists? To deny that in the neo-colonial states forces with social democratic policies cannot undertake armed struggle against dictatorships is patently absurd. For Petras' overview of the Nicaraguan struggle, see his *Class, State and Power in the Third World* (London 1981) pp. 265-74.
8.   Jaime Wheelock, *Imperialismo y Dictadura* (Mexico 1975) pp. 141-76; Julio López C., Orlando Nuñez S., Carlos Fernando Chamorro Barrios and Pascual Serres, *La Caida del Somocismo y la Lucha Sandinista en Nicaragua* (San Jose 1980) pp. 79-85.
9.   Weber, p. 43.
10.   Millett, passim.
11.   For Chamorro's position, see his major work on the dictatorship, *Estirpe Sangrienta: Los Somoza* (Managua 1979).
12.   Harald Jung, 'Behind the Nicaraguan Revolution' (*New Left Review*, no.

117, Sept.-Oct. 1979) p. 82.

13. A fuller picture of the shifts of alliance and balance of forces can be obtained from Black, pp. 107-53; Weber, pp. 41-9; Jung, pp. 75-85. A detailed *sandinista* version is given in López *et al.*, which also reprints the programmes of the major parties.

14. This appreciation extends well beyond the ranks of the FSLN. It is shared by Weber, whose book is a concise and spirited depiction of the revolution and defence of *sandinismo* from a position that is not Leninist but employs Marxist terminology in its argument that the FSLN can and very likely will lead a socialist revolution. The same position is held by the United Secretariat of the Fourth International, which placed its local affiliate under the direction of the FSLN, to which it gives whole-hearted support, Pedro Camejo and Fred Murphy (eds), *The Nicaraguan Revolution* (New York 1979) pp. 7-23. For a faithful *sandinista* view that remains largely unencumbered by such concerns, see Black, whose book is neither short nor analytical but full of useful information and unlikely to be superseded as the authoritative English language narrative of the revolution.

15. *Observer*, 23 April 1979.

16. *Pueblo*, no. 3, July 1979, pp. 4-6; Menjívar, *Eslabón*, p. 54.

17. LAPR, 9 March 1979; *Latin American Economic Report*, 26 Oct. 1979.

18. Gdn, 11 May 1979.

19. Ibid., 25 Aug. 1979.

20. Menjívar, *Eslabón*, p. 59.

21. *Pueblo*, no. 5, Jan. 1980, pp. 1-2.

22. Ibid., no. 6, Feb. 1980, p. 11.

23. Quoted, in Spanish, in Tomás Guerra, *El Salvador: Octubre Sangriento* (San José 1979) pp. 9-11.

24. Quoted in ibid., p. 11.

25. Details of the programme of the *Foro* are given in López Vallecillos and Orellana, pp. 189-90.

26. Pearce, pp. 153-4; Guerra, p. 12.

27. The full document is reproduced in Menjívar, *Eslabón*, pp. 143-7.

Chapter 9

1. Nicos Poulantzas, *Fascism and Dictatorship* (London 1974) pp. 313-30.

2. Carolyn Forché, 'The Road to Reaction in El Salvador' in *The Nation*, *El Salvador: The Roots of Intervention* (Marion, Ohio 1981) pp. 7-8.

3. Ibid., p. 9.

4. Guerra, p. 18.

5. Quoted in Tommy Sue Montgomery, 'Politica Estadounidense y Proceso Revolucionario: El Caso de El Salvador' (*Estudios Centroamericanos*, XXXV, March-April 1980) p. 243.

6.   Heather Foote, 'United States Policy towards El Salvador: September 1979 to the Present' (mimeo, Washington July 1980) p. 8.

7.   *New York Times*, 29 Oct. 1979.

8.   Vallecillos and Orellana, p. 194.

9.   *El Salvador: Alianzas Políticas y Proceso Revolucionario* (Mexico 1980) pp. 26-30.

10.   Ibid., pp. 64 ff.

11.   *International Herald Tribune* (henceforth referred to as IHT), 25 October 1979.

12.   Guerra, pp. 17-18.

13.   Ibid., pp. 30-1.

14.   Ibid., pp. 52-7; IHT, 31 October 1979.

15.   Guerra, pp. 62-3.

16.   'Por qué las Ligas Populares 28 de Febrero nos retiramos del Foro', reprinted in Menjivar, *Eslabón*, pp. 157-8.

17.   *Le Monde* (henceforth referred to as LeM), 18 Oct. 1979; IHT, 18 Oct. 1979; Gdn, 22 October 1979.

18.   *Alianzas*, pp. 21-5.

19.   Ibid., pp. 46-7.

20.   Ibid., pp. 17-18.

21.   Ibid., pp. 50-2.

22.   Guerra, pp. 119-24.

23.   Ibid., p. 72; Gdn, 8 Nov. 1979.

24.   Guerra, pp. 30-1.

25.   Interview with the Centro Internacional de Información Latinoamericana (CIILA), quoted in ibid., pp. 141-2.

26.   IHT, 2 Nov. 1979; LAPR, 2 Nov. 1979; Guerra, pp. 40-1.

27.   Guerra, pp. 79-80.

28.   Ibid., p. 72; LAPR, 9 Nov. 1979.

29.   Forché, p. 8.

30.   Foote, p. 12.

31.   Forché, p.9.

32.   The full text is given in Menjivar, *Eslabón*, pp. 177-84.

33.   See ibid., pp. 195-207.

34.   Menéndez, p. 154.

35.   Francis Andrés Escobar, 'En la Linea de la Muerte' (*Estudios Centroamericanos,* XXXV, Jan.–Feb. 1980) p. 26.

36.   Ibid., p. 31; Gdn, 24 Jan. 1980.

37.   A full English translation is given in 'El Salvador – a Revolution Brews' (*NACLA*, XIV, no. 4, July-Aug. 1980) pp. 31-4.

38.   Anon., 'El Salvador en la Hora de la Decisión' (mimeo, Mexico 1980) p. 20.

39.   Forché, p. 10.

40.   ANEP, 'Posición del Sector Productivo Salvadoreño ante el Nuevo

Esquema de Gobierno', reprinted in Menjivar, *Eslabón*, pp. 219-22.

41.   LAPR, 25 Jan. 1980; ibid., 7 March 1980.

42.   'Consideraciones del General José Alberto Medrano', *La Prensa Gráfica*, 20 Feb. 1980.

43.   LAPR, 22 Feb. 1980.

44.   Ibid., 2 Jan. 1980.

45.   Ibid., 11 Jan. 1980.

46.   Montgomery, p. 246.

47.   Ibid.

48.   IHT, 25 Feb. 1980.

49.   Ibid., 26 Feb. 1980; Gdn, 26 Feb. 1980.

50.   LAPR, 18 April 1980.

51.   Congressional Record No. 99, Part II, Washington D.C., 17 June 1980, cited in Philip Wheaton, *Agrarian Reform in El Salvador: A Program of Rural Pacification* (Washington 1980) p. 17.

52.   Quoted in ibid., pp. 11-12.

53.   Cynthia Arson, 'Background Information', pp. 5-7.

54.   Quoted in Wheaton, p. 12.

55.   'Reforma Agraria: Estrategia de Radio' (confidential memorandum, San Salvador March 1980) p. 3, quoted in ibid., p. 13.

56.   Ibid.

57.   NACLA, 'A Revolution Brews', p. 17.

58.   Quoted in Wheaton, pp. 13-14.

59.   *El Salvador en la Hora de la Decisión*, p. 22.

60.   Gdn, 20 March 1980.

61.   The full text is given in Pearce, pp. 230-1.

62.   LAPR, 22 Feb. 1980.

63.   Quoted in *Revolt in El Salvador* (New York 1980) p. 21.

64.   LAPR, 17 April 1980.

65.   Quoted in Wheaton, p. 18.

66.   Ibid., p. 16.

67.   *New York Times*, 7 March 1980.

68.   The best study of the reform is Laurence R. Simon and James C. Stephens, *El Salvador: Land Reform 1980-81* (Boston 1981).

69.   Ibid., p. 22; Wheaton, p. 15.

70.   Simon and Stephens, pp. 27-31.

71.   Wheaton, p. 15.

72.   Statement before Congressional Sub-Committee on Inter-American Affairs, 11 March 1981.

73.   Simon and Stephens, pp. 55-7.

74.   Interview in *Development of the People's Struggle*, p. 30.

75.   *Pueblo*, Jan. 1980, pp. 29-30.

76.   *Newsweek*, 9 March 1981, p. 22; ibid., 15 Feb. 1982, p. 21.

Chapter 10

1. LAPR, 16 May 1980.
2. El Salvador Solidarity Campaign, *Newsletter*, May 1980.
3. *Le Monde Diplomatique*, January 1981; *Sunday Times*, 22 Feb. 1981.
4. LAPR, 6 June 1980; LeM, 10 June 1980.
5. LAPR, 27 June 1980.
6. Ibid., 20 June 1980.
7. Intercontinental Press (New York), 7 July 1980; LeM, 26 June 1980.
8. IHT, 27 June 1980.
9. *El Salvador: Un Pueblo en Lucha* (New York 1980) p. 17.
10. Gdn, 15 Aug. 1980; IHT, 15 Aug. 1980.
11. *The Guardian* (New York), 1 Oct. 1980.
12. LAPR, 29 Aug. 1980.
13. LeM, 19 Aug. 1980.
14. The fullest English-language account of the division is by Robert Armstrong, writing in *The Guardian* (New York), 24 Sept. and 1 Oct. 1980. See also LAPR, 26 Sept. 1980; Intercontinental Press, 13 Oct. 1980.
15. Francisco Quinoñez, 'Informe sobre la insubordinación de las Fuerzas Armadas de El Salvador' (mimeo, n.p., n.d.).
16. IHT, 29 Nov. 1980; *The Guardian* (New York), 10 Dec. 1980.
17. IHT, 6 Dec. 1980; *Washington Post*, 16 July 1981.
18. IHT, 6 Dec. 1980.
19. The document is dated 11 November 1980 and marked 'To: Dissent Channel. From: ESCAFT/D. Re: DM-ESCA No. 80-3.'
20. IHT, 19 March 1981.
21. In many respects the paper coheres with the alternative 'preventive' strategy suggested by Richard Feinberg, 'Central America: No Easy Answers' *(Foreign Affairs,* Summer 1981) pp. 1121-46. This is by no means to impute authorship of the 'Dissent Paper' to Feinberg, who had already left government service.
22. *Miami Herald*, 24 August 1980.
23. Gdn, 11 Dec. 1980.
24. IHT, 11 Dec. 1980.
25. Ibid.
26. Ibid., 17 Dec. 1980.
27. IHT, 20 Dec. 1980.
28. Pearce, p. 247; *El Salvador: Un Pueblo en Lucha,* p. 34; Agence Latino-Americaine D'Information (ALAI), *Bulletin* (Quebec), 30 Jan. 1981.
29. Intercontinental Press, 16 March 1981.
30. Gdn, 29 Dec. and 30 Dec. 1980.
31. IHT, 5 Jan. 1981.
32. LeM, 10 Jan. 1981.

33.   *El Salvador Libre* (Mexico), no. 8, Jan. 1981.

34.   See, for example, the analysis of Juan Ramón Medrano in ibid., no. 12, March 1981. This formulation was used very soon after the offensive, as pointed out in LAPR, 23 Jan. 1981. See also Gdn, 23 March 1981.

35.   Gdn, 15 Jan. 1981; LeM, 16 Jan. 1981.

36.   LeM, 16 Jan. 1981.

37.   LAPR, 16 Jan. 1981.

38.   IHT, 5 Jan. 1981; 17 April 1981; 7 May 1981.

39.   Ibid., 23 Feb. 1981; Gdn, 23 Feb. 1981.

40.   United States Department of State, Bureau of Public Affairs, 'Communist Interference in El Salvador, February 23 1981'.

41.   *Washington Post*, 14 March 1981.

42.   Konrad Ege, 'El Salvador: White Paper?', *Counterspy* (New York), May–July 1981.

43.   See, in addition to Ege, the excellent piece by James Petras, 'White Paper on the White Paper', *The Nation*, pp. 1-7, also reprinted in *Le Monde Diplomatique*, April 1981.

44.   *Wall Street Journal*, 8 June 1981.

45.   Gdn, 19 Feb. 1981.

46.   IHT, 6 March 1981.

47.   Gdn, 16 Feb. 1981.

48.   IHT, 26 Feb. 1981.

49.   Gdn, 3 March 1981.

50.   Quoted in LeM, 22 March 1981.

51.   Ibid.

52.   *People's Daily*, 27 Feb. 1981, quoted in LeM, 28 Feb. 1981.

53.   Gdn, 3 March 1981.

54.   Center for International Policy Studies, Aid Memo, April 1981.

55.   LeM, 27 April 1981.

56.   Pearce, p. 241.

57.   IHT, 22 April 1981.

58.   Quoted in Morton Halperin (ed.), *Report on Human Rights in El Salvador* (Washington 1982) p. 198.

59.   *La Prensa Gráfica,* 22 June 1981, quoted in ibid., p. 198.

60.   Gdn, 4 March 1981.

61.   Gdn, 6 March 1981; LAPR, 13 March 1981.

62.   IHT, 18 March 1981; 19 March 1981.

63.   Ibid., 13 May 1981.

64.   Gdn, 29 Jan. 1982; 1 Feb. 1982; 2 Feb 1982.

65.   Gdn, 6 Nov. 1981; 5 Dec. 1981.

66.   *Presencia* (La Paz), 24 Sept. 1981.

67.   Rubén Zamora, address to El Salvador Solidarity Campaign, London, 31 Oct. 1981.

68.   LeM, 27 April 1981.

69.   *The Guardian* (New York), 10 Feb. 1982.
70.   Gdn, 2 Feb. 1982.
71.   IHT, 9 Feb. 1982.
72.   Ibid., 13 Feb. 1982.
73.   Ibid., 15 Feb. 1982.
74.   LeM, 23 Feb. 1982.
75.   Gdn, 8 March 1982.
76.   Ibid., 25 Feb. 1982.
77.   *New York Times*, 9 Jan. 1982.
78.   Gdn, 1 March 1982.
79.   Ibid., 6 March 1982.
80.   IHT, 13 March 1982.
81.   Gdn, 12 March 1982.
82.   *Newsweek*, 22 March 1982.
83.   IHT, 3 Feb. 1982.
84.   *Newsweek*, 1 March 1982.
85.   *New York Times*, 21 March 1982.
86.   Gdn, 8 March 1982.
87.   Ibid., 16 March 1982.
88.   *Newsweek*, 15 Feb. 1982.
89.   Intercontinental Press, 1 March 1982.
90.   IHT, 22 Feb. 1982.
91.   Ibid., 19 Feb. 1982.
92.   Gdn, 11 March 1982.
93.   IHT, 9 March 1982.
94.   LeM, 6 Feb. 1982; *Wall Street Journal*, 8 Feb. 1982.
95.   Gdn, 29 March 1982; Martin Bell, 'Nine O'Clock News' (BBC), 28 March 1982.
96.   *Newsweek*, 29 March 1982.
97.   Letter to Peter Thomas MP, quoted by John Pilger in a letter to the *Guardian*, 9 Feb, 1982.
98.   Gdn, 24 March 1982.
99.   *Newsweek*, 22 Feb. 1982.
100.   Ibid., 29 March 1982.
101.   ITN, 'News at Ten', 27 March 1982.

Conclusion

1.   IHT, 11 Feb. 1982.
2.   Michael Löwy, *The Politics of Combined and Uneven Development* (London 1981) p. 161.

SELECT BIBLIOGRAPHY

Alegria, C. and Flakoll, D.J., *La Encrucijada Salvadoreña* (Barcelona 1980)

Anderson, Thomas P., *Matanza. El Salvador's Communist Revolt of 1932* (Lincoln, Nebraska 1971)

Anon., *El Salvador en la Hora de la Decisión* (Mexico 1980)

Arias Gómez, Jorge, *Farabundo Martí. Esbozo Biográfico* (San José 1972)

Badía, Roberto, 'Consideraciones Básicas para una Politica de Población en El Salvador. Aspectos de Salud' (*Estudios Centroamericanos,* XXXV, no. 329, March 1976)

Bravo, Oscar, 'Modernización Industrialización y Politica en América Central: El Salvador, Guatemala y Honduras' (Occasional Paper, Institute of Latin American Studies, Stockholm, August 1980)

Bloque Popular Revolucionario, *Combate Popular*, 1977–8.

———, *Boletín Internacional*, 1979–80

Browning, David, *El Salvador. Landscape and Society* (Oxford 1971)

Cable, Vincent, 'The "Football War" and the Central American Common Market' (*International Affairs*, XLV, 1969)

Calvo, Lee, 'El Salvador: Elections of an Elite' (mimeo, Washington 1978)

Cardoso, Ciro F. and Pérez Brignoli, Héctor, *Centro América y la Economia Occidental (1520-1930)* (San José 1977)

Centro América Hoy (Mexico 1976)

Colindres, Eduardo, *Fondements Economiques de la Bourgeoisie Salvadorienne dans la Periode 1950 à 1970* (Paris 1975)

———, 'Periodos de la historia económica de El Salvador' *(Estudios Centroamericanos,* XXXI, no. 329, March 1976)

Contribución al Estudio del Conflicto Hondureño Salvadoreño (San Salvador 1969)

Dalton, Roque, *Miguel Mármol* (San José 1977)

Domenech, Mauricio, *et al.*, 'The Basis of Wealth and Reaction in El Salvador' (mimeo, San Salvador 1976)

Downing, T.J., 'Agricultural Modernization in El Salvador, Central America' (Occasional Paper 32, Centre for Latin American Studies, University of Cambridge, 1978)

Ege, Konrad, 'El Salvador: White Paper?' (*Counterspy*, New York, May–July 1981)

Elam, Robert E., 'Appeal to Arms: The Army and Politics in El Salvador, 1931-1964' (unpublished PhD, University of New Mexico 1968)

El Proceso Político Centroamericano (San Salvador 1964)

El Salvador: Alianzas Políticas y Proceso Revolucionario (Mexico 1980)

El Salvador: Un Pueblo en Lucha (New York 1980)

Escobar, Francis Andrés, 'En la Linea de la Muerte' (*Estudios Centroamericanos*, XXXV, Jan.-Feb. 1980)

Feinberg, Richard, 'Central America: No Easy Answers' (*Foreign Affairs,* Summer 1981)

Foote, Heather, 'United States Policy towards El Salvador: September 1979 to the Present' (mimeo, Washington July 1980)

Forché, Carolyn, 'The Road to Reaction in El Salvador' in The Nation, *El Salvador: The Roots of Intervention* (Marion, Ohio 1981)

Forché, Carolyn, and Wheaton, Philip, *History and Motivations of US Involvement in the Control of the Peasant Movement in El Salvador, 1970-1980* (Washington 1980)

Frente de Acción Popular Unificada, *Pueblo. Boletin Internacional*, 1979–80

_____, *Polémica Internacional*, 1980

Frente Democrático Revolucionario, *El Salvador Libre*, 1981—

_____, 'Plan General del Gobierno Democrático Revolucionario' (mimeo, San Salvador 1980)

Galván Bonilla, C. and Mancia Vides, P., *La Historia del Cafe en El Salvador* (San Salvador 1978)

Gualán, A., 'Years of Valiant Struggle (35 years of the Communist Party in El Salvador)' (*World Marxist Review*, vol. 8, no. 6, June 1965)

Guerra, Tomás (ed), *El Salvador: Octubre Sangriento* (San Jose 1979)

Halperin, Morton (ed.), *Report on Human Rights in El Salvador* (Washington 1982)

HMSO, *El Salvador: Review of Commercial Conditions* (London, various years)

Institute of Policy Studies, 'Background Information on the Security Forces in El Salvador and US Military Assistance', ed. Cynthia Arnson (Washington 1980)

Jung, Harald, 'Class Struggles in El Salvador' (*New Left Review*, 122, July–Aug. 1980)

Karush, G.E., 'Plantations, Population, and Poverty: The Roots of the Demographic Crisis in El Salvador' (*Studies in Comparative International Development*, vol. 13, no. 3, 1978)

Kennedy, Paul P., *The Middle Beat: A Correspondent's View of Mexico, Guatemala and El Salvador* (New York 1971)

La Inversión Extranjera en Centroamérica (San José 1975)

Latin America Bureau, *Violence and Fraud in El Salvador* (London 1977)

———, *El Salvador under General Romero* (London 1979)

Lateinamerika Nachtrichten, *El Salvador. Ein Land im Kampf um seine Befreiung* (Berlin 1980)

LeoGrande, William M., and Robbins, Carla Anne, 'Oligarchs and Officers: The Crisis in El Salvador' (*Foreign Affairs*, Summer 1980)

López Vallecillos, Italo and Orellana, Victor Antonio, 'La Unidad Popular y el Surgimiento del Frente Democrático Revolucionario' (*Estudios Centroamericanos*, XXXV, March–April 1980)

Luna, David Alejandro, 'Un heroico y trágico suceso de nuestra historia' in *El Proceso Político Centroamericano* (San Salvador 1964)

———, 'Análisis de una Dictadura Fascista Latinoamericana. Maximiliano Hernández Martinez, 1931-44' (*La Universidad*, año 94, no. 5, Sept.–Oct. 1969)

———, *Manual de Historia Económica de El Salvador* (San Salvador 1971)

Martin, Percy F., *El Salvador of the XXth Century* (London 1911)

Martz, John D., *Central America: The Crisis and the Challenge* (Chapel Hill 1959)

Menéndez Rodríguez, Mario, *El Salvador: Una Auténtica Guerra Civil* (San José 1980)

Menjivar, Rafael, *Crisis del Desarrollismo. Caso El Salvador* (San José 1977)

———, *El Salvador, El Eslabón Más Pequeño* (San José 1981)

NACLA, 'El Salvador – A Revolution Brews' (XIV, no. 4, July–Aug 1980)

Nation, The, *El Salvador: The Roots of Intervention* (Marion, Ohio 1981)

Partido Comunista de El Salvador, *Fundamentos y Perspectivas* (San Salvador 1979)

———, *Voz Popular*, 1979–

———, *Boletín Exterior*, 1979–

Partido Revolucionario Salvadoreño, *El Salvador: Une Perspective Revolutionaire* (Algiers 1977)

Pearce, Jenny, *Under the Eagle. US Intervention in Central America and the*

Caribbean (London 1981)

Petras, James, 'White Paper on the White Paper' in *The Nation* (1981)

Quiñoñez Reyes, Francisco, 'Informe sobre la insubordinación de las Fuerzas Armadas de El Salvador – 8 de Septiembre de 1980' (mimeo, n.p., n.d.)

Resistencia Nacional, *Por la Causa Proletaria* (San José 1978)

Revolt in El Salvador (New York 1980)

Ruhl, Arthur, *The Central Americans* (New York 1927)

Ruiz, Santiago, 'La Modernización Agricola en El Salvador' (*Estudios Centroamericanos*, XXXI, no. 330, April 1976)

Salazar Valiente, Mario, 'Esbozo histórico de la dominación en El Salvador: 1920-74' (*Avances de Investigación*, no. 17, Universidad Nacional Autónoma de México, 1975)

Sánchez, J., 'Social Developments in El Salvador and the Policy of the Communist Party' (*World Marxist Review*, vol. 8, no. 8, August 1980)

Schlesinger, Jorge, *Revolución Comunista* (Guatemala 1946)

Selva, Mauricio de la, 'El Salvador: Tres Décadas de Lucha' (*Cuadernos Americanos*, no. 21, Jan.–Feb. 1962)

Shafik Handal, Jorge, 'El Salvador: A Precarious Balance' (*World Marxist Review*, vol. 6, no. 6, June 1973)

Simon, Laurence R. and Stephens, James C., *El Salvador: Land Reform 1980–81* (Boston 1981)

Torres Rivas, Edelberto, *Interpretación del Desarrollo Social Centroamericano* (Santiago, Chile 1968)

Tricontinental Society, *El Salvador: The Development of the People's Struggle* (London 1980)

———, *Revolutionary Strategy in El Salvador* (London 1981)

United Nations, *La Transformación del Campo y la Situación Económica y Social de las Familias Rurales en El Salvador* (New York 1976)

United States, Department of State, *Communist Interference in El Salvador* (Washington 1981)

Webre, Stephan, *José Napoleón Duarte and the Christian Democratic Party in Salvadoran Politics, 1960–78* (Baton Rouge 1979)

Wheaton, Philip, *Agrarian Reform in El Salvador: A Program of Rural Pacification* (Washington 1980)

White, Alastair, *El Salvador* (London 1973)

———, 'Squatter Settlements, Politics and Class Conflict' (Occasional Paper no. 17, Institute of Latin American Studies, University of Glasgow, 1976)

Wilson, Everett Alan, 'The Crisis of National Integration in El Salvador,

1919–1935 (unpublished PhD, Stanford University 1970)
Woodward, Ralph Lee Jnr, *Central America: A Nation Divided* (New York 1976)

APPENDIX ONE
CHRONOLOGY

1821	Independence from Spain
1823	United Provinces of Central America declared independent from Mexico
1833	Peasant rebellion led by Anastasio Aquino
1847	El Salvador declared a sovereign republic
1859	Gen. Barrios (1859–63) introduces first measures to encourage coffee cultivation
1879–82	Expropriation of communal lands under Zaldívar regime (1876–85)
1909–31	Political power monopolised by Meléndez–Quinoñez clan
1931	Amid rising social conflict and economic crisis, liberal President Araujo overthrown by Gen. Hernández Martínez
1932	Peasant rebellion inspired by PCS and suppressed with great loss of life by Martínez, who consolidates his dictatorship
1944	Martínez foils coup attempt but is forced to resign (April); replaced by Gen. Menéndez, who calls elections. Coup (October) led by Col. Aguirre allows Gen. Castaneda Castro to win poll
1948	Coup (December) gives power to Col. Osorio
1954	Guatemalan regime of Col. Arbenz overthrown (June) by CIA-backed invasion
1956	Elections bring Col. Lemus to power
1960	Coup (26 October) gives power to military–civilian junta, which calls free elections
1961	Coup (25 January) overthrows junta, which is replaced by a 'Directorate' controlled by Col. Rivera. Alliance for Progress declared. Bay of Pigs leads to complete break between US and Cuba
1962	Rivera 'elected' president; PCS attempt at guerrilla fails

236

1967	Col. Sánchez Hernández 'elected' president
1969	War with Honduras (14–18 July)
1970	Attempt at partial agrarian reform blocked by oligarchy; PCS splits and FPL formed in clandestinity
1972	Fraudulent elections (20 February) rob UNO of victory; Colonel Molina 'elected'; coup attempt to reverse result (25 March) fails. FPL undertakes first actions; ERP established
1974	FAPU established
1975	BPR established; ERP splits and FARN founded
1976	Effort to introduce agrarian reform blocked by ANEP and FARO
1977	Elections (20 February) won by Gen. Romero after extensive fraud; defeated UNO candidate Col. Claramount leads occupation of central plaza of San Salvador (24 February); riots in capital violently repressed. LP–28 established. UGB persecution of Jesuits; US military aid rejected and economic aid withdrawn. Economic aid restored (August) following Romero's inauguration. Law for the Defence of Public Order introduced (November); repression increases
1978	Conflict between FECCAS and ORDEN in San Pedro Perulapán; violence in countryside rises. Escalation of guerrilla activity (November and December). First major FSLN offensive against Somoza (September)
1979	*March:* Strike movement leads to repeal of Law for the Defence of Public Order
	May: Martial law imposed; massacre of BPR militants outside cathedral
	July: FSLN overthrows Somoza
	August: Vaky and Bowdler attempt to persuade Romero to relax control and introduce minor reforms
	September: Demonstrations and occupations multiply; *Foro* founded
	October: Carter establishes 'Caribbean Contingency Task Force'; Romero visits US (13th); coup removes Romero (15th); military occupation of major centres and attacks of factory occupations; ERP attempts uprising in San Salvador suburbs (16th); colonels accept *Foro's* terms for joining government (19th); popular demonstrations repressed with high casualties; LP–28 and FENASTRAS quit *Foro* (24th); BPR occupies ministries (24th)

November: US sends $205,000 in military aid; BPR occupation lifted and 30-day truce declared

December: US sends military survey team; truce expires with no reduction in repression; civilians in regime send ultimatum to COPEFA to end violence (27th)

1980   *January:* Civilian ministers' ultimatum rejected (1st); ministers resign; FPL, RN and PCS unite guerrilla forces (10th); popular organisations unite to form CRM (11th); march to mark 48th anniversary of 1932 uprising draws 250,000 people and is attacked with many dead. Christian Democrats join government

February: CRM issues Programmatic Platform; D'Aubuissón and Medrano threaten to stage coup but are stopped by US; Robert White appointed US Ambassador

March: Agrarian reform and state of siege declared (6th); PDC splits; CRM calls general strike (17th); Archbishop Romero assassinated (24th)

April: Establishment of FDS (4th) and FDR (18th); D'Aubuissón attempts coup, is arrested and exiled; US Congress approves $5.7 million in 'non-lethal' military aid

May: Expropriations under agrarian reform halted (14th); Salvadorean high command meets Honduran and Guatemalan counterparts; Rió Sumpul massacre (15th); Majano removed from post as joint-commander of military; guerrillas form DRU

June: Second International recognises FDR; 24-hour general strike (24th)

August: 3-day general strike (13th-15th); STECEL strike (21st); FARN leaves DRU

September: Majano group loses dispute over 'Battle Orders'; death of Ernesto Jovel of FARN

October: FARN rejoins guerrilla front; FMLN formed

November: Dissent Paper criticises US policy; leadership of FDR assassinated (28th); Reagan wins US presidency

December: US missionaries killed (4th); US cuts military and economic aid; Bowdler and Rogers visit San Salvador; junta reorganised, Majano ousted and Duarte made president; FMLN makes advances in Chalatenango and Morazán

1981   *January:* FMLN offensive (10th–16th); White claims Nicaraguan intervention; US aid restored (14th); $5 million

worth small arms sent without congressional approval; 20
military advisers sent; US AIFLD employees killed; Reagan
comes to power and White sacked

February: State Department alleges Cuban and Nicaraguan
intervention (23rd); US diplomatic campaign rebuffed; EEC
sends aid to refugees

March: Further military aid of $25 million sent; military
advisers increased to 54; Duarte formally freezes reforms
announced in October 1979

April: Military counter-offensive against FMLN loses
momentum

May: Major demonstration in Washington against US
intervention

June: White Paper discredited by admissions of author

July: FMLN opens operations against economic targets;
new military offensives in north and east fail to dislodge
guerrillas

September: Franco-Mexican recognition of belligerent
status of FMLN–FDR; US Congress approves new aid
package provided the administration certifies every six
months that the regime is endeavouring to improve human
rights; Gen. Galtieri, Argentine army commander, refuses to
rule out sending of troops

November: Haig issues unprecedented strong threats to
Cuba and Nicaragua; US refuses to rule out sending of
troops, increasing fears of a regional escalation of conflict

December: Junta calls elections for a constituent assembly in
March 1982; FMLN withstands military offensives in
Chalatenango, Morazán and Guazapa

1982　　*January:* Reagan certifies junta is making progress in
curbing violations of human rights; 800 people killed by the
National Guard in Mozote, Morazán; FMLN destroys half of
the regime's airforce at Ilopango; US government releases
$55 million extra in military aid to make good the loss; 1,500
troops taken to US for training; foundation of Central
American Democratic Community; Reagan announces
$305 million regional development plan, with El Salvador to
receive $100 million

February: FMLN attacks Usulután; Haig rebuts parallels
with Vietnam; US adviser ordered home for possessing rifle

in combat zone; Reagan says there are no plans for the sending of troops; Britain, alone of EEC countries, agrees to send observers to elections; FMLN attacks Santa Ana, San Miguel and San Vicente in start of pre-election offensive; Mexican president López Portillo announces plan for regional negotiations in Managua: Reagan announces 'Caribbean Basin' aid plan; President Galtieri of Argentina agrees to sell weapons to junta; US navy starts monitoring the Gulf of Fonseca

March: NATO naval exercises in the Caribbean; Gen. Garcia announces army on verge of major victory in Guazapa; FMLN breaks out without major loss; 100 congressmen write to Reagan urging changes in policy; *Newsweek* poll shows administration's line on El Salvador unpopular; FMLN escalates actions in San Miguel and San Vicente, embarks on operations in San Salvador; US spyplane photos produced by State Department to prove belligerent attitude of Nicaragua, but fail to convince that it is aiding FMLN; Nicaraguan prisoner presented in Washington rejects claim of Nicaraguan and Cuban intervention; confronted by failure of diplomatic campaign US reconsiders Mexican peace plan; revealed that administration allocated funds for destabilisation of Nicaragua, which declares state of emergency; D'Aubuissón wounded in election campaign but maintains higher profile than Duarte; official military candidate, Gen. Guevara, wins Guatemalan elections; coup in Guatemala; FMLN offensive fails to halt elections; poll produces no overall winner but parties of the extreme right form coalition to control assembly

APPENDIX TWO
THE LANDED OLIGARCHY

1. Production of Coffee, Cotton and Sugar (1970/1)

Family	Coffee (quintales of 46 kg)	Cotton (quintales)	Sugar (tons)
Regalado	85,000		105,000
Guirola	72,107	67,000	9,000
Llach and Schonenberg	50,000	27,000	
Hill-Llach Hill	49,500	77,000	
Dueñas	45,500	124,000	44,000
Alvarez Lemus	42,000		
Meza Ayau	41,100		
Sol Millet and Luis Escalante	36,500		
Daglio	35,500	18,000	
Alvarez	33,000		
Salaverria	31,500	31,000	10,000
W. Deininger	22,000		
Alfaro	22,000		48,000
Dalton	21,500	35,000	
Lima	20,000		
García Prieto	20,000	92,000	
Avila Meardi	19,000	18,000	
Liebes	18,000		
Battle	18,000		
Alvarez Dews	16,000		22,000
Quinoñez	14,500		45,000
De Sola	13,500		22,000
Kriete	13,000	100,000	

Family	Coffee (quintales *of 46 kg*)	Cotton (quintales)	Sugar *(tons)*
Christian Burkard	12,500	79,000	51,000
E. Salaverría	12,000	10,000	
Bonilla	10,000		
Schwartz	8,500		
Bustamante	8,000		123,000
Alvarez Meza	8,000		
Soler	7,500		
Henriquez	7,500		
Rengifo	6,500		
Duke	6,500	34,000	
Homberger	6,000	29,000	
Sol Meza	6,000		
Belismelis	5,500		

2. Export of Coffee (1974, per cent)

Family/Firm	%
1. H. De Sola e hijos	14.37
2. Cia Salvadoreña de Cafe	8.16
3. Exportadora Liebes	7.03
4. Daglio y Cia	6.66
5. Prieto	5.92
6. Mauricio Borgonovo	5.76
7. Cafeco S.A.	4.15
8. Battle Hermanos	3.93
9. Miguel Dueñas	2.88
10. Llach	2.87
11. Salaverría Durán y Cia	2.80
12. Christian Burkard	1.80
13. Agro Industrias Homberger	1.79
14. José Antonio Salaverría	1.64
15. Salmar	1.59
16. Rodrigo Herrera Cornejo	1.55
17. Arnoldo Castro Liebes	1.46
18. Industrias de Cafe S.A.	1.41
19. Bonilla hijos	1.32

Family/Firm	%
20. Esther de Rengifo Nuñez	1.15
21. Regalado Hermanos	1.10
22. Armando Monedero	1.09
23. J. Hill	1.07
24. Empresa Cafetalera Sol Millet	1.02
25. Carlos Schmidt	0.92

3. Families Possessing over 1,000 Hectares (alphabetical order)

Family	Area (hectares)
Aguilar	1,488.2
Alfaro	6,138.8
Alvarez	4,602.7
Alvergue Gomez	2,048.5
Barrientos Sarmiento	1,530.6
Baum	3,034.4
Beneke	1,083.6
Borja	5,905.0
Bustamante	6,816.8
Carranza Martinez	1,545.8
Daglio	1,869.8
Dalton	1,480.4
Deininger	3,295.9
De Sola	2,581.2
Dueñas	5,713.0
Regalado Dueñas	6,424.7
Gallardo	1,484.8
Giammattei	5,490.2
Guirola	13,682.6
Gutiérrez Diaz	2,464.5
Hernández	1,140.6
Langeneger de Bendix	1,452.5
Letona de Trigueros	1,152.0
Magana	13,778.1
Martínez	1,234.7
Meléndez	1,306.6
Mendoza de Cross	1,477.6

Family	Area (hectares)
Menéndez Castro	1,176.8
Menéndez Lorenzo	1,546.5
Menéndez Salazar	1,968.6
Meza (Ayau, Alvarez, Sol, Calderón, Quinoñez)	4,247.1
Milla Sandoval	1,349.6
Orellana	2,717.9
Padilla y Velasco	1,626.5
Palomo	1,316.0
Parker	1,893.3
Peña Acre de Espinoza	1,054.8
Romero Bosque	1,831.1
Saca	2,072.0
Salaverría	7,808.0
Salguero Gross	1,091.0
Sandoval Langeneger	1,175.8
Schmidt (Moron, Herrera)	1,054.1
Schonenberg	1,018.2
Sol Castellanos	2,864.8
Sol Millet	2,146.9
Urrutia Fantolli	1,555.3
Venutulo	3,005.8
Vilanova Kreitz	2,407.0

Note: Table 3 refers to properties held only in the following departments: Santa Ana; Sonsonate; Ahuachapán; Chalatenango; La Libertad; San Salvador; Cuscatlán.

Source for all Appendix Two: Eduardo Colindres, *Foundements Economiques de Bourgeoisie Salvadorienne*, pp. 43–4.

APPENDIX THREE
GLOSSARY OF MAJOR
CONTEMPORARY
ORGANISATIONS

AGEUS	Asociación General de Estudiantes Universitarios Salvadoreños/General Association of Salvadorean University Students
ANDES	Asociación Nacional de Educadores Salvadoreños/ National Association of Salvadorean Education Workers
ANEP	Asociación Nacional de Empresas Privadas/ National Association of Private Enterprises
ANSESAL	Agencia Nacional de Seguridad Salvadoreña/ Salvadorean National Security Agency
ARENA	Alianza Republicana Nacionalista/Nationalist Republican Alliance
ATACES	Asociación de Trabajadores Campesinos Salvadoreños/ Association of Salvadorean Farm Workers
BPR	Bloque Popular Revolucionario/Revolutionary Popular Bloc
CCS	Central Coordinadora de Sindicatos–José Guillermo Rivas/Trade Union Co-ordinating Centre–Jose Guillermo Rivas
CGS	Confederación General de Sindicatos/General Confederation of Trade Unions
CGTS	Confederación General de Trabajadores de El Salvador/ General Confederation of Workers of El Salvador
CONDECA	Consejo de Defensa Centroamericano/Central American Defence Council
COPEFA	Consejo Permanente de las Fuerzas Armadas/ Permanent Council of the Armed Forces

CRM	Coordinadora Revolucionaria de Masas/ Revolutionary Co-ordinator of the Masses
CUTS	Confederación Unificada de Trabajadores Salvadoreños/United Confederation of Salvadorean Workers
ERP	Ejército Revolucionario del Pueblo/People's Revolutionary Army
FALANGE	Fuerzas Armadas de Liberación Nacional – Guerra de Exterminación/Armed Forces of National Liberation – War of Extermination
FAN	Frente Amplio Nacional/Broad National Front
FAPU	Frente de Acción Popular Unificada/United Popular Action Front
FARN	Fuerzas Armadas de Resistencia Nacional/ Armed Forces of National Resistance
FARO	Frente de Agricultores de la Región Oriental/ Eastern Farmers Front
FDN	Frente Democrático Nacional/National Democratic Front
FDR	Frente Democrático Revolucionario/Democratic Revolutionary Front
FDS	Frente Democrático Salvadoreño/Salvadorean Democratic Front
FECCAS	Federación Cristiana de Campesinos Salvadoreños/Christian Federation of Salvadorean Rural Workers
FENAPES	Federación Nacional de Pequeños Empresarios/ National Federation of Small Businessmen
FESINCONTRANS	Federación de Sindicatos de Construcción, Transportes y Similares/Federation of Construction, Transport and Allied Trade Unions
FESTIAVECES	Federación Sindical de Trabajadores de la Industria de Alimentos, Vestidos y Similares de El Salvador/Trade Union Federation of Food, Clothing and Allied Workers of El Salvador
FMLN	Frente Farabundo Martí para la Liberación Nacional/ Farabundo Martí National Liberation Front
FPL–FM	Fuerzas Populares de Liberación–Farabundo

	Martí/ Popular Liberation Forces–Farabundo Martí
FUDI	Frente Unido Democrático Independiente/ Independent United Democratic Front
FUSS	Federación Unitaria Sindical Salvadoreña/ Salvadorean Unitary Trade Union Federation
ISTA	Instituto Salvadoreño de Transformación Agraria/ Salvadorean Institute of Agrarian Transformation
LP–28	Ligas Populares–28 de Febrero/Popular Leagues – 28th February
MERS	Movimiento Estudiantil Revolucionario de Secundario/ Revolutionary Movement of Secondary Students
MJM	Movimiento de la Juventud Militar/Military Youth Movement
MLP	Movimiento de Liberación Popular/Popular Liberation Movement
MNR	Movimiento Nacional Revolucionario/National Revolutionary Movement
MPSC	Movimiento Popular Social Cristiano/Popular Social Christian Movement
ORDEN	Organización Democrática Nacionalista/ Democratic Nationalist Organisation
PAR	Partido de Acción Renovadora/Party of Renovative Action
PCN	Partido de Conciliación Nacional/Party of National Conciliation
PCS	Partido Comunista de El Salvador/Communist Party of El Salvador
PDC	Partido Demócrata Christiano/Christian Democrat Party
PPS	Partido Popular Salvadoreño/Salvadorean Popular Party
PRS	Partido Revolucionario Salvadoreño/Salvadorean Revolutionary Party
PRTC	Partido Revolucionario de Trabajadores Centroamericanos/ Central American Workers' Revolutionary Party
RN	Resistencia Nacional/National Resistance

STECEL	Sindicato de Trabajadores de la Empresa Comisión Ejecutiva Electrica de Río Lempa/Rio Lempa Electrical Company Workers' Trade Union
UCA	Universidad Centroamericana/Central American University – José Simeon Cañas.
UCS	Unión Comunal Salvadoreña/Salvadorean Communal Union
UDN	Unión Democrática Nacionalista/Democratic Nationalist Union
UGB	Unión Guerrera Blanca/White Warriors' Union
UNO	Unión Nacional Opositora/National Opposition Union
UPT	Unión de Pobladores de Tugurios/Union of Tugurio Dwellers
UR–19	Universitarios Revolucionarios – 19 de Julio/ Revolutionary University Students – 19th July
UTC	Unión de Trabajadores del Campo/Union of Rural Workers

APPENDIX FOUR
THE ORGANISATION OF THE OPPOSITION

FMLN ————————— FDR

	CRM	FDS
1. FPL	BPR	MNR
	FECCAS	MPSC
	UTC	UES (National University)
	ANDES	
	MERS	AGEUS
	FUR–30 (United Revolutionary Front-30th July)	MIPTES (Independent Movement of Professionals and Technicians)
	UR–19	
	CCS	AEAS (Assoc. of Bus Companies)
	MCP (Popular Culture Movement)	
		FESTIAVECES
	UPT	FSR (Revolutionary Federation of Unions)
2. RN	FAPU	
	MRC (Revolutionary Rural Workers Movement)	FUSS
		STISS (Union of Social Security Workers)
	FUERSA (United Front of Revolutionary Students)	STIUSA (Union of United Industries Workers)
	ARDES (Revolutionary Assoc. Secondary Students)	
	VP (Proletarian Vanguard)	*Observers*
	OMR (Revolutionary Teachers Movement)	FENAPES (withdrew 1980)
		UCA
	FENASTRAS	

3. *ERP/PRS*　*LP–28*
　　　　　　LPC (Rural workers)
　　　　　　LPS (Secondary students)
　　　　　　LPO (Workers)
　　　　　　LPU (University students)
　　　　　　ASOTRAMES (Assoc. of
　　　　　　　　Market Workers)
　　　　　　OB–LP–28 (*Barrio*
　　　　　　　　committee)

4. *PCS*　　*UDN*
　　　　　　AESS (Assoc. of High School
　　　　　　　　Students)
　　　　　　FAU (University Action
　　　　　　　　Front)
　　　　　　ATACES
　　　　　　CUTS

5. *PRTC*　*MLP*
　　　　　　BTC (Brigade of Rural
　　　　　　　　Workers)
　　　　　　CBO (Workers' Rank and
　　　　　　　　File Committee)
　　　　　　BRES (Revolutionary
　　　　　　　　Brigade of High School
　　　　　　　　Students)
　　　　　　LL (Leagues for Liberation)

Source: Derived from Institute of Policy Studies.

APPENDIX FIVE
PROTECTING CIVILISATION

According to *Socorro Jurídico*, the church human rights organisation, 12,501 people died in 1981, bringing the total number of deaths since October 1979 to over 30,000. The great bulk of people who have lost their lives are not combatants but innocent workers and peasants deemed to be 'subversives' by the armed forces. Young people are uniformly suspected of aiding the opposition, and have been the main sector of the population to suffer at the hands of the military, particularly the paramilitary forces – the *Guardia Nacional* and the *Policía de Hacienda*. The two *denuncias* printed below should suffice to illustrate the manner in which the civil war is being fought by one side. Copies of these statements are on file at the Library of the Center for National Security Studies, Washington D.C. and are reprinted in Morton Halperin (ed), *Report on Human Rights in El Salvador*.

At 2.30 a.m. on April 7 (1980) my son, Luis Alonso Quintanilla Sánchez, and my husband, Luis Alonso Quintanilla Perdomo, were arrested at our home on the main street north, Guadelupe district, House number 3, Apopa (a town ten miles from San Salvador). The arrest was made by properly-uniformed Treasury Policemen, who came to the house in three pick-up trucks. The first was a white Toyota, and the other two were blue and red respectively. There were approximately 30 Treasury Policemen. We were all asleep at the time. Since the house is still under construction, it does not have a door. In place of a door, we had put up a table, which was forcibly shoved aside when approximately twelve of them entered. The rest stayed outside the house. At the time of these events, I was with my eight children and my husband. We were all immobilized by this since the Treasury Police entered noisily, screaming insults and threats. Once inside, they found another table used by the family and one of the Treasury Policemen yelled, 'Get up, you son of a bitch and come here and remove this table.' The father of the children got up and said, 'I'm coming'. He took away the table and went back to bed.

At that point a policeman approached his bed and shined a light on him and said, 'Get up, you son of a bitch. Show me your papers. We are the armed forces.' He got up, went to get his papers and said, 'Here they are'. The same policeman said, 'Get out the weapons, son of a whore.' Luis Alonso Quintanilla Perdomo replied, 'I don't have weapons. If you want, search for them.' Then a thin, white policeman sat on one of the dining room chairs and said to him, 'You bastard, get them.' He replied, 'I don't have anything.' The same thin, white policeman said to another policeman of the same physical description, 'What do we do with this one, do we take him or do we leave him alone?' The other replied, 'Let's take him, they're all guerrillas.' Then I said to them, 'Look, gentlemen, we don't have any weapons.' And the same policeman who had forced my husband to get up said, 'What are you talking about? Everyone here is a guerrilla', and even pointed at the children. They began to search the house, lifting mattresses, cushions and pillows and everything they found in their path. They even shined a light into the toilet looking for weapons. They went to my children's bedrooms. They did not find my son Jorge Alberto Quintanilla Sánchez. He was getting ready to leave by the backdoor, but before going he told one of his younger brothers that he was doing it so that everyone wouldn't be taken. But at the very moment that he was saying goodbye, one of the policemen realized and yelled, 'Hey, look, one of them is getting away.' He then connected an apparatus that looked like a large searchlight and when an orange light lit up, the policeman released a burst of machinegun fire, aimed at my son. Since the boy had already left the house, when the policemen outside the house saw and heard the other policemen's weapons, they fired their machineguns. One could hear the boy calling, 'Help!' One of the policemen outside yelled, 'Kill the son of a bitch; don't let him get away.' The others obeyed, and killed him. After this, one of the policemen said to Luis Alonso Quintanilla Sánchez and his father Luis Alonso Quintanilla Perdomo, 'Go on, get out of here. I don't want to kill any more here.' They shoved them outside and kicked Luis Alonso Jnr. when he refused to walk. They also kicked his father when he said to the policeman, 'Just let me put on my pants.' The policeman who had killed one of his children . . . said to him, 'Why, just go that way.' When they had taken them, I left the house to give my husband his pants. Five agents had my husband, while three had my son. They were tying together their thumbs and their wrists. My son said to them, 'Why are you taking me, I haven't done anything.' The policeman who had murdered his brother said to him, 'We are taking you in as a guerrilla.' And the youth repeated, 'I am not anything.' The police did not reply and put him inside the white Toyota pick-up after having tied him securely. When I came outside to give my husband his pants, one of the policemen grabbed me and told me, 'If you don't want us to kill them here, you'd better go to bed.' I obeyed and went inside the house. Earlier he had warned us not to come outside because they were going to leave two policemen outside the house.

When I heard the vehicles start up, I saw that they headed in the direction of San Salvador. Inside the house, I and my six children cried and my youngest daughter told me not to cry, because she was afraid that they would come and kill everyone. She could see the policemen I mentioned earlier. So we decided to wait until after the curfew to look for the body of my son, Jorge Alberto. Shortly after 5 a.m. that morning, I went out to see whether my son was dead and found him with his skull crushed and his brains exposed. He had bullet wounds in his left cheek, nose, ear and right leg. They had robbed a watch he carried. I didn't know what had happened to my other son and my husband until five that afternoon when a friend had located their bodies at the El Recuerdo funeral home. The man that identified them had seen them in the San Nicolás District. Since the funeral home was in that area, I went to get them and the man in the funeral home told me that they were ripped to pieces, especially in the back. That same day, an item appeared in the paper *El Mundo*, which stated that 21 bodies had appeared in the San Nicolás District, known as the Monte Carlo de Soyapango District, near a house whose address was not known; *El Mundo* went on to say that the individuals had died in a confrontation with the Treasury Police, which had uncovered a guerrilla cell. When the guerrillas saw the security forces, the confrontation occurred and it was there that the individuals in question died. This is false, since my husband and son, who were among the 21 bodies, had been taken away by the Treasury Police in the early morning hours that same day in Apopa, and taken under arrest to San Salvador, after those had killed my son Jorge Alberto Quintanilla Sánchez, at the scene of the arrest. According to witnesses and statements, the event reported in *El Mundo* and in the Official Bulletin of the Treasury Police did not occur in the manner reported, rather, just as my husband and son, those 21 individuals had been taken from their homes, moments before they were killed.

On Thursday, February 28 1980, two truckloads of police and National Guardsmen in civilian dress arrived. With them were Napoleón Alvarenga Fuentes, Baudilio Galdamez and Saúl Casco Noyola, Cinquera members of ORDEN. These three and other members of ORDEN are those who were in charge of leading the security forces and the Army to the homes of those people whom they believed belonged to some popular organisation. That day they came to Cinquera at around seven in the morning, and they went to the home of Aida Escalante. They threatened all the members of the family. They tied her up and forced her into a truck. They took her in the direction of San Nicolás. There they forcibly arrested Félix Rivera. Then they returned to the district of La Escopeta where they fired their weapons, seached two houses and stole a number of articles. They also took a number of sacks, put Aida and Félix in them, and then sat on them. They took them away to the National Guard station at Suchitoto, where Aida and Félix were tortured to death. I say they were brutally tortured because Aida's body did not have a single bullet wound, but her nose and her teeth were broken and her lip was missing . . . She had a hole in her head but I do not know how they did that; it was so large that a hand could fit in easily; they had removed her fingernails. Her fingers were shrivelled. Her entire body had been soaked in some kind of acid. She also showed signs of having been raped . . . On Sunday, at around five in the morning, six truckloads of soldiers, Guardsmen, police and members of ORDEN entered Cinquera. They got out and then went to El Cacao; there they took Isabel Barahona. At her home they murdered a young boy from Sitio de Niño who had arrived the day before to visit her. They took Isabel about one block from her home. A heavyset policeman grabbed her by the hair and swung her around three times. When she hit the ground they shot her three times. Then they went to the other side of the district and took a young girl by the name of Guadelupe Monge; from then they began to beat me. One of my daughters, Lucia Juárez, tried to defend me, but the Guardsmen grabbed her by the arms. One Guardsman whose face was covered by a handkerchief slapped her in the face; she fainted and they took her to a grove of coffee trees, where they raped and murdered her with four machete strokes to the head. After killing her, they returned to my house and told me that we should stop causing problems; that because of us many Guardsmen had died. They left, but they returned shortly thereafter to burn the body and to order us to leave if we didn't want what happened to my daughter to happen to us. We left and headed for the mountains, where we spent the night. On the way, we saw that the Guardsmen and members of ORDEN were setting fire to a number of ranches. The next day we left for San Salvador.

INDEX